Race Tech's Motorcycle
Suspension Bible

Paul Thede and Lee Parks

Dedication

This book is dedicated to those with an open mind and a thirst for knowledge.
For the enthusiast who wants to go faster or smoother or safer or all of the above.

Inspiring | Educating | Creating | Entertaining

Brimming with creative inspiration, how-to projects, and useful information to enrich your everyday life, Quarto Knows is a favorite destination for those pursuing their interests and passions. Visit our site and dig deeper with our books into your area of interest: Quarto Creates, Quarto Cooks, Quarto Homes, Quarto Lives, Quarto Drives, Quarto Explores, Quarto Gifts, or Quarto Kids.

© 2010 Quarto Publishing Group USA Inc.
Text © 2010 Paul Thede and Lee Parks

First Published in 2010 by Motorbooks,
an imprint of The Quarto Group, 100 Cummings
Center, Suite 265-D, Beverly, MA 01915, USA.
T (978) 282-9590 F (978) 283-2742
QuartoKnows.com

Motorbooks titles are also available at discount for retail, wholesale, promotional, and bulk purchase. For details, contact the Special Sales Manager by email at specialsales@ quarto.com or by mail at The Quarto Group, Attn: Special Sales Manager, 100 Cummings Center, Suite 265-D, Beverly, MA 01915, USA.

10 9 8

ISBN-13: 978-0-7603-3140-8

Digital edition published in 2010
eISBN: 978-1-61059-166-9

Publisher: Zack Miller
Senior Editor: Darwin Holmstrom
Editor: Peter Bodensteiner
Creative Director: Michele Lanci-Altomare
Design Managers: Brad Springer, Jon Simpson, James Kegley
Designer: Danielle Smith

"Race Tech," "Gold Valve," "Emulator," and other trademarked Race Tech products used by permission of Race Tech.

Printed in China

About the authors

Paul Thede is widely considered motorcycling's preeminent suspension guru. He is the owner and chief engineer of Race Tech, the largest motorcycle suspension modifier in the world. Paul lives in Corona, California.

Lee Parks is the best-selling author of *Total Control*. Based on his internationally renowned Total Control Advanced Riding Clinics, *Total Control* is considered by many to be the riding skills bible. Parks lives in Apple Valley, California.

Contents

Authors' Notes

I first swung a leg over a mini bike at the age of 10 and was hooked. My life instantly had direction. I raced professional motocross, studied hard in school because I wanted to work in the industry, went to college and studied harder, graduating summa cum laude with a bachelor of science degree in mechanical engineering from California Polytechnic University in Pomona. I started a business with partners building high-performance motors and suspension and then opened Race Tech in 1984.

It didn't take long to realize I could drop lap times far faster by setting up suspension than by building superfast motors. Somewhere in this timeline I realized I wasn't going to be the next national champ, and while I continued to race, I really enjoyed helping others go fast and stay on the rubber side.

Back in the early 1990s, we turned our attention to road race and street bikes and were blown away with the results. I invented the Gold Valve and the Gold Valve Cartridge Emulator back then and started to produce products—including a line of suspension tools—that would help others tune suspension. In 1994 I created the first Technical Edge Suspension Seminar and have taught more than 100 seminars and thousands of students around the world.

Through the years I've had the privilege of working with many top-level riders like Doug Dubach, Gary Denton, Mike Beier, Jeremy McGrath, Tallon Vohland, Rodney Smith, Ty Davis, Danny "Magoo" Chandler, Jamie James, James Randolph, Tom Kipp, Lee Parks, Rich Oliver, David Anthony, Micky Dymond, Darryl Atkins, Benny Carlson, Josh Brooks, Mike Metzger, Jordan Szoke, Bonneville legend Paul Livingston, Mike and Jeff Alessi, Jake Weimer, Eric and Ben Bostrom, Kerry Peterson and the Peterson gang, Malcolm and Alexander Smith, Brandon Thede (my six-year-old son), and riders like you.

In the following pages, I promise to avoid big words as there is very little value in you being impressed with my vocabulary. In some cases, you may want to read a section more than once, and in fact, you may want to read the book many times. I encourage you to use the forms available to download free on www.racetech.com. Refer to the Troubleshooting and Testing chapter as you are testing, because it can "jog the marbles." Use our website to look up suggested spring rates and see what's available for your model. Feel free to contact Race Tech and ask questions about your specific bike—we have great technical support. Lastly, if you are really intrigued, take advantage of our suspension seminars—many of the world's top tuners have done just that.

It has been my experience over the years that much of the information available on suspension was hard to understand, incomplete, or contradictory. In fact, much of the most important information was simply not out there for public consumption. For that reason, most people find suspension tuning a "mysterious black art." My goal is to help you understand this challenging subject at a higher level than you do now. Be willing to learn something new, and keep in mind that there is always a "next level" of understanding as well as suspension performance. There's always room for improvement. "The best you've ridden is the best you know."

It is my opinion that almost any brand of suspension can be made to work well. This depends mostly on setup. However the maximum potential can be limited by its design. I have immense respect for other suspension manufacturers and tuners and my hope is that this book complements and enhances their work too.

People with many different levels of interest and understanding will read this book. Perhaps you simply want a little clarity on a mysterious subject, or maybe you are reading this because your kid races. On the other hand, you might work on suspension for a living (or you may want to). If you want to become a great suspension tuner, you will need to be many things: a detective, a salesman, a psychiatrist, a technician, and most of all, a student (like my son Brandon).

Good luck and great riding.
—*Paul Thede*

Authors' Notes

To understand the genesis of the *Race Tech's Motorcycle Suspension Bible* is to peer into the minds of three enthusiasts who love all things that go fast and smell of hot oil: Paul Thede, Al Lapp, and myself.

In my first book, *Total Control*, it was my mission to demystify the art of advanced riding—as part of that project, I took the bold step of including two chapters on suspension theory and setup. I did this because so much of proper riding technique is about minimizing suspension movement so that the limited amount of wheel travel remains available to maintain traction. It seemed obvious then that part of the advanced riding equation would be to help riders get their suspension systems set up properly. And, because I'm a big believer in teaching people how to fish as opposed to simply giving them a fish, we spend an entire hour on suspension in my Total Control Advanced Riding clinics (www.totalcontroltraining.net).

When consulting an expert to help design this portion of the clinic's curriculum, there was really only one choice—Paul Thede. Paul has forgotten more about suspension than most people will ever know. His ability to make that knowledge understandable in a real-world context is surpassed only by his exhaustive understanding of mechanical engineering. My challenge was to take a small piece of Paul's depth of knowledge and create a book that regular motorcyclists would understand.

A true pioneer in motorcycle suspension, Paul shares his knowledge in a most unselfish way. He teaches many of his most treasured secrets to those who attend his internationally acclaimed Race Tech Suspension Seminars (www.racetech.com). This means he has trained a huge majority of his future customers as well as his competitors. It's virtually impossible to see a modern suspension company in business today that has not been significantly influenced by him.

As a former professional photographer, I knew I'd have no problem with the many how-to photos in the studio, but there was one more critical part that the book needed—technical illustrations. For this mammoth task I needed someone with tremendous talent—enter "Big Al" Lapp. Al is a longtime friend, racing buddy, and incredibly talented illustrator. Fortunately he is also a big time gearhead, equally at home at the controls of a welder or lathe as he is with the tablet of his Mac. Al was able to make the words and ideas come alive in ways only someone who both understood and loved the material could.

Mark Kalan videotaped Paul's six day seminar, which was used as the basis for the book. Many people spent countless hours transcribing, whittling down, and editing the information and photos into workable-sized chunks. I would like to thank Matt Wiley, Tracy Martin, Michael "Pilot" Nelson, Rachel Westfall, Jim Barg, and Lenny Albin for their sizeable contributions to the project.

Finally, I hope that when you complete this treatise on suspension, you will not so much be impressed with what *we* know, but be genuinely impressed with what *you* know. Too many authors of technical books have forsaken the average reader in the hopes of impressing their peers. While I hope that we can achieve both, we have gone to great lengths to make this material accessible to the layman as well as thought provoking to the engineering elite. If we have failed at either one, it was not for a lack of effort.

—*Lee Parks*

Chapter 1
Suspension Basics

Why do we need suspension anyway? After all, go karts go pretty darn fast without any. The simple answer? Bumps. (Well, holes too.)

Back in the beginning, the wheel was revolutionary, but wooden wheels and solid axles didn't give the most comfortable ride. Springs were added and that was much better, but the wheels still kind of bounced around a bit. Pneumatic tires were a huge breakthrough in both comfort and grip, but the wheels still bounced around too much. Next, the damper was added to control the oscillations, and the modern suspended system was born.

THE GOAL

If we were to describe the ideal suspension, it would have maximum traction, minimal harshness (or maximum plushness), controlled bottoming, consistency (it would not fade), control the pitch (front-to-back movement) of the bike, have a proper "feel" for the road, and so on. Note that some of these characteristics are contradictory—like minimizing harshness and resisting bottoming—and you'll see that we've got quite a challenge on our hands.

The basic goals of suspension are the same in every vehicle, from a motorcycle to a car to a semi truck. Of course, we wouldn't set up a cruiser the same as a superbike, and we wouldn't set up a trail bike like a supercrosser, but the description of the perfect ride is the same—a bump is a bump and traction is traction.

Let's start with the definitions of *sprung* and *unsprung mass*. Sprung mass is the mass above the spring. This includes the engine, most of the frame, the gas tank, seat, rider, and so on. The unsprung mass is the mass that goes up and down with the wheel. This includes the wheels, axles, lower slider on a telescopic fork, brake caliper, part of the swingarm, and so on.

The two essential components in the suspension—the spring and the damper—can take many forms, but they all have the essential job of isolating the sprung mass from the ground.

In general, in the perfect world, the sprung mass should move along in a straight line (or a smooth arc around a turn), and the unsprung mass should move up and down, following the ground. Ideally, when going over bumps, the load between the tire and the ground should remain constant, with the same load on the up side as the down side. (One of the few exceptions to this is in supercross "whoop" sections where the fastest way across is to get "on top" of the bumps and never let the wheel drop into the low points between bumps.)

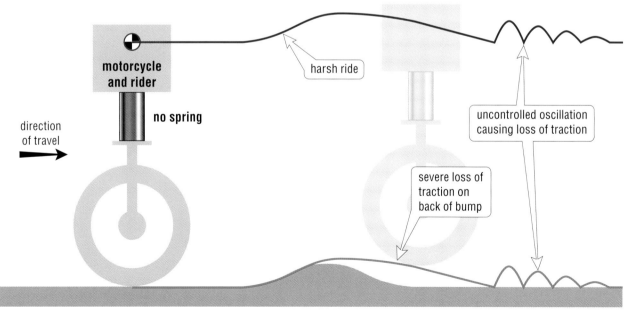

motorcycle
and rider

no spring

harsh ride

direction
of travel

uncontrolled oscillation
causing loss of traction

severe loss of
traction on
back of bump

1.1 Without suspension the wheel is solidly attached to the chassis. When the wheel hits a bump, the chassis is displaced violently (it's harsh). It continues upward past the crest of the bump. The wheel loses contact with the ground. When it comes back down, it bounces.

The technology required to create the perfect ride is still not here (this is particularly true for motorcycles), but this is the goal.

Now for the million-dollar question: how do we accomplish this? To begin, let's look at the forces involved with suspension. Certainly there are inertial forces—both linear and rotational—but let's focus on the three main forces in suspension components: spring forces, damping forces, and frictional forces. That's it. That's all there is. Suspension is simple! Now before you skip to the end of the book to see how it turns out, let's take a closer look.

SPRING FORCE

The two basic types of springs are mechanical and air. Mechanical springs come in three different forms: coil, leaf, and torsion bar, with coil springs being the most common on motorcycles. The force of a coil spring depends on wire diameter, coil diameter, number of coils, and materials.

Air springs, on the other hand, have properties like initial pressure, compression ratio, and effective piston area. *The main thing to know about spring force is that it is dependent on position, meaning the distance the spring is compressed.*

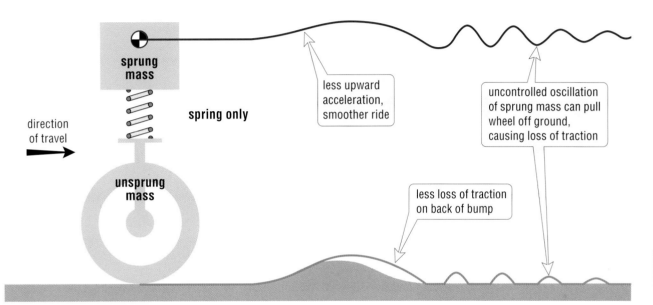

1.2 When a spring is added, notice that the chassis initially moves upward but not as much as without suspension. It is not as harsh. Once it moves initially, it oscillates uncontrollably. The wheel still loses contact with the ground but not as much. When it comes back down, it doesn't bounce quite so much.

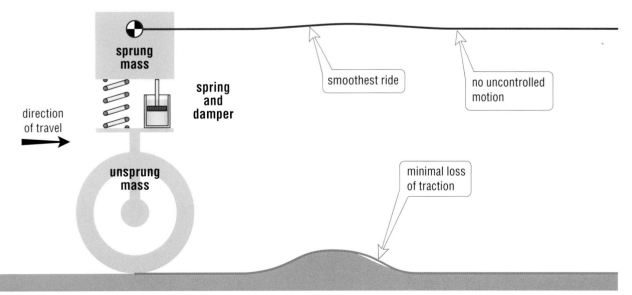

1.3 When a damper is added, notice that all the unpleasant characteristics are minimized but they're not gone. The sprung mass only moves upward slightly. The wheel still loses contact with the ground but for a much shorter time. When it comes back in contact with the ground, it remains in contact.

DAMPING FORCE

Damping forces depend on oil viscosity, orifice sizes, piston size, valving, shim configuration, and most of all, *velocity*. It is worthwhile to note that we are referring to *damper* velocity—how fast the damper compresses or rebounds—not *vehicle* velocity.

FRICTION FORCE

Frictional forces depend on the materials in contact (the coefficient of friction), the normal force (the force perpendicular to the surfaces in contact), and whether there is movement or not (if the forces are static or dynamic).

ENERGY

On the energy level, springs store energy. In other words they turn kinetic energy (energy due to motion) into potential or stored energy. Dampers and friction both turn kinetic energy into heat. Why in the heck are we looking at energy? At a basic level suspension setup is force and energy management.

A subtle note at this point, if the shock gets hot during use, it's doing its job. More damping means more heat. The more and the bigger the bumps are and the faster you hit them, the more energy is converted into heat. The more heat, the hotter the shock gets. Many riders have mistakenly thought that if the shock gets hot, something is wrong.

In the following pages we will take some of the mystery out of the black art of suspension. Keep in mind that "suspension is simple." That may seem like a joke, but once you get a clear grasp of the fundamentals, it will be much easier to comprehend the more complex aspects. Let's start with springs.

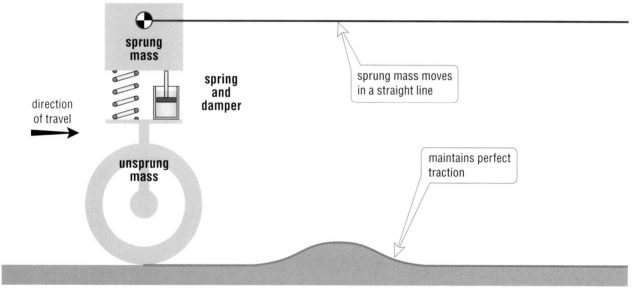

1.4 In the perfect world, the center of gravity of the sprung mass doesn't move vertically. The wheel remains in contact with the ground at all times. This can only be achieved with active suspension where the wheel is sucked up on the face of the bump and pushed down on the back side. The technology to do this is not here yet, but this is the ideal ultimate goal.

Chapter 2
Springs

While everyone knows basically what a spring is, few understand how spring forces affect suspension action. In the following pages, we'll take a closer look at spring forces and the different types of springs used on motorcycles.

SPRING FORCE

Spring force is the first of the three forces in suspension we will look at. When setting up your suspension, getting the correct spring rate and preload is crucial, so it should be done before any other changes are made.

The most important thing to know about springs is that the spring force is dependent on how much the spring is compressed—this is referred to as *spring displacement*. For example, if it takes 10 kilograms(kg) of force to compress a spring 1 millimeter(mm), the spring's rate would be 10kg per mm. So if you want to compress this particular spring 5mm, how much force would it take? The answer is 50kg. Ten millimeters of spring compression would take 100kg of force, and so on. Thus, the amount of force the spring pushes back is dependent on how far it's being compressed. It's important to remember that springs are displacement (or position) sensitive.

The total spring force created in telescopic front forks is a bit more involved. This is because there is a volume of air trapped inside the fork tubes that acts like an additional spring. When front forks are compressed, the air pressure inside the fork increases, even if no initial air pressure was used in the fork. The more the fork compresses, the more progressive the "air spring" becomes. Basically, the front forks have two spring forces: 1) the mechanical spring force, and 2) the air spring.

SPRING RATE

Spring rate is the "stiffness" of the spring, commonly measured in kilograms per millimeter (k/m), pounds per inch, or newtons per millimeter. One way to test spring rate is to first measure the spring's "free length" (the uninstalled length), then put a known amount of weight on the spring, and measure the amount it compresses. Spring rate is calculated by dividing the force by the displacement. Note: Spring rate is more commonly measured by compressing it in displacement increments and measuring the additional load.

By placing increasingly heavier weights on the spring and measuring how much it compresses, a graph of force versus displacement can be plotted. If we place a 10kg weight on the spring and it displaces 20mm, the spring rate is calculated as follows: 10kg/20mm = .5kg/mm. A 1kg/mm spring would displace 10mm with the same 10kg weight added: 10kg/10mm = 1kg/mm. More on this in the section on measuring spring rates.

2.1 One way spring rate can be calculated is by applying a known amount of force and then dividing that amount by the distance the spring travels.

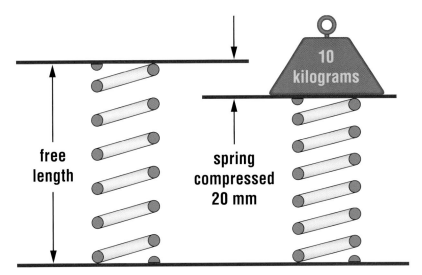

$$K \text{ (spring rate)} = \frac{10 \text{ kg}}{20 \text{ mm}} = .5 \text{ kg/mm}$$

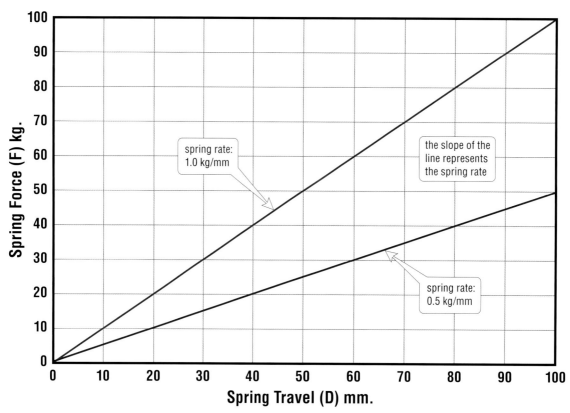

2.2 This is a force-deflection curve for two different-stiffness springs. The blue spring requires 5kg additional force for each 10mm increment through its entire range. The red spring is twice as stiff, so it has twice the slope, requiring an additional 10kg for each 10mm increment.

There are three basic types of spring designs: straight-rate, dual-rate, and true progressive. A straight-rate spring maintains a constant rate throughout its travel and is very common in racing applications. The coils on a straight-rate spring are spaced evenly. Each additional displacement increment (millimeter or inch) takes the same amount of additional force to compress it as it goes through its entire travel.

Progressive springs, by contrast, change their rate in relation to where they are in the travel. Progressive springs come in two main varieties: dual-rate and true progressive. A dual-rate spring commonly has two different coil spacings along its length—one is closer together, while the other end has the coils spaced further apart. As the spring compresses, all the coils compress at the same time. The closer-spaced coils run out of travel sooner (the coils touch each other and therefore have no travel remaining). They are then "blocked out," making the spring stiffer. Stacking two different springs on top of each other can also create a dual-rate spring.

A true progressive spring has coils that start out close together, and then are spaced progressively further apart with each successive coil. Initially, the spring force changes only a small amount with each incremental change in displacement. As the spring compresses, the coils are progressively blocked out, making its rate change gradually. A progressive rate can also be accomplished by using tapered wire, but at a much higher cost.

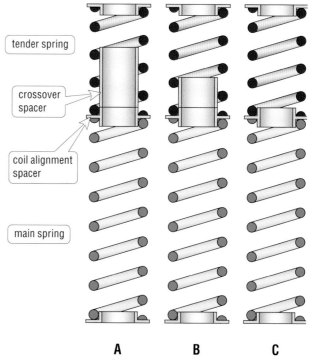

2.3 One method of creating a dual-rate spring is to stack two springs on top of each other. We can control the crossover point with different length spacers that block out the secondary or "tender" spring.

10

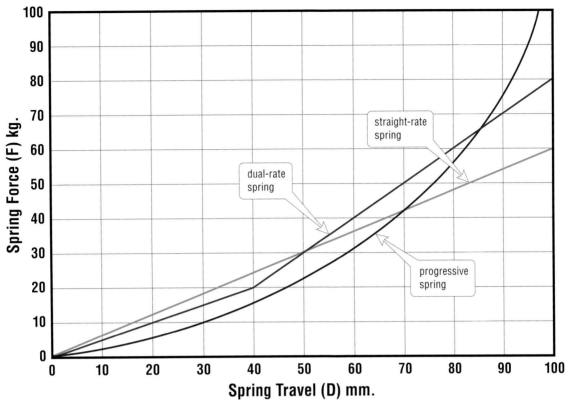

2.4 Progressive springs gradually increase force through their travel, while dual-rate springs have a distinct "crossover point" where they change rates. Straight-rate springs have a constant spring rate.

From left to right: straight-rate, single spring dual-rate, stacked dual-rate, and true progressive rate springs.

Which spring type is better is a matter of application as well as opinion, but Race Tech recommends straight-rate springs in most telescopic forks. Here's why. When setting up the spring rates on suspension, the ideal setup is one that is progressive enough yet not too progressive. A spring rate that is not progressive enough will tend to be a compromise. It may have a tendency to feel too harsh on small bumps and additionally may bottom out when hitting a large bump.

A spring rate that is too progressive will cause the suspension to drop through its travel too easily during the first part of movement, causing a mushy feeling. Additionally, as the suspension continues to compress, it may become too stiff too fast and feel harsh.

Remember that in telescopic forks there are two main spring forces: the mechanical coil spring and the air spring. By its very nature the air spring is very progressive and can easily be tuned with oil level. Race Tech has found that the combination of a straight-rate spring and the naturally occurring, progressive air spring offers the best combination of front suspension progressiveness. In fact, if more progressiveness is desired, a simple increase in fork oil level may be all that is necessary.

On the rear of dirt bikes and ATVs with no linkage, testing has shown that progressively wound springs or even dual- and triple-rate springs perform the best. This can make the wheel force curve similar to that of a linkage setup. Street and road race rear suspension does not require much, if any, rise in rate and work fine with straight-rate springs.

Straight-wound springs are also easier to understand in terms of their spring rate. Conversely, the only way to actually see how the force of a progressive spring changes is by using a spring tester to map out the spring forces.

For example, if a simple dual-rate spring is marked as a 0.5 to 1.0kg/mm spring, its initial rate is 0.5kg/mm. But there's a problem: where does the 1.0kg/mm rate start? Without consulting the manufacturer or testing it yourself, you wouldn't know.

Many people mistakenly ask what the initial and final rates are. This information is very misleading. To illustrate this problem look at Figure 2.5. We have plotted three dual-rate springs. All of them start with the same initial rate of .5kg/mm and all of them end with a rate of 1.0kg/mm. They are, however, dramatically different, simply by virtue of having different crossover points. (The crossover point is the point in the travel where the rate changes.) Notice that without this information, the initial and final rates are almost worthless in describing the spring. Where the rate change occurs causes a huge difference in how the suspension reacts, so it's not so simple.

A straight-rate spring is much easier to understand (a 0.5kg/mm spring will always take an additional 0.5kg of force to move it each additional millimeter), so you end up with suspension that is easier to tune.

Keep in mind that we want enough progression but not too much. On the rear of motorcycles, there are linkages with very little rise in rate as they are compressed. Some front A-arms on ATVs have the same problem. In these cases a progressive or dual-rate spring—or even a triple-rate spring—can be appropriate.

How do you know what spring rate is correct for your motorcycle? Use the methods outlined in the "how to measure sag" section later in this chapter to determine if the existing spring rate is too high or too low, and then take an educated guess as to what your ideal spring rate should be.

An easier way is to go to www.racetech.com and use the online spring rate calculator—just look up the make, model, and year of the motorcycle you want for a spring rate calculation. Select the type of riding and enter the rider's weight without any gear. The recommended spring rate shown on the calculator should be within a few percent of the ideal spring rate, though it may not be exact. Just select the available rate that is closest to the recommended rate. The stock rate is shown as well for comparison.

STACKING SPRINGS

A number of design parameters affect spring rate. One of these is the number of coils. By increasing the number of spring coils, the spring rate becomes softer. This is contrary to what many riders think about springs—they think that more coils (spring material) should equal a stiffer spring rate, but the opposite is true. Imagine that you have a spring with a rate of 10kg/mm and you put 10kg of force on it—it would compress 1mm.

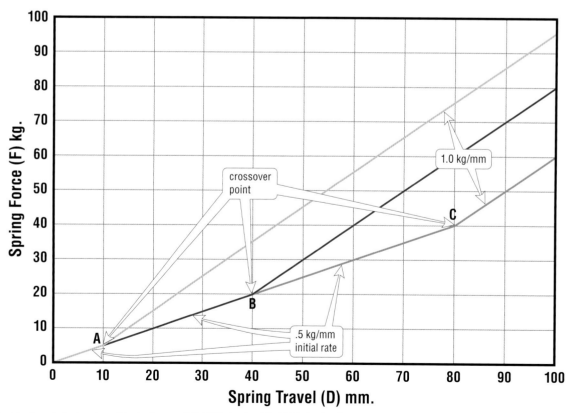

2.5 Shown are three dual-rate springs all having the same initial (0.5kg/mm) and final (1.0kg/mm) spring rates but having different crossover points. This illustrates the challenge of naming these springs. Note: This could also be created with stacked springs instead of being built into individual springs.

Imagine taking another identical 10kg/mm spring and stacking it on top of the first. If we put 10kg on the first spring, both springs will compress 1mm for a total of 2mm. Thus, the combined spring rate would be 5kg/mm (K = force/displacement or 10kg/2mm = 5kg/mm). The combination of both springs *lowers* the overall spring rate. This is called springs in series.

The formula that governs this is:

$$\frac{1}{K_t} = \frac{1}{K_1} + \frac{1}{K_2} + \frac{1}{K} \ldots$$

K_t - Total Spring Rate
K_1 - Spring Rate of First Spring
K_2 - Spring Rate of Second Spring
$K \ldots$ - Etc. Spring Rate

In our example of the two stacked 10kg/mm springs, the formula would look like this:

$1/K = 1/10 + 1/10 = 0.1 + 0.1 = 0.2$
$K = 1/0.2 = 5kg/mm$

Perhaps it's easier to visualize a torsion bar spring like the one used in the VW Beetle rear suspension. The spring is not a coil but a straight, round steel bar. Imagine the torsion bar was clamped in a vise and the other end had a hex nut welded to it. You could put a torque wrench on the end and apply a specific torque and then determine the spring rate by recording the amount of rotation. Now if the bar were the same diameter but twice as long, it would rotate twice as far with the same amount of torque applied.

The length of the torsion bar relates to the number of coils in a spring—the fewer the coils (or the shorter the piece of bar stock), the stiffer the rate. The greater number of coils (or the longer the bar stock), the softer it is. Again, when two springs are stacked, the number of total coils is increased, causing the spring rate to be reduced.

Conversely, removing coils makes the rate stiffer. Race Tech has a triple-rate fork spring kit that illustrates the concept. The kit is not made to be progressive, as it would first seem. Rather, it is made to provide more than one rate. It comes with one main spring—a regular, full-length, main fork spring, and two short, secondary springs that can be stacked on top of the main spring. This allows the user to choose different combinations of springs and change the spring rate. Using the main spring by itself provides the stiffest spring rate (0.46kg/mm in this example). If one of the smaller springs is added to the main spring, the new spring rate is 0.43kg/mm. If all three springs are stacked up, the resulting rate is about 0.40kg/mm. With the addition of each spring, the combined rate becomes softer. By removing springs, the rate gets stiffer.

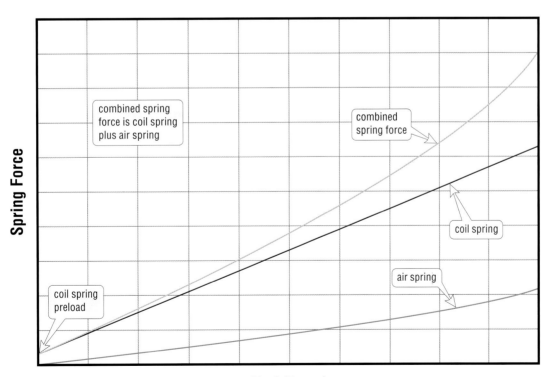

2.6 The total spring force is a combination of mechanical spring and air spring.

It's interesting and important to note that two springs placed in parallel (as used on front forks) add to each other, stiffening the overall or combined spring rate. If you are running two .46kg/mm springs in your dirt bike front end, the combined rate is .92kg/mm. This technique is commonly used to "split" rates. A .95kg/mm spring in one leg and a 1.0 kg/mm spring in the other gives a total of 1.95 overall. This is equal to two .975 springs.

AIR AS A SPRING AND OIL LEVELS

All telescopic motorcycle forks contain an air space—as the fork is compressed, the air space gets smaller and its pressure increases. When oil is added in the fork tube, the air space is reduced, and the compression ratio is increased. The air spring inside the fork tube works in parallel with the mechanical springs, and therefore the fork oil level has a direct relationship to the overall stiffness.

On motorcycles with air valves built into the fork caps, it is not generally recommended to use air as anything more than an emergency tuning variable. This is because adding air can increase harshness noticeably (due to additional seal drag or excessive topping out) and, unless the added pressure is excessive, only yields a relatively small benefit in bottoming resistance. Adding air is almost like adding spring preload (not spring rate). On touring bikes, however, the use of additional air pressure is quite effective for temporarily changing the load-carrying capacity for riding two-up. The air valve also is handy for bleeding off excess air pressure that can build up because of temperature and altitude changes as well as air leakage past the seals.

Changes in oil level affect the total spring force. Due to the progressive nature of the air spring, the change in spring force will be noticed more in the last part of the stroke as the fork reaches the bottom.

SPRING DESIGN AND MANUFACTURE

Coil-type springs are used in most motorcycle suspension. However, springs can take on many forms, including torsion springs (round bar stock twisted axially), leaf springs (flat or curved metal bars, mostly used on older cars and trucks), Belleville diaphragm springs (conical washer-shaped springs that are used on some motorcycle and automobile clutches), and finally air or nitrogen bladders or chambers.

Springs can be made of a variety of materials, including steel, titanium, or even carbon fiber. Heat-treated steel springs are by far the most common on motorcycle and other powersport vehicles.

High-performance springs are the most desirable and the most difficult to produce. Our definition of a high-performance spring is one that is physically light for its given rate. The following is the formula that manufacturers use to design coil springs using round cross-section wire:

$$K = \frac{d^4 \times G}{8\,D^3 \times N}$$

K - Spring Rate
d - Wire Diameter
G - Modules of Rigidity, a material property
   (G for chrome silicon spring steel—8,102kg/mm^2
   or 11.5×10^6 lbs/in^2)
N - Number of Active Coils
(Squared and Ground subtract 2 Coils)
D - Mean Coil Diameter (mid coil)

This can look a bit complicated, but if we take a moment, it can explain a lot. Notice that wire diameter is in the numerator (top of the fraction). This means as we increase wire diameter, the rate gets stiffer. Notice also that N (number of active coils) is in the denominator (bottom half of the fraction). This means that the more active coils a spring has, the softer it is (we discussed this when we talked about stacking springs in series). This means springs can be designed very differently and end up with the same rate. Two designs, one with heavy gauge wire and lots of coils or a second design with thin wire and few coils, could be the same stiffness.

How is this important in the real world? First, think about how much the spring actually weighs. The spring with the heavy gauge wire and lots of coils would be considerably heavier than the light gauge wire with fewer coils—thus; the first design would not be preferred. Secondly, the spring with the light gauge wire with fewer coils will have more travel.

The downside to small wire diameter is that much higher quality (and more expensive) material must be used. Also, because oil level is generally measured with the spring out, this difference in volume affects the air compression ratio in the fork (a spring that weighs more takes up more volume = higher compression ratio = higher effective oil level).

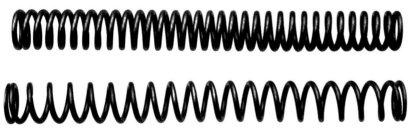

The top spring here has heavy-gauge wire and a lot of coils and is a low-performance spring. The lower spring is a high-performance spring that has small-gauge wire and fewer coils. It may be surprising, but these two springs have identical spring rates.

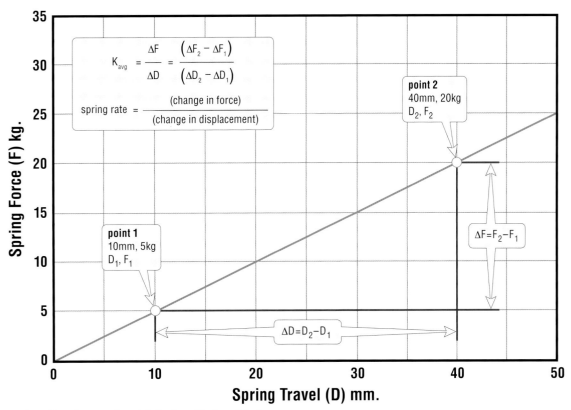

$$K_{avg} = \frac{\Delta F}{\Delta D} = \frac{(\Delta F_2 - \Delta F_1)}{(\Delta D_2 - \Delta D_1)}$$

$$\text{spring rate} = \frac{(\text{change in force})}{(\text{change in displacement})}$$

point 2
40mm, 20kg
D_2, F_2

point 1
10mm, 5kg
D_1, F_1

$\Delta F = F_2 - F_1$

$\Delta D = D_2 - D_1$

2.7 Calculate Spring Rate - Average spring rate is the slope of the force-deflection curve.

Here is a rather obscure real-world example of why using a high-performance spring can really make a difference. Old 35mm Harley-Davidson forks are pretty small in diameter for a 600-pound motorcycle, so the fork tubes have really thick walls to help support all that weight. With a small tube and very thick walls, there is little room inside to accommodate the spring and maintain the correct oil level.

Some aftermarket springs that are manufactured for these forks use thick wire: they are low-performance, but less expensive to make. The problem is that these springs take up too much volume, so much that there isn't enough volume left inside the fork for the oil to cover the damping rod. If you use the recommended oil level and the suspension is compressed, the air space is used up and the fork "hydraulic locks." This means that the suspension bottoms on the oil even though there should be suspension travel left.

This brings us to a very fine point. A spring takes up a certain volume within the fork depending on its dimensions—if the spring is changed, and the new spring displaces a different volume, the oil level will have to be adjusted accordingly.

To calculate the volume the spring displaces, you could weigh it and divide by its density. For example, if a steel spring weighs 292 grams and the density of steel is 7.87 grams per cc then, you would divide 292 grams by 7.87 grams, to get 37.1cc. In 41mm forks, 10cc is equal to approximately 10mm

of oil level. If you were to swap in springs that displace more—going from 37cc to say 67cc—this equals a 30cc change. The result is like changing your oil level 30mm. That's a lot.

Another thing that is critical to spring performance is rate tolerance. "Industry standard" spring rate tolerance is plus or minus 5 percent (+/- 5 percent). This means if a shock spring is rated at 5.0kg/mm, the spring could actually have a spring rate between 4.75 and 5.25kg/mm. A spring marked 5.2 could be 4.94 to 5.46. As you can see, the rates can overlap. The only accurate way to confirm the actual spring rate is with the use of a calibrated spring tester. Race Tech springs are stringently tested, so our tolerances are much, much tighter. This provides significantly more consistency and easier suspension tuning but also obviously costs us a bit more.

Sometimes springs will get shorter with use—this is known as spring sacking. This used to be quite a problem, and consequently service manuals commonly have a minimum spring length tolerance for reference. It is important to note that sacked-out springs have not lost their rate, only their length. (This is not true for engine valve springs: they sack because of exposure to high temperatures.)

If the length decreases, the preload decreases and the suspension feels softer. Race Tech springs are pre-set (sacked out) at the factory, so they won't change lengths when in use. The process of pre-setting a spring involves compressing the spring to coil bind (this occurs when all the spring's coils touch each other) a few times until the spring "sets" to its final length. Once a spring takes a set, it is done sacking. This virtually eliminates the problem.

MEASURING SPRING RATE

The following table and graph will help you understand how to measure spring rate. If we test a spring on a spring tester we measure travel (displacement) and force. Unlike the first example, we measure the force at incremental known displacements. (Previously, we put on a fixed weight and measured how much it compressed.) Average spring rate between two points (K) is defined as the change in force divided by the change in displacement.

Calculating Average Spring Rate between Two Points from Test Data

$$K_{avg} = \frac{\Delta F}{\Delta D} = \frac{(F2 - F1)}{(D2 - D1)} = \frac{\text{(change in force from point 1 to point 2)}}{\text{(change in displacement from point 1 to point 2)}}$$

We have arbitrarily decided to use 10mm increments for displacement. The first point is zero displacement. At this point the load cell would show the weight of the spring. We subtract this weight off of all measurements by "zeroing" the load at this point.

If you are serious about working with suspension for a living, Intercomp makes this compact digital spring tester. A fork spring tester kit can be added on to this base unit as well.

Next we crank the spring down 10mm and read the force. In this example it reads 5kg. If we compress it to 20mm, it reads 10kg. If we compress it to 30mm, it reads 15kg, and so on. This force data goes in the "force" column.

Once we have displacement and force data, we can plot the data on the graph and calculate the spring rate. In the table to the right, we've done the math. The ΔD column is the incremental change in displacement. The Greek symbol delta (Δ) is quite often used to designate "change." We also calculated the incremental change in force in the ΔF column.

Spring rate K is equal to the change in the force divided by the change in the displacement. As you can see, the rate in this example is 0.5kg/mm. It is important to note that we are actually calculating the slope of the line. Notice this is a straight-rate spring as the line is straight. In this "perfect-world" example, we could have used any two points and gotten the same 0.5kg/mm result.

With a straight-rate spring, the force increases as you compress it, but the rate doesn't change.

We plotted two springs on Figure 2.2. With the blue plot, when we crank this spring down 10mm, we'll have 10kg of force. If we crank the spring down 40mm, we have 40kg. Putting this data into the formula, we calculate that the spring has a rate of 1.0kg/mm. As previously mentioned, the spring rate is the slope of the line—if the spring has a steeper slope, it is a stiffer spring. In the case of the spring on the graph, it is twice as stiff (and thus the line is twice as steep) as the softer spring shown.

SPRING PRELOAD

Spring preload is one of the most misunderstood concepts when discussing suspension. Often we hear riders talk about adjusting their motorcycle's spring preload to make the spring stiffer or softer. This is a misconception: changing spring preload does not change the spring rate at all. The spring has the same rate regardless of how the preload adjustment is set.

Let's look at what really happens. When a spring is installed in either the front or the rear suspension, the spring is typically compressed a small amount. The length the spring is compressed is referred to as *preload*. Specifically it is defined as the distance the spring is compressed from its free (or uninstalled) length to its installed length with the suspension fully extended, Most vehicles, including motorcycles, use positive spring preload (negative preload means the suspension compresses before hitting the spring). This is true even for bikes that don't have external preload adjusters. Even suspension with the external preload adjusters backed out all the way commonly still have some preload.

Let's now introduce the concept of preload force (which is different than preload length). Preload force is the initial force the spring exerts on the end of the fork tube—or the spring collars of a rear shock—with the suspension fully extended. This force is easy to calculate:

Force = Spring Rate × Displacement

SPRINGS

Point	Displacement (mm)	Force (kg)	Change in D (ΔD)	Change in F (ΔF)	ΔF/ΔD	Spring Rate
1	0.0	0	–	–	–	–
2	10.0	5	10–0=10	5–0=5	5/10	0.5kg/mm
3	20.0	10	20–10=10	10–5=5	5/10	0.5kg/mm
4	30.0	15	30–20=10	15–10=5	5/10	0.5kg/mm
5	40.0	20	40–30=10	20–15=5	5/10	0.5kg/mm
6	50.0	25	50–40=10	25–20=5	5/10	0.5kg/mm
7	60.0	30	60–50=10	30–25=5	5/10	0.5kg/mm
8	70.0	35	70–60=10	35–30=5	5/10	0.5kg/mm

2.8 Theoretical "perfect world" spring test data.

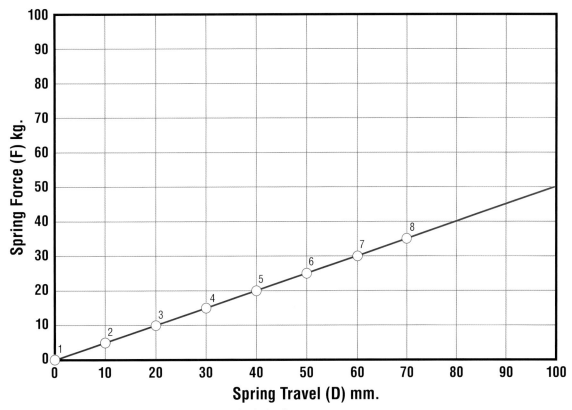

2.9 This graph shows the theoretical raw data points and a line "connecting the dots."

With a given amount of preload force on the spring, it will take that same force to initiate suspension movement when the suspension is fully extended. As preload is increased, it takes more force to cause the fork or shock to begin to compress. When preload force is decreased, less force is required to cause movement. It is important to note that when the motorcycle is resting on the ground with the rider on board, the suspension is compressed. When preload is changed the sprung mass is held higher or lower. This means more preload does not require more force to initiate movement once the weight of the bike has compressed the suspension.

A consequence of too much spring preload that results in the suspension being too extended is that there will not be enough travel available for the suspension to extend into holes. This can cause tires to lose traction as they skip over depressions in the road's surface. On the other hand, too little preload squanders ground clearance in corners and can cause the suspension to bottom out more easily.

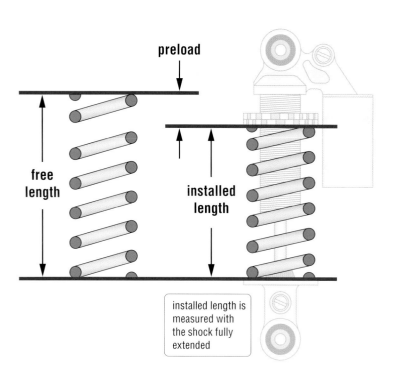

preload

free
length

installed
length

installed length is
measured with
the shock fully
extended

2.10 Preload is the amount the spring is compressed when installed with the suspension fully extended. It is the difference between the free length and set length of the spring.

Graph 2.12 (page 20) shows the difference between adding preload to a softer spring (blue line) compared to a stiffer rate spring (red line). Notice that the two lines cross at the 30mm fork travel mark. This means that both of these setups provide the same amount of force to hold the bike up at 30mm in the travel. The stiffer spring builds force at a faster rate (it is stiffer) but starts off at a lower initial force. It will actually "feel" more progressive than the softer spring with more preload. Remember, however, that more progressive is not necessarily better.

SUSPENSION SAG

The main thing spring preload adjustments really do is change the ride height. A change in ride height affects what percentage of suspension travel is available for absorbing bumps and for extending into holes or dips in the road surface. To understand how this affects the suspension's ability to handle bumps and dips in the road, you must first understand suspension sag (or race/static sag). Note also that it affects chassis geometry and handling. See the geometry chapter for more details.

The concept of sag is simple. When a rider sits on a motorcycle, the suspension moves downward, or "sags" under the rider's weight. Sag is the amount that the motorcycle's suspension compresses from fully extended with the rider on board. How much the bike sags depends on the spring rate, the sprung weight of the bike and rider, and the preload.

Referring to Figure 2.13, the line at the bottom represents a level road surface. Above the surface of the road are potential bumps that will be absorbed by the suspension during compression. Below the road surface are potential dips, or depressions, which the suspension will extend into as the motorcycle moves forward. The illustration shows the effect of a three-step preload adjuster.

Imagine that with only the weight of the bike acting on the suspension (far left of figure) it is nearly "topped out," meaning 95 percent of the suspension's travel is available for absorbing bumps. Notice that the three-step ramped preload adjuster is set to its middle setting.

When the weight of the rider is added (second from left), the suspension sinks downward, or sags. Now 75 percent of suspension travel can absorb bumps, and 25 percent is left to extend into holes. In the next drawing, the preload adjuster has been set to its lowest, or softest, setting. This moves the point of compression and extension downward so that 65 percent of the travel is now available for compression and 35 percent for extension. (It is important to note that the total amount of suspension travel always remains the same at 100 percent.)

In the last of the series of drawings, the preload adjuster has been moved to its highest, or stiffest, setting. The point of compression and extension has been moved up, and now 85 percent of the travel is available to absorb bumps and 15 percent can extend into holes.

The correct sag for motorcycle suspension can depend on a number of things—including chassis geometry and type of use—but in general it should be somewhere around ⅓ of the suspension's total wheel travel. This number changes with application (see table on page 21) but it is important to keep in mind that all these numbers are derived through testing. When we test enough bikes, we find trends. The trends help shorten the testing process, but don't fall in love with a particular number. Every situation has unique elements, and the correct number depends on the specific application and rider.

Note that a particular sag number can be achieved with dramatically different spring rates. Perhaps a spring rate that is too soft using lots of preload, or a really stiff spring using very little preload. With either of these scenarios, the quality of the ride will suffer. The spring with a rate that's too soft will dive and bottom easily. The spring with a very stiff rate will feel harsh, as it builds force too fast and will not move enough when hitting bumps.

By taking a few sag measurements, the ballpark spring rate can be determined: we'll discuss that in more detail later on in this chapter. In general, at the time of this writing, most street bikes are set up with fork springs that are too soft for aggressive riding even on the street though there are exceptions. Racers generally use higher spring rates with less preload than street riders.

Personal preference, riding conditions, and type of riding are all important factors to consider when setting up spring rates and suspension sag. The stock suspensions of modern MX bikes are all over the place rate-wise as to the ideal rider weight. Trail bikes are generally undersprung. Don't make the mistake of trying to set up your street bike like a racer, or your enduro bike like a supercrosser. When in doubt, consult www.racetech.com or a good suspension tuner.

So far we've only discussed static sag. Dynamic ride height, the amount the suspension displaces when you are riding, is actually more important for optimal performance. As we've discussed, static sag is measured when the motorcycle is stationary. Dynamic ride height, as the name would suggest, is measured while the bike is in motion. Because the motorcycle is moving, dynamic ride height is hard to measure without data acquisition like a Race Tech ShockClock and Dynamic Geometry software, but the concepts are important to understand. Static sag measurements, on the other hand, are relatively easy to figure out: all it takes is an assistant and a tape measure.

The main thing preload adjusters do is change the geometry of the bike when it is being ridden (see the geometry chapter).

Let's say the bike is set up perfectly. If a heavier rider gets on the bike, the preload adjusters can be used to compensate for the increased weight. If the preload is not changed, the bike would sag more—both statically and dynamically—when in use. This would affect ground clearance as well as rake and trail on the front end and anti-squat on the rear. Preload does affect bottoming resistance, but if you are experiencing bottoming and the sag is in the recommended ballpark, you probably are not going to cure the problem with preload. If the rider weight change is excessive, the spring rate should be changed.

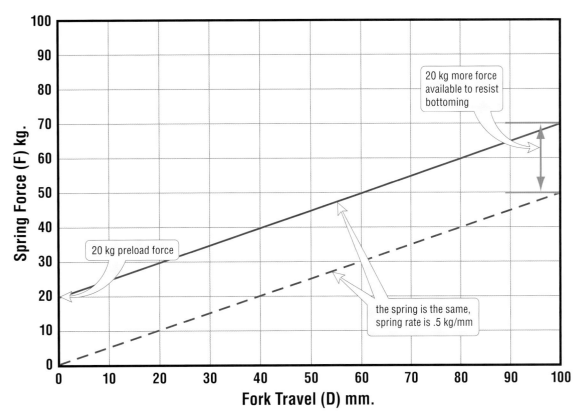

2.11 This graphically displays the effect of preload. The curve is displaced vertically upward. Notice the spring rate (slope) remains the same. In order to get 20kg preload force we had to put on 40mm preload on this .5kg/mm spring. Notice the x-axis is now labeled Fork Travel not Spring Travel.

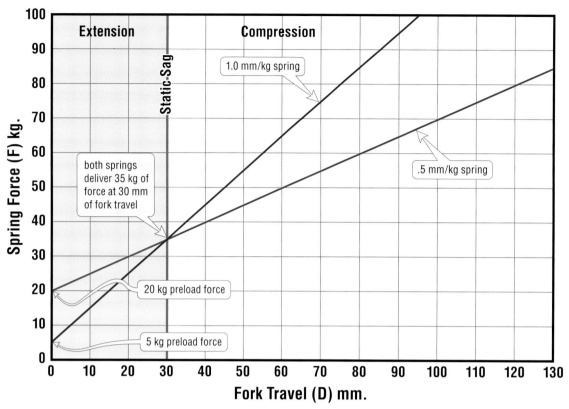

2.12 In the graph the .5kg/mm spring has 20kg preload force from 40mm preload while the 1.0kg/mm spring has 5kg preload force from 5mm preload. Notice they both create the same force to hold up the bike at 30mm travel.

MEASURING STATIC SAG THE RACE TECH WAY

At first glance, measuring static sag seems pretty simple. Extend the suspension and measure between the axle and a near-vertical point on the bodywork/frame on the rear of a motorcycle or the exposed chrome on the front end. Have the rider get on the bike and bounce the suspension several times, then take another measurement. The difference between the two measurements is the static sag.

Unfortunately, this process will not get you any type of consistent measurement. The culprit? Friction.

Friction is one of the three forces in suspension. All moving parts in a suspension system have friction. On front suspension, fork tubes slide through bushings and fork seals slide over fork tubes, all creating friction. Friction is present in the rear suspension as well. Swingarm bearings, shock linkages, rear shock seals, and internal pistons all have friction.

There are two types of friction: static and dynamic. Static friction is the friction that must be overcome to initiate suspension movement. Static friction is easy to demonstrate. Stand next to your motorcycle, hold the front brake, and slowly load the front suspension through the bars. Notice that it doesn't move right away. It takes a certain amount of downward force to get the forks to move. Once they just start to move, the static friction of the seals and bearings has

been overcome. Dynamic friction, on the other hand, is the resistance encountered during motion. Dynamic friction is typically less than static friction.

All this friction creates problems in suspension performance as well as when measuring sag. If the previous method for measuring sag is used, the measurement will not be repeatable because each time the rider sits on the motorcycle, the suspension can stop at a different position (within a certain range). Fortunately we can isolate the effect of the friction and remove it from the results using the "Race Tech Method." Instead of using just two measurements (fully extended and rider on board), we will take three. The following procedure will give you more accuracy and consistency.

Length One (L1) is the first measurement. To obtain L1, the rear wheel must be off the ground. If the bike has a centerstand, this task is simple; if not it may help to have a few, friends around to lift the bike. If you're measuring a road race bike, don't use a swingarm stand—even though the tire will be off the ground, the weight of the motorcycle will still be pushing down on the suspension, causing it to compress.

For the rear suspension measurement, use a measuring tape or a Race Tech Sag Master to measure the distance between the wheel axle and some point directly above it on the bodywork or frame. To measure the front suspension, the distance between the axle and lower triple clamp or the exposed chrome length can be used. This value is the L1 measurement.

(These same locations will be used for all three measurements. Use a tape measure that reads in millimeters, as it is much easier to do the math when calculating static sag.)

The L2 measurement is next. Put the motorcycle back on the ground and place the rider on board. Have the rider grab onto something to balance or use a wheel chock, like the Condor Pit-Stop, while the rider is in position. Now push down on the suspension about 25mm (about an inch) and *very slowly* let the suspension rise back up and stop. If there were no friction in the suspension, it would continue to come up further. Where the suspension stops is the L2 measurement (measure between the same two points as L1). It's important that the rider does not move or jiggle around as this will cause the L2 measurement to be inaccurate.

Where the rider is positioned on the motorcycle is critical when measuring static sag. On off-road bikes the rider should be standing on the footpegs for consistency. If the rider sits on the seat, there is no telling where he is going to plop his butt down, and this will throw the numbers off. On street bikes, have the rider sit down in a normal riding position.

Now lift the sprung mass of the motorcycle up about 25mm and very slowly let it sink back down until it stops. Where it stops is L3. Again, if there were no friction, it would drop a bit more. The midpoint between L2 and L3 is where it would be without friction. Next average L2 and L3 and subtract that result from L1 to find static sag. Static Sag = L1 - ((L2 + L3)/2)

If you carefully use this three-step method to calculate sag, you will be consistent within one millimeter every time. In addition to obtaining an accurate sag measurement, the three-step measuring method provides other valuable information about the suspension's condition (see Stiction Zone).

What's the ideal sag? It depends on the type of motorcycle and rider preference. Our testing shows the ideal sag is about ¼ to ⅓ of the suspension's total travel. Typically for a sportbike, sport-touring, or standard motorcycle, sag should be around 35mm, front and rear. Road race bikes may have less sag, usually between 25–35mm. Some cruisers and custom motorcycles with limited suspension travel could have 25mm or less, especially in the rear. Off-road bikes, with their much longer suspension travel, are between around 60–75mm on the front and 95–105mm at the rear. Race Tech, however, has used numbers anywhere from 85mm to 115mm on the rear, depending on what kind of geometry is needed. Off-road, 80cc minis can have 55–60mm at the front and 75–80mm at the rear.

Keep in mind that these numbers have come from testing and are very general. Each setup must be specific to the bike and rider.

FREE SAG

Free sag is the amount the bike compresses from fully extended under the bike weight only—*without* the rider on board. This measurement, also known as bike sag, is used primarily during rear shock setup.

If there is too much sag in the suspension when maximum spring preload is used (you run out of preload adjustment range), a stiffer spring may be needed. Similarly, if the preload has been reduced to its minimum and there is still too little sag, it may indicate you need a lower spring rate. But, supposing the range of preload adjustment allows the sag to be in the ballpark, how can you tell if the spring is close to the correct spring rate? Checking the free sag can help.

For example, if we set the static sag on the rear of a dirt bike to 100mm and then measure the free sag to be 5mm, what would we do? The sag chart below says the rear free sag for a dirt

Recommended Sag Measurements

Front

	Road Race	Street	Dirt – full size	Dirt – mini 80cc
Sag	25–35mm	30–35mm	60–75mm	55–65mm
Preload	5–25mm	10–35mm	3–15mm	3–10mm
Stiction Zone	5–15mm	5–15mm	10–25mm	10–20mm
Rear				
Sag	25–35mm	30–35mm	95–100mm	80–85mm
Free Sag, Top-out Bumper	2–8mm	2–8mm	15–40mm	10–25mm
Free Sag, Negative Spring	10–15mm	10–15mm		
Stiction Zone	2–5mm	2–5mm	2–5mm	2–5mm

These guidelines are good starting points and are not set in stone.

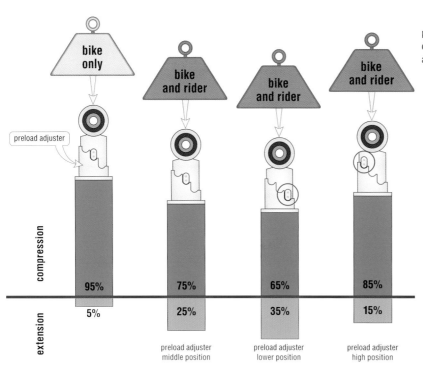

2.13 This figure shows the relationship between spring preload and sag. It also illustrates how changing preload changes the percentage of the suspension's travel that is available for compression and extension.

bike should be 15–40mm, so we are out of the recommended range. Would we need a stiffer or softer spring? The answer is a *stiffer* spring but with *less* preload. This is because the original spring is too soft and we cranked in an excessive amount of preload to get the static sag in the ballpark. This excessive preload is holding the bike up when the rider is off the bike. As you can see, suspension setup can be counterintuitive until you understand the physics involved.

Keep in mind that free sag should be measured when the static sag is already set. In other words, if the static sag is way off, the free sag doesn't mean much.

Note: These are good *starting points*. They are not written in stone!

Lately there is a trend for suspension manufacturers to use long, soft, top-out springs. In both forks and shocks these are called negative springs and they fight the main spring. Top-out springs will skew the free sag numbers. To further complicate things, keep in mind that many different rates and lengths of top-out springs have been used by suspension manufacturers.

If they are very stiff, the free sag numbers will be very similar to a standard elastomer or rubber top-out bumper. If the negative spring is very, very soft, it may be similar to a top-out bumper as well if it completely tops out with just the spring preload. When the negative spring is long and fairly soft, it will have a measurable effect.

Put your bike on a center or chassis stand, hold onto the chassis, and push down on the swingarm at the axle with your foot. If it extends 5 or 10mm, you've got one of these shocks (or else the swingarm is so flexible you should swap it out for something stronger—like spaghetti noodles). If you

have determined you have a bike with a negative spring and it has a significant effect, then use the free sag guidelines for a negative spring in the chart on page 21.

In general, suspension should not top out under the bike weight only (zero free sag). One exception for the no-top-out rule is when setting up shocks for adults riding pit bikes like KLX 110s. They are commonly topped out under their own weight because of the fact that the bike is fairly light compared to the weight of the rider. Some of these riders can be well over 200 pounds on bikes originally designed for kids.

STICTION ZONE

The difference between the L2 and L3 is an indication of the amount of friction present in the suspension components. We call it the stiction zone. The size of the stiction zone is an excellent indicator of the condition of the suspension. In general, the difference in the measurements for a properly functioning front suspension is 10–20mm. If the measurement is more than 40mm, there is a significant problem. This could be caused by bent fork tubes, worn-out components (fork tubes, bushings, seals), or a misaligned front fork caused by improper installation or a crash. See the chapter on troubleshooting for more information.

Good numbers for rear suspension are much lower—2mm is considered good and more than 6mm indicates something's wrong. Excessive friction in the rear suspension could be caused by a dirty or worn-out shock linkage or swingarm pivot bearings, or a bent rear shock shaft or bad seal. The front suspension's stiction zone is greater than the rear's because of the basic design of telescopic front forks. Even when the bike is just sitting on its wheels, there is a side load (actually forward load) on the fork bushings that tries to lock up the forks. Added to this is the relatively large area of the fork seals.

If you have more than the recommended stiction, stop, do not pass GO, do not collect $200, and give some attention to your suspension components.

Luggage should also be taken into account. If a backpack or fanny pack is used, its weight must be present for accurate sag measurements. The fuel-carrying capacity of the motorcycle is also a consideration. Gasoline weighs around seven pounds per gallon, so the amount of fuel present during sag measurements will make a difference—especially on a dual-sport motorcycle with an oversized fuel tank. Testing with half a tank of gas is a good compromise. Rear axle position can also affect these measurements. Be sure to check sag after gearing changes.

SETTING PRELOAD

Setting preload on a shock is pretty straightforward. Referring back to Figure 2.10, start by measuring the spring free length, installing the spring on the shock and tightening the spring preload collars until the set length is shorter than the free length by the amount of the preload.

Telescopic forks can be a little more involved. There are two structural styles of forks: right side up (conventional) and upside down (inverted). There are two basic designs of top-out springs: internal and external. The first thing you must know is which type of top-out spring you have. Damping rod forks are always external and right side up. Upside down forks are always internal top-out cartridge forks.

The only uncertain design is a right-side-up cartridge fork as it could be either. This is easy to determine when the fork is apart by looking for the top-out spring location. If the fork is together, unscrew the fork cap. Hold the lower slider and pull up on the fork cap. If it is springy, it has an internal top-out. If it is not springy, it is an external top-out. This type should be springy when you pull up on the chrome tube.

External top-out. Figure 2.15 shows the external top-out spring in this right-side-up damping rod fork. The easiest way to measure preload is to hold the chrome fork tube in the soft jaws of a vise. Unscrew the cap and let it rest on the spring or spacer. Measure from the top of the chrome tube to the sealing lip on the cap (the part of the cap that will stop on the top of the tube). This is a direct measurement of preload. Make sure the preload adjuster is backed out all the way before you do this.

Internal top-out. This type requires you to measure the set length. The set length is the installed length of the spring with the fork fully extended. First, set the preload adjustment to minimum (if available).

Measuring the set length is best accomplished with the cartridge out of the fork, however, it can be done with the fork spring out and cap unscrewed from the outer tube but still attached to the damping rod. Collapse the fork tube. The set length is measured from the point the spring touches on the top of the cartridge to the point the spring touches on the cap with the rod fully extended. (Sometimes the point the spring touches on the cap is actually a special washer or spacer.) A tape measure can be put down the fork tube with the spring removed, if you are careful to make sure the tape is resting on the flange when measuring.

Once the set length is recorded, measure the length of the spring and subtract. If the spring is longer than the set length, this is the preload. Be sure to include spring washers.

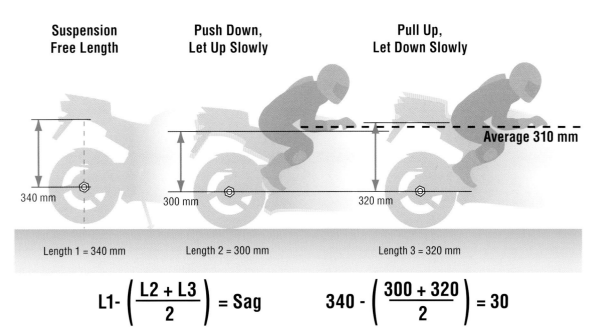

$$L1 - \left(\frac{L2 + L3}{2} \right) = Sag \qquad 340 - \left(\frac{300 + 320}{2} \right) = 30$$

2.14 This shows the RT method of setting sag. The Stiction Zone is the difference caused by friction when pushing down to get L2 and pulling up to get L3. The Stiction Zone can give you clues as to whether there is a problem with the linkage or suspension components.

External Top-Out Spring

preload

spacer length

free length

set length

external top-out spring (outside the damping rod or cartridge)

Internal Top-Out Spring

preload

set length

free length

internal top-out spring (inside the cartridge)

2.15 To setup spring preload the first thing you must identify is which type of top-out spring you are dealing with. Shown are the two styles. Pay particular attention to the method of measuring preload. Another variation of internal top-out spring design is a negative spring. See figure 2.16.

If additional washers need to be added, make sure they are located properly. This can be done with a flange on a special washer or spacer or by putting them on the bottom of the spring on an upside down fork.

RELAXED PRELOAD

Back-in-the-day life was easy. Measuring preload was simple (Figure 2.15). All you did was measure the free length of the spring and subtract the set length to calculate preload.

Life is harder now (tell Mom and Dad). The latest development for sport bikes is "long, soft, top-out springs" aka "negative" springs as in Figure 2.16. This means when you install the spring, the fork or shock gets longer or "grows". If the set length grows, the amount of preload you calculated using the previous method is incorrect (the actual installed preload is less than calculated)!

In the old days the top-out spring was so stiff the fork barely grew at all, so we didn't have to account for this. What to do, what to do?

Let's define some new terms:

- **relaxed set length**—the measured installed length without the spring installed (easy to measure)
- **relaxed preload**—the calculated preload using the relaxed set length (easy to calculate)

  relaxed preload = free length - relaxed set length

- **actual installed set length**—the length of the spring installed (can be hard to measure)
- **actual preload**—the length the spring is compressed from its free length when it is installed with the suspension fully extended. (hard to calculate because the actual set length has grown)

actual preload = free length - actual installed set length

One way to deal with this is to measure the growth of the cartridge when the spring is installed and subtract this amount from the calculated relaxed preload. With the spring out, the fork cap on, and the fork tube fully collapsed, measure from the top of the fork tube to the fork cap. Install the spring and measure the distance between these same two points. The difference is the growth.

When getting preload recommendations from the DVS valuing section on Race Tech's website, we give relaxed preload because it is much easier. We usually give a note in the Product and Valving Search to notify you that you are dealing with long soft top-out springs. The difference can be as much as 40mm!

In most cases we recommend replacing the stock "long, soft, top-out springs" with our Reactive Spring Series. They are not as stiff as the old days but are not nearly as soft or as long as the new fangled ones. Testing has shown the proper top-out spring can drastically affect traction particularly when leaned over in the turns.

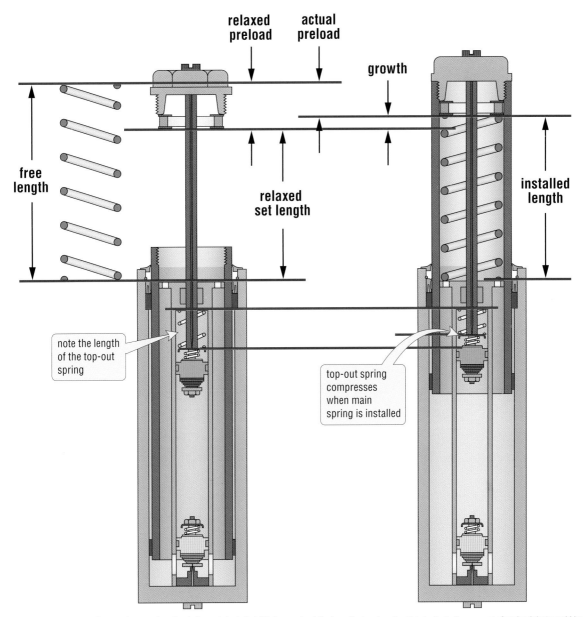

relaxed preload

actual preload

growth

free length

relaxed set length

installed length

note the length of the top-out spring

top-out spring compresses when main spring is installed

2.16 Forks with soft top-out springs get longer when the fork cap is installed. We have coined the term "relaxed preload" to indicate the amount of preload that would be created if the fork didn't grow. Actual preload is the installed preload.

RIDER WEIGHT

When measuring sag and adjusting preload, both the rider's weight and the weight of his/her riding gear must be taken into account. The rider must be wearing all his riding gear. Typically a road racer's leathers could weigh as much as 35 lbs. A motocross racer typically wears 10–20 lbs. of gear, and street riders could be all over the place.

Chapter 3
Damping

When it comes to overall ride and handling characteristics, many professional tuners consider damping to be the most critical factor. It's a complex subject, so we'll start with the basics. Damping is viscous friction. It turns kinetic energy into heat and is sensitive only to damper velocity and not suspension stroke position. This makes it fundamentally different than a spring, which stores energy and is only sensitive to the position in the stroke.

Damping in modern motorcycle suspension components is created in different ways, but it almost always involves a fluid. The configuration can be as simple as forcing oil through a hole—as with old-style damping rod forks—or can be as sophisticated as a multi-stage, bending shim stack configuration in combination with externally adjustable, low- and high-speed compression and rebound circuits.

All forms of damping accomplish one thing: they slow down the movement of the suspension. Compression damping slows down the suspension as it compresses when the wheel encounters a bump, and rebound damping slows the action of the suspension as the suspension extends.

DAMPING AND ENERGY

As we discussed previously, springs store energy as the wheel encounters a bump. When traveling down the back side of the same bump, the spring releases this same amount of stored energy. Damping, however, changes the kinetic energy of suspension movement into heat. Because energy can only be changed from one form to another (Newtonian physics— let's leave quantum physics alone for now), the total amount of energy remains the same.

This conversion of energy from one form into another is easy to observe. When a motorcycle is ridden over bumps it is the damping action that causes the shock to get hot. Suspension damping converts energy into heat only when the suspension is moving.

POSITION AND VELOCITY

Let's look at what happens when a wheel hits a bump. Initially the travel starts out at the static ride height at zero suspension velocity. When the wheel hits the bump, the suspension compresses. Somewhere the middle of the stroke the compression velocity is at its maximum and then slows down to zero velocity at maximum compression. The suspension continues to compress even slightly past the crest of the bump. The front wheel goes airborne and, when it is done compressing, the suspension starts to extend. It accelerates to a maximum rebound velocity and then slows down to zero at full extension.

It remains at zero velocity at full extension until the wheel hits the ground. It then accelerates to its maximum velocity and slows down to zero at maximum compression. It rebounds a bit slower this time, because the wheel is in contact with the ground instead of free falling in the air. It overshoots on rebound a bit then finally compresses back to the static ride height and zero velocity.

SUSPENSION OIL

One important factor that affects damping is oil or suspension fluid. Oil is incompressible (well, not really, but to a great extent we can think of it that way). When pressure is applied to a chamber filled with oil, the pressure is exerted equally in all directions. If there is an opening for the oil to get out of a chamber, there will be flow and viscous friction (damping or resistance to flow). The degree of damping is determined in large part by the flow rate—more damping means less flow and vice versa.

Oil viscosity is a measure of a fluid's resistance to flow. It is commonly thought of as equivalent to the fluid's thickness (sometimes called "weight"). The more viscous the oil, the more resistance there is to flow.

One measurement of oil viscosity is called Seconds Saybolt Universal (SSU) or Saybolt Universal Seconds (SUS). It is named after Edward Saybolt who arrived at his method to measure oil viscosity around 1898. He took 60cc of oil, placed it in a specific vat, and heated it to 210 degrees Fahrenheit. He then opened a calibrated hole at the bottom and timed how long it took to drain out.

The Saybolt Seconds measurement indicates the number of seconds it took to drain: the thicker the oil, the longer the time, and vice versa. When a specific oil is measured, it will have a specific number of Saybolt Seconds: 75, for example.

When the Society of Automotive Engineers (SAE) got together, they decided it would make more sense to create viscosity ranges: that is 5W, 10W, 20, 30, and so on.

This method of measuring oil viscosity is actually a measurement of kinematic viscosity. (For the purposes of this book it is not important to get into a discussion of absolute versus kinematic viscosity.)

In the SI System (International System of Units— better known as metric) kinematic viscosity is commonly measured in centistokes (cSt). The ISO (International Organization for Standardization) has grouped oil viscosities into ranges labeled as the midpoint of the range, that is 22, 32, 46, etc.

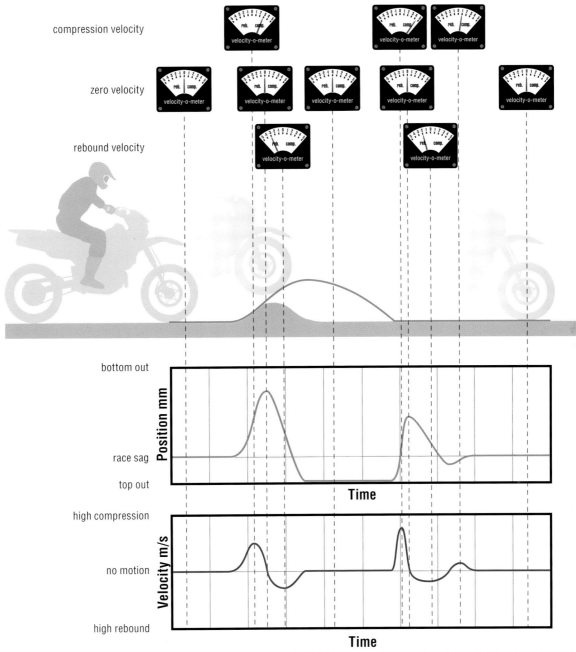

3.1 This motorcycle hit a bump or jump, went airborne, then landed and recoiled. When it initially hit the bump, the compression velocity spiked then slowed down and stopped. It rebounded to full extension until it landed and the compression spiked again, this time to maximum. It then rebounded again and settled in to somewhere close to the static ride height.

Oil viscosity changes with temperature. Oil thins out as it heats up and thickens as it cools. The viscosity index is a number that tells us how stable the viscosity is with temperature: the higher the viscosity index, the more stable it is.

The viscosity index is determined by measuring the viscosity at two temperatures, 210 degrees F and 100 degrees F. The 100 degree reading is where the "W" (or "winter") designation is measured. (Contrary to popular opinion, "W" doesn't mean weight.) The viscosity index number is then assigned based off these two measurements. In engine oil terminology, if the oil falls into the 10W range at the low testing temperature and a 30 range at the high temperature, it is designated as a 10W30 oil and is called "multi-grade."

Oil can be made more temperature, stable using viscosity index modifiers, including certain long chain polymers. You can think of some of these long chain polymers as looking like spiders with long legs. When the oil is cold, the spider legs are wrapped around their bodies and their presence does not affect the resistance to flow. When the oil heats up, the spider legs expand and increase the resistance to flow. This causes the oil's viscosity to become thicker than it would be without the viscosity index modifier added.

For example, if we start with a 10W unenhanced petroleum-base oil, it has the viscosity of a 10 weight at 100 degrees F. If we heat the oil to 210 degrees F, it is thinner and is still a 10. We could call it a 10W10 at this point. But if we add viscosity index modifiers, this same oil can become as thick as a 30 at the higher test temperature (10W30).

In viscosity index numbers, the petroleum-base, straight-rate, unenhanced oil has a viscosity index of around 100. The example of a 10W30 has a viscosity index of about 140. Engineered synthetic oils commonly have a viscosity index well over 150 without additives. With viscosity index modifiers, it can exceed 400.

The base oil is thin, but the viscosity index modifier adds to the viscosity. As the oil wears out, the long polymer chains break. It's like having the spider legs chopped off, and the multi-grade oil starts to revert back to its base oil properties (in the case of a 10W30, it degrades to a straight 10W10 or 10 weight). This degradation of the viscosity index is one reason suspension oils have to be changed periodically. These oils also suffer contamination from internal wear (adding things like aluminum oxide) as well as external contamination past the seals.

As mentioned previously, standard oil viscosity ratings are ranges, not specific viscosities. This means oil viscosity ratings can vary within a range between manufacturers. A 2 weight oil from one manufacturer might actually be thicker than a 5 weight oil from a different company. Trying to compare suspension oil from different companies is futile unless you actually test them. This is compounded by the fact that suspension oils are not governed by the same laws of classification that engine oils are—suspension oil manufacturers can call their oil anything they want. For these reasons it is important to choose a brand and stick with it for consistent results when making internal changes.

Which oil is the best oil to use for motorcycle suspension? After much testing with various manufacturers, Race Tech eventually had its own Ultra Slick suspension fluids blended back in the mid-1990s and has continued to refine them over the years. These fluids use synthetic-base oil along with high-end friction modifiers. They are very slippery, temperature-stable, retain their viscosity index for a long time, have high thermal oxidation resistance, and provide a long service life.

MEASURING DAMPING

Let's take a closer look at damping. As we discussed earlier, damping is sensitive to damper shaft velocity. A spring is easy to measure, but how can we measure a damper? Imagine we have a really long shock: hold it horizontally, placing the end of the shock on a scale resting against a wall, then compress the shock at a steady rate. The scale in our scenario would indicate the amount of damping being created at that velocity.

If we then increase the rate of compression in increments and record the corresponding damping in a table, we could plot these damping numbers against the different velocities. For this example we have arbitrarily defined compression as a positive velocity and compressive force as positive.

For rebound we would have to replace the scale with a pull scale. We could then start the process over, measuring rebound damping at incremental velocities. To plot this data we would recognize that extension is a negative direction and rebound damping force is negative. Next we would

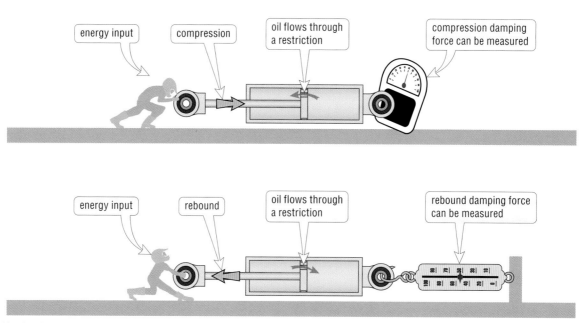

3.2 Making damping the old-fashioned way! In reality a shock dyno is used to cycle the shock rapidly while taking data at a very high rate.

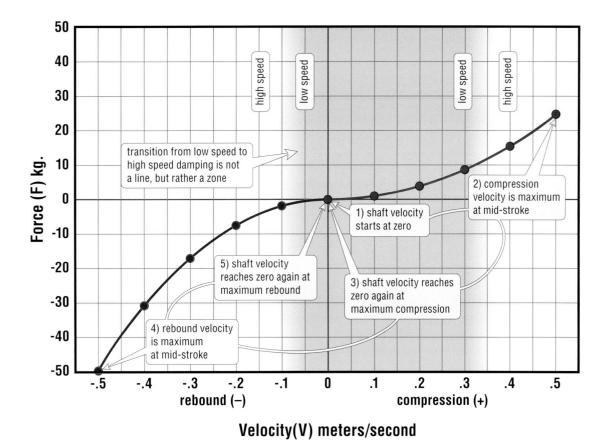

Velocity(V) meters/second

3.3 This is a damping curve going through one complete cycle. Notice the curve starts from fully extended at zero velocity then accelerates as it compresses—going to the right—up to a maximum velocity (in this case .5m/sec). It then starts slowing—retracing the curve back to zero velocity at full compression. It changes direction and starts rebounding up to a maximum rebound velocity at mid-stroke of .5m/sec then retraces the rebound curve as it slows down to zero again at full extension.

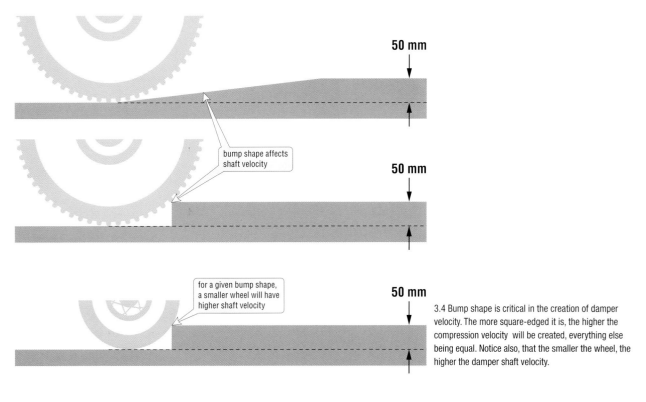

3.4 Bump shape is critical in the creation of damper velocity. The more square-edged it is, the higher the compression velocity will be created, everything else being equal. Notice also, that the smaller the wheel, the higher the damper shaft velocity.

connect the dots, as in Figure 3.3, estimating the real curve by smoothing the data. The combination of the smoothed compression and rebound curves is the total damping curve.

Real shock dynos typically use a crank on an electric motor, hydraulic cylinder, or linear electric motor to stroke the shock in and out. They measure velocity and load at very high sampling rates. In one full cycle of the shock it starts out at zero velocity, compresses to a maximum velocity, slows down and stops, reverses direction, starts extending up to a maximum rebound velocity, then slows down to zero. This gives us a lot of data in a single cycle. On the graph this cycle starts at the origin (0 velocity, 0 force). It heads up the curve to a peak then heads back down to the origin. It then goes to a maximum rebound velocity and heads back again to 0, 0 (origin).

In actual use the entire damping curve (the full measured range) is not used on every bump. If the maximum velocity of a particular compression hit is very low, it doesn't go up the compression curve very far. On the rebound side, energy is stored in the spring, so the further it is compressed, the faster the maximum rebound velocity will be.

When tuning the suspension damping, it is vital to know what velocities are occurring. Particularly on compression, the shape of the bump has as much to do with the velocity as the size of the bump. Bumps can be square-edged, rounded, ramped, or somewhere in between. The more square-edged a bump is, the faster the suspension must move to allow the wheel to travel over the bump while keeping the tire pressed on to the road's surface. Even at a relatively slow vehicle speed, riding over a square-edged bump creates a great deal of velocity—consider an aggressive parking lot speed bump that abuses you at relatively low speeds.

Conversely, a rounded bump will cause the suspension to move more slowly as seen in Figure 3.5. Bump shape aside, as vehicle speed increases, so does the suspension velocity. Double the vehicle speed and you'll double the shaft velocity. (Well, not exactly; there are other factors like tire compression, but you get the idea.) You may not have the luxury of a ShockClock or other data acquisition system, but it is a good idea to start estimating whether the actual velocities are low or high speed.

How much damping is best? Well that depends on how you're riding, where you're riding, and what type of motorcycle we're talking about.

Sometimes the answer is counterintuitive. Most people think that racers (both MX and road race) need more damping than trail riders or street riders. Think about the back side of the bump when the wheel is trying to get back on the ground: the faster you are going, the quicker it needs to extend. This means we could actually benefit from *less* rebound damping at higher speeds. Hmmm . . .

In fact, when magazines evaluate a new sportbike at a racetrack, they often write something like: "We wanted to lay down a really hot lap at Willow Springs, so we added a bunch of compression and rebound damping to help control wallowing at the high speeds." While this definitely controls wallowing, there may be a much greater price paid in traction. When Race Tech technicians provide suspension support at the track, they find that many racers use way too much damping, and as soon as damping is reduced, their lap times improve.

Let's turn to dirt applications. Supercross requires bottoming resistance as a primary consideration, particularly for lesser-experienced riders that overshoot or undershoot landings. SX whoop sections also benefit from a fairly high level of compression stiffness to maintain chassis geometry and help a rider "get on top of the bumps." Though it helps in the whoop sections, this high level of stiffness is counterproductive on braking and acceleration bumps. Many tuners feel that a lot of rebound damping is also beneficial, but there is really no reason to have more than that required for outdoor MX.

Most current sportbikes have external adjustments for both compression and rebound damping, as well as for spring preload. Many forks use a screw adjustment located on the top of the leg for rebound damping (not to be confused with the spring preload adjuster). Another screw on the bottom, near the axle, usually adjusts compression damping. Sometimes two adjustments are provided for low- and high-speed compression damping.

A few street bikes use one fork leg exclusively for compression damping and the other exclusively for rebound damping: these will be labeled as such. The side used for compression damping usually has the letters "Comp" stamped on the fork cap. Rebound damping is indicated as "Reb," or often as "Ten" which is short for tension.

Most modern dirt bikes with twin chamber forks have the adjusters reversed. The compression damping adjustment is on the top of the fork legs and rebound adjustment is on the bottom. The main point is that it's very important to check

Most cartridge forks have the rebound damping adjuster on the fork cap. It will often be labeled with the letters "Ten" (tension) or "REB" (rebound). A few models, such as the 2009 Yamaha R1s, FZ1s, and many Moto Guzzis, have one fork cap for compression and the other for rebound.

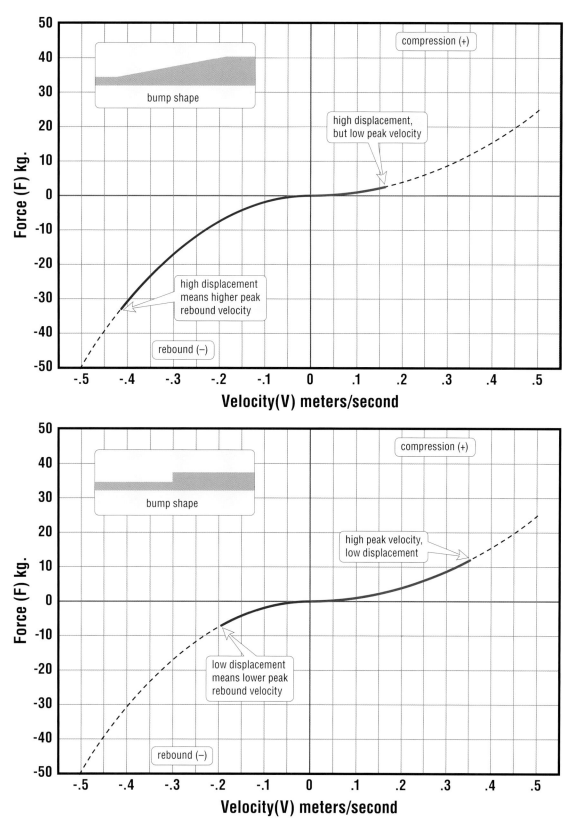

3.5 This illustration shows the effect of the shape of the bump given equal bike speeds. Notice the bumps are the same height as well. The ramped bump will not create as high of compression velocities as the square-edged one. This is shown by the compression not climbing up the compression damping curve as far. On the rebound stroke this shows the effect of the wheel deflecting off the square edge on compression causing it to use less travel. Less travel used means less energy stored in the spring, so lower peak rebound velocity will result.

for these markings or consult the owner's manual before you start making adjustments.

On rear shocks, the adjusters on the reservoir typically are for compression and the one on the shaft near the eyelet is for rebound damping. These adjusters—often referred to as "clickers"—have their limits and typically affect only a small portion of the entire damping range. Tweaking external adjusters will never make up for poor internal valving.

Most external rebound damping adjusters adjust low-speed damping. If there is only one compression adjuster, it is usually low-speed. If there are two compression adjusters, one is low-speed and the other is high-speed. Making external damping adjustments can never compensate for worn-out damping components or worn-out suspension oil. So, if your bike is wallowing like a '62 Cadillac with blown-out shocks, you might want to do some suspension rebuilding or replacement before you spend the rest of your life playing with the clickers.

REBOUND DAMPING

Let's take a closer look at rebound damping. Changes in rebound damping affect traction, the feeling of control, and ride plushness. If you look at Figure 3.6, you will see that all of these factors are plotted.

First let's look at plushness. With less rebound damping, the wheel moves quickly and the ride quality is plush even to the point of being "loose." As rebound is increased, the feeling of plushness drops off until, at the extreme end, the ride feels harsh.

Notice that there are no numbers on either axis, as the purpose of the graph is to communicate the concept. Also, the feeling of control is largely subjective, so it is hard to assign numbers to. Having said that, these charts are based on years of testing both on- and off-road machines and hold true in theory for virtually every type of vehicle. Keep in mind most riders don't ride at the limit of traction, and if you're not at the limit of traction, it can be quite difficult to tell if you've lost traction.

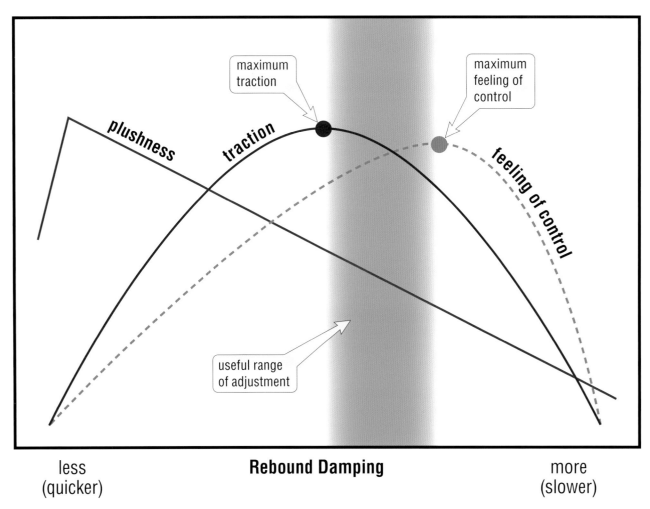

DAMPING

3.6 This shows the relationship between rebound damping and traction, control, and plushness. Note that when traction is falling off as rebound is increased, the feeling of control is still increasing. Most riders will benefit from using less rebound damping than they are used to.

Looking at the graph, you will notice that with too little rebound damping, there is very little traction available. When the tire hits a bump, the suspension compresses and the spring stores some of the energy. On the back side of the bump, the stored energy in the spring pushes the tire back down in an uncontrolled way. The tire is free to oscillate and can become so light as it bounces that it literally comes off the ground. Undamped oscillation is the enemy of traction. If the motorcycle is traveling in a straight line, the loss of traction will merely be uncomfortable. However, if this happens when the bike is leaned over in a turn, the loss of traction can cause the bike to slide out and crash.

Similarly, with an excess of rebound damping there is very little traction available. In this case, as the tire travels up the bump the spring is, again, storing energy. This time, however, when the tire attempts to move down the back side of the bump—pushed by the stored energy in the spring—the movement is slowed down excessively by the rebound damping. If the action is slowed enough, the tire will not be able to follow the downside of the bump fast enough to maintain consistent contact with the ground. This will cause a reduction or complete lack of traction.

When suspension with too much rebound damping encounters a series of bumps, it can lead to packing. This means the suspension doesn't return far enough, not reaching its original starting point. The available travel to absorb bumps becomes less and less, and at the same time it requires more and more force to initiate movement. This can reduce traction as well as make for a harsh ride.

Now let's suppose the initial rebound setting is already at the peak of traction. If we increase the rebound damping and the test rider has a leisurely pace on a racetrack or through a canyon, the resulting loss in traction may not be recognizable. However most riders will feel like there is more control.

Most riders believe that a bike is in control when they don't feel it wiggling around in the corners. Less wiggles feels like more traction, and more wiggles feels like less traction. It is important to note on the chart that the point at which the bikes feels the most "in control" is not when it has the highest amount of traction. Therefore, at the point of highest traction, the bike will wiggle around a little more than feels comfortable for many riders.

The main reasons why the point of maximum feeling of control and the point of maximum traction are so far apart for both dirt and pavement riders is because most riders are not riding on the "edge" of traction. And secondly, most don't relate decreasing rebound damping with improving traction.

For dirt, there is also the symptom of "kicking." It is the most commonly misdiagnosed problem on the rear end. It is thought to be a lack of rebound damping while in fact it is usually caused by either excessive stiffness or excessive bottoming. So the bike kicks and, to fix it, they slow the rebound. The rider will likely think the "kicking" is solved, and especially if the rider is prone to thinking that slowing

the rebound will cure the problem. The rider never recognizes that he lost traction and *gets used to the new feel*. And, in fact, any less damping than this will make the bike feel "loose" to him. The rebound is never sped back up: after all why would anyone want it to "kick" again? Hmmm . . .

On the paved end, many street riders and road racers "test" their suspension settings on perfectly smooth roads that hardly even need suspension. In such a scenario, an overabundance of damping provides the least amount of wiggling, additional pitch control (front to back movement), and, for them, the maximum feeling of control.

The job of the suspension engineer and tuner is to make the two peaks—max traction and max feeling of control—as close as possible. This is done by reshaping the damping curve and requires an understanding of high- and low-speed damping. However, some riders are so used to excessive rebound damping, you likely will never get the two curves to peak at the same point.

So where do you want to set rebound? Some would say where the curves cross, but this is not a measurable point. The useable range is between the two peaks. If the setting is to the left of the traction peak, you lose both traction and the feeling of control. If you are to the right of the feeling of control peak, you are losing both traction and control. Now, if the rider can get used to a little looser feeling, the gains in traction will improve lap times and tire life, and his "ideal feel peak" would be closer to the traction peak. Some riders cannot handle the looser feeling and end up closer to the control peak.

Sometimes it's possible to "see" differences in traction on dirt bikes. By trying different rebound settings in the same corner (particularly one with poor traction) you may notice a different level of roost coming off the rear tire. The rider must use the same line and the same gear and enter the corner at the same speed as much as possible. While many think a big roost looks like traction, the opposite may actually be true.

Go back to our earlier discussion of energy. Energy is the ability to do work and can be changed from one form to another. Power is the rate of doing work. The power created in the engine has to go somewhere: it can be turned into either projectiles or propulsion. Mathematically: $P = P + P$ or Power = Projectiles + Propulsion (silly but true).

All kidding aside, the message is important. After a certain point, more dirt flying off the back tire means less acceleration for the vehicle, and vice versa. Keep in mind that being in too low of a gear—particularly on an open bike—will cause the wheel to spin and throw up quite a roost. This may look and sound fast but in fact is quite the opposite.

A word of caution: being at the limit of traction is a delicate position to be in, and it is often not possible to tell any difference in traction without pushing traction to its limit. Under these circumstances it's easy to go too far and crash. Keep in mind that different brands or models of tires react differently at the edge of traction. Some are very forgiving and some go away abruptly. While testing, it is vitally important to keep in mind that while slowing rebound down you might be giving up traction.

We know that too little rebound damping and too much rebound damping can be equally bad when it comes to both traction and a feeling of control. At the very least, the optimum range of rebound settings is somewhere between the peak of traction and the peak of the feeling of control. While there is no owner's manual that can tell you where to set the adjusters for maximum traction, testing to find this setting can be quite rewarding.

HOW TO TEST REBOUND DAMPING

So how do you find the point at which the rebound damping settings will provide maximum traction?

The first method is a "push test." This test requires that the spring setup is in the right range. Also, it is vital that friction is minimal: if the suspension suffers from an appreciable amount of friction, this test is worthless. (Telescopic forks on the front end are notorious for excessive friction, so be aware.) The push test can be very useful, but it may require quite a bit of testing to get the feel of it.

We'll discuss how to test the rear suspension, but the procedure is basically the same for the front. Start by measuring sag, paying particular attention to the "stiction zone." If stiction is excessive, you will not be able to use this method.

Stand next to the motorcycle with the front wheel pointed straight ahead. Push down on the seat fairly aggressively and watch what happens when the suspension rebounds, or moves upwards. Let your hands follow the seat as it comes up: this means you are not holding it down nor are you letting your hands completely off the seat. You are looking for two things: how fast the suspension rebounds and the number (if any) of bounces that it takes just after it reaches the top of its stroke.

Too much rebound damping looks like this: you push down on the seat and you can see the suspension move upward slowly. As it slowly reaches the top of the rebound stroke it stops all movement.

Too little rebound damping looks somewhat different: you push down and the suspension rebounds nearly as fast as you can remove your hands. In addition to a quick upward movement when it reaches the top of its stroke, it moves back down again and oscillates two or more times.

Here is what a good starting point for rebound damping looks like: after the suspension is compressed, it will rebound. When the suspension reaches the top of its stroke, it will barely overshoot and settle down to its free sag point (a very small, single bounce).

Keep in mind you can only feel low-speed rebound damping with this test and not high-speed.

If friction is excessive, it will appear that there is more rebound damping than there actually is, and this test will be misleading! A considerable number of vehicles out there have so much linkage or bearing friction that you can literally take all the oil out of the shocks, lift up the wheel, and it will stay where you place it. In this case the friction feels very similar to damping and can fool you. This is where a measurement of the stiction zone can be invaluable.

Another thing that can change the feel is the stiffness of the seat. If the seat is soft, the compression will feel softer and the rebound will feel slower. You may want to find something harder to push on, like a tail section. Using the tail section instead of the seat will give you more leverage and the spring and compression damping will feel softer. Having said this, if you do enough push tests and correlate them with track testing, you can get quite good at initial setup.

The second, and best, way to adjust rebound damping is to go testing and make a series of runs with different rebound adjustments. Create a bracket of settings by changing the adjustment in one direction until it gets worse. Then go in the other direction until it gets worse. If you do this, your setting in the middle was the best. But remember: if you are not on the edge of traction, you may not be aware of the change. This is not easy. As you are testing, pay attention to how the feeling of control changes and select a setting that gives you the balance you like.

On some bikes with adjustable rebound damping, you can change the settings and work up to this point. Not all rebound damping adjusters are equal, however. On some motorcycles the range of adjustment is too far one way or the other. For example, sometimes when the rebound adjuster is set to the maximum (slowest) setting, the resulting rebound damping is still too quick. This is quite common on street forks particularly in the 1990s and early 2000s. On dirt bikes it is just as common to see rear shocks with too much rebound damping even at minimum settings. This is a telltale sign the suspension needs to be modified internally. Virtually all motorcycles can benefit from aftermarket valving and personalized setup.

If you own a motorcycle without rebound damping adjustment, you may still be able to make it better simply by changing the oil. As we discussed previously, most oil's viscosity will break down with use and the oil will become thinner, or less viscous. This is quite often overlooked. It's also worth noting here that rear shocks on some bikes are not rebuildable and therefore cannot have their oil changed.

Because you may not know what weight to put in (stock weights may not be viscous enough, or in some rare cases, too viscous), a quick check at www.racetech.com will usually provide the information. Unfortunately, while increasing oil viscosity may improve rebound damping by slowing it down, it will also increase compression damping. This may result in excessive compression damping, but fortunately there are fixes for this.

Remember that external rebound adjusters are typically low-speed adjusters. Even if you get a good setting for traction using them, there may be huge gains to be had from internal valving changes as well. Not only is it possible to move the

DAMPING

peaks closer together, you can also improve control when using large amounts of travel—like on big bumps or whoop sections in the dirt—or make improvements in pitch control, particularly on the front end of a street or road race bike.

COMPRESSION DAMPING

Compression damping is one of the most misunderstood components of suspension tuning. Understanding how compression damping affects ride quality goes a long way toward demystifying the "black art" of how suspension works.

A fundamental difference exists between compression and rebound damping. Compression damping has to deal with a much wider range of velocities generated by bumps of different sizes and shapes. Rebound damping, on the other hand, primarily has to control the energy of the compressed spring and, therefore, its adjustments are easier to perform.

Compression velocity—and therefore damping—is affected by the shape, as well as the size, of the bump as well as the speed at which you hit it. Bumps that have a more square or sharp-edged shape cause the suspension to move rapidly upward, while a bump with a gradual slope, or more rounded shape, causes slower suspension movement. This is the reason for separate low- and high-speed compression damping. Remember, the terms *high-* and *low-speed damping*

refer not to the forward speed of the motorcycle, but rather the velocity of the suspension movement.

In the past, many suspension tuners have considered compression damping a necessary evil, meaning that less was better. Perhaps this way of thinking stems from the limitations of old-style damping rod forks. Damping rod forks have what is known as "orifice-style" damping, which can be both too harsh and too mushy at the same time. (More on this in a moment.)

With the advent of cartridge-type forks found on most sportbikes and Race Tech Gold Valve Cartridge Emulators (aftermarket damping control valves for damping rod forks), the ability to control the shape of the compression-damping curve has improved dramatically.

To study the effects of compression damping we'll first look at compression damping as a whole and leave the details of high- and low-speed for later. Compression damping is vitally important as it affects traction, plushness, and bottoming resistance as well as control. (See Figure 3.7.)

Let's first consider bottoming resistance as it relates to plushness. Notice that the more compression damping there is, the more resistance the suspension has to bottoming out. Compression damping force is added to the spring forces to help resist bottoming. At the same time that bottoming resistance increases, the feeling of plushness decreases making the ride harsher.

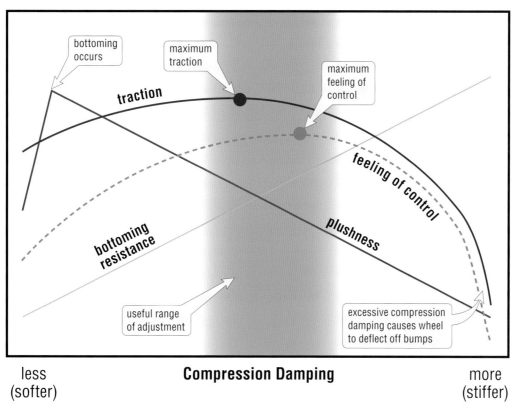

3.7 Notice that, as with rebound damping, both traction and control drop off as compression damping is increased. It doesn't fall off as rapidly as with rebound. Notice also that the peak for control is to the right of traction once again.

As compression damping is decreased (left side of the graph), plushness increases up to a point. In extreme cases, when very little compression damping is used, the plushness can actually decrease. This occurs on big bumps when the suspension bottoms and feels harsh. In this case many riders are not aware that the harshness is a result of bottoming. In fact, I would estimate only 50 percent of riders (even really good ones) can tell if the front end bottoms and only 1 in 20 can tell when the rear is bottoming.

On smaller bumps, less damping results in a plusher ride. It may seem obvious, but you need to have the right amount of compression damping—not too much, nor too little. Bottoming resistance and ride plushness are a compromise. You may need to sacrifice one for the other. The job of a suspension designer/tuner is to have the least amount of compromise in both areas. More on this later.

So, more compression damping means more bottoming resistance: pretty simple. But the creation of damping requires velocity, so in a situation like bottoming mid-turn on a road racer where there is very little suspension velocity (the suspension is being compressed due to centripetal acceleration), compression damping is not the answer to this particular bottoming problem—springs are.

Let's examine the effects of compression damping on traction. Imagine you're riding along and you hit even a small bump. If there is too little compression damping, the suspension will not have enough resistance to upward wheel movement. This means that the wheel still has vertical inertia at the crest of the bump, so it will continue to move upward. Remember Newton's First Law of Motion: "Every object in a state of uniform motion tends to remain in that state of motion unless an external force is applied to it." As the wheel continues to move upward, it continues compressing the suspension past the crest of the bump. This causes the tire to unweight and possibly even lose contact with the road surface as it crests the bump, causing a loss of traction.

At the other extreme, excessive compression damping will give too much resistance to suspension movement, thereby compressing the tire and deflecting the sprung mass upward. Not only can this cause an uncomfortable or harsh ride, but this upward velocity of the chassis unweights the wheel, just like having too little compression damping. In extreme cases of too much compression damping and a large or square-edged bump, the wheel comes entirely off the ground as it skips over the bumps, causing a dramatic loss of traction. In bumpy turns at extreme lean angles, you may experience difficulty holding a line as the bike will tend to drift to the outside of the turn due to the loss of traction.

If you're hitting a series of bumps with too much compression damping, the suspension can actually pump up as the wheels hit successive bumps. This is the opposite of packing caused by too much rebound damping. As the traction curve shows on the graph, traction falls off much more quickly with too much compression damping. So if you

have to guess how much compression damping to use, err on the side of too little.

Dive is a term used to describe the front end compression that occurs during braking. In this case, compression damping controls the rate of downward movement. The maximum amount of travel used in the forks is determined by a combination of the spring force (including air pressure) and the compression damping (along with friction of course). More damping makes the forks compress slower and may use less suspension travel. Less compression damping causes the forks to compress faster and use more suspension travel.

One of the biggest misconceptions about compression damping is that the faster you ride, the more you need. It is true that the faster you go, the harder you hit bumps—you may need more compression damping to control bottoming. It is also true that some racers that are more abrupt with the application of the brakes and the throttle may prefer a slower compression response rate. However, if you are not bottoming and you can learn to apply the brakes and throttle more smoothly, you may not need any more compression damping.

Our preferred method is to first determine proper spring rates (see the spring chapter or the charts at www.racetech.com) and then use only as much compression damping as you need for pitch control (rocking of the chassis front and back during acceleration and braking) and bottoming control.

Keep in mind that the shape of the damping curve is critical. In this section we simplified our description of symptoms and talked about damping as a whole, but in real life the bike may need more low-speed damping and less high-speed to achieve the best setup (or vice versa). The compression side is what good tuners spend a lot of their time on—they're always seeking the right curve to maximize bottoming resistance while maintaining plushness and providing a good "feel" for the ground.

HOW TO TEST COMPRESSION DAMPING

Unlike rebound damping, it is hard to push the suspension down fast enough by hand to tell a lot about compression damping. Therefore, you will need to find a suitable road or section of dirt to use for testing. Ideally it will have both large and small, rounded- and sharp-edged bumps on it.

When there is too much compression damping, you will feel the bike hitting the front sides of bumps somewhat like the way a suspensionless bicycle reacts when it hits bumps. The ride will also feel harsh over moderate and even small bumps. Keep in mind, however, that excessive friction or binding can feel the same way.

In the case of too little compression damping, the front end will tend to dive quickly under braking (lack of pitch control). It can have an overall mushy or vague feel and may bottom out easily. If the suspension bottoms excessively on the front side of a bump, it can launch the bike and rider into the air. This can feel like excessive compression damping—it can be very difficult to tell the difference. More information on this distinction is available in the troubleshooting chapter.

On a dirt bike it can be valuable to watch the roost off the rear wheel. If you have a rough straightaway with the type of dirt that will show a visible roost, watch for an even stream coming off the back wheel as the bike is ridden over the bumps. If the roost starts and stops, it is not maintaining traction. Often, this is because the compression is too stiff and the suspension is deflecting. This can also be caused by a too soft compression setting. Next make a change in the direction you think is best and see if it gets better or worse. Remember, too, that rebound damping can cause this phenomenon.

Another clue on dirt bikes can be gathered with your ears. On a rough, choppy section, listen for evenness of the engine. If the rpm are going up and down a lot, the wheel is not on the ground much. The two most likely reasons are that it may be deflecting off the bump because it is too stiff, or it could be skipping over the bumps because the rebound is too slow.

Personal preference has a lot to do with the "ideal" setup, as some riders like a firmer ride with more bottoming resistance while others like it plusher. It is not about right or wrong, it's just personal preference and what will make that rider the fastest they can be.

DAMPING ROD FORKS (ORIFICE DAMPING)

We've discussed compression and rebound damping, including what each does and why they are necessary to maintain traction. Now we'll move on to the various types of fork and shock designs that are used to control damping.

The most common fork design is the damping rod. I know, I know: damping rods? Why damping rods? If you understand damping rods and their limitations and solutions, it will be easier to understand cartridges. Once you understand cartridges, it will be easier to understand shocks. This way, once we get to shock design, it won't take much effort to cover the subject.

Damping rod forks have been around for years and today can be commonly found on most cruisers, standards, trail bikes, dual-sports, minis, and most vintage bikes. Damping rod forks are less expensive to manufacture but don't offer much sophistication in the way of damping control.

DAMPING ROD ANATOMY

Figure 3.8 shows the components of a damping rod fork design. The fork slider at the bottom is attached to the motorcycle's front axle and the fork tubes are inserted into the upper and lower triple clamps. Inside the forks are the springs and damping rods. The main fork spring is located directly on top of the damping rod that is fastened to the fork slider with a bolt at the bottom. The main spring supports the sprung mass of the front of the motorcycle and rider. There is another smaller spring called a top-out spring located between the bottom of the damping rod and bottom of the fork tube. The top-out spring keeps the fork tube from banging into the

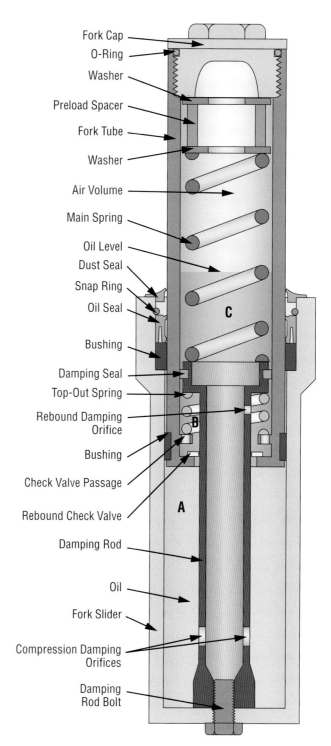

3.8 Damper Rod Components

damping rod as the forks extend fully. Most modern damping rod forks use a top-out spring.

The top of the damping rod is a piston and has a piston ring that seals on the inside of the fork tube. The piston ring keeps suspension oil from passing between the damping rod and the inner fork tube.

DAMPING ROD COMPRESSION STROKE

When the fork is compressed (Figure 3.9), you can picture the fork tube (the upper portion) moving downward into chamber A. The volume of oil displaced is that which the fork tube displaces. (This means the wall thickness, not the outer diameter or inner diameter.)

As the fork compresses, the volume in chamber A is getting smaller while the volume in chamber B is getting larger. This means the oil pressure in chamber A increases while the pressure in chamber B decreases. However, as soon as movement occurs, the rebound check valve opens and allows fluid to pass easily into chamber B. This means the pressure in chamber B is only slightly less than in A, and you can practically consider chambers A and B to be one chamber (AB).

At this point, the volume the fork tube displaces still needs to get out of chamber AB. It escapes through the compression damping holes located at the bottom of the damping rod, up through the center of the damping rod, and out into chamber C. It can also travel out through the rebound hole(s) in chamber B, but this is a much smaller volume.

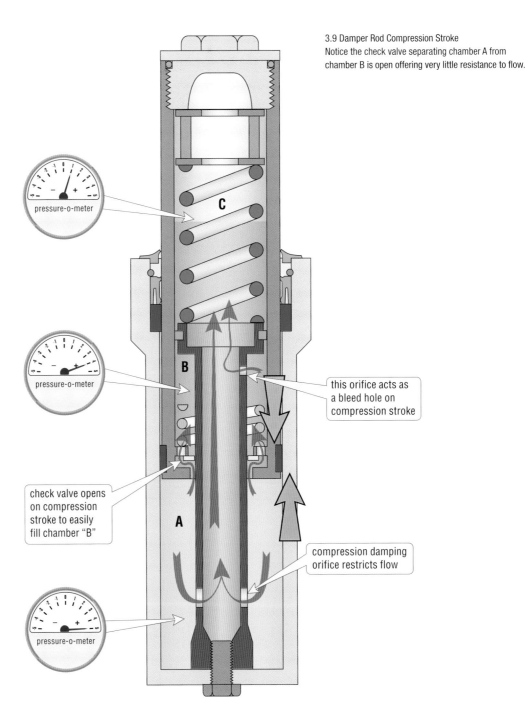

3.9 Damper Rod Compression Stroke
Notice the check valve separating chamber A from chamber B is open offering very little resistance to flow.

pressure-o-meter

pressure-o-meter

pressure-o-meter

this orifice acts as a bleed hole on compression stroke

check valve opens on compression stroke to easily fill chamber "B"

compression damping orifice restricts flow

DAMPING

38

Compression damping is controlled by the number and size of the compression damping holes and the rebound damping hole(s) along with the oil viscosity. Note that the rebound holes actually *reduce* the overall compression damping caused by the compression holes. This type of damping is referred to as orifice-style damping because the resistance is created by forcing oil through holes.

It is also important to note that the pressure in chamber C builds as the air volume decreases. This pressure in chamber C is dependent on the initial pressure, the compression ratio (oil level), and the travel.

As long as the compression stroke is not too rapid, orifice damping can provide a reasonably comfortable ride as the front wheel hits small bumps. Unfortunately, not all bumps are rounded and small in size—when a square-edged or large bump is encountered, orifice damping can create a very harsh ride. Because oil is not compressible, the faster the fork compresses, the faster the oil is forced through the compression damping holes.

Orifice-style damping increases very rapidly as velocity increases. In fact, the damping force increases with the square of the velocity. This means every time the velocity doubles, the damping increases by four times. We have illustrated this (see Figure 3.10) by showing the thick flow arrow being squeezed at the entrance of the small orifices on a high-speed hit.

You can see the compression stroke displayed on a shock dyno graph in Figure 3.11. Notice that as the speed builds, the force builds. This happens slowly at first but then increases rapidly before going nearly vertical. It is almost as if the oil flow—and therefore the fork velocity—reaches a speed limit. This is not absolutely true, of course, but because the damping force becomes very high, the maximum velocity the fork reaches, in practice, becomes limited. This causes the wheel to deflect off of square-edged bumps and the ride gets harsh, indicated by the curves going into the "pain zone."

Another drawback of orifice damping occurs in the low-speed range of movement. When braking, the front

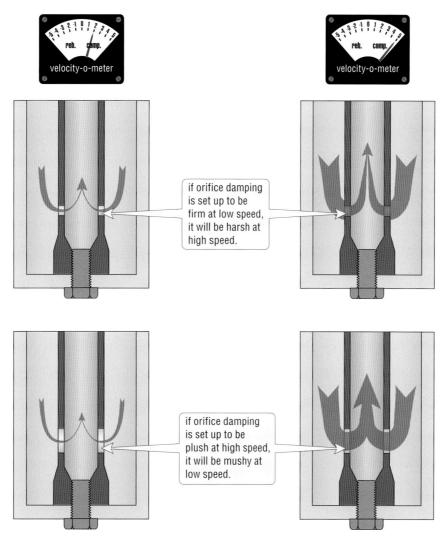

3.10 The down-side of orifice damping is it is either too mushy and soft at low speeds or way too harsh on high speed hits.

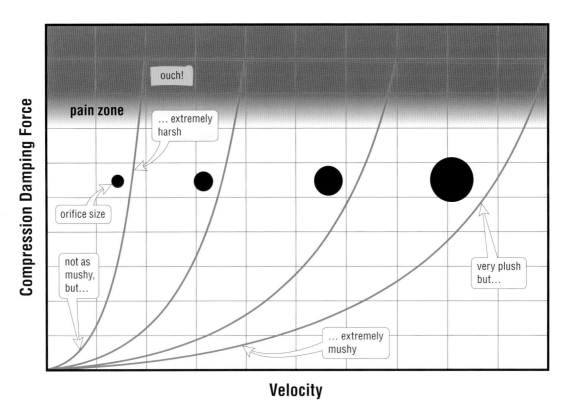

3.11 This figure displays damping curves for four compression hole sizes. Notice the characteristic "fish hook" shape remains for all the curves. Notice also the tradeoffs involved.

end dives rather slowly in comparison to the high velocities created on an abrupt hit of a square-edged hole or rock at high vehicle speed. At these low damper velocities there is not much resistance to flow and the forks feel mushy and dive relatively rapidly. In fact, when going through long duration dips or gullies—even if they are not very deep—the forks can bottom.

Perhaps you've considered increasing the compression damping hole size as the solution for the harshness problem. This change in orifice size is illustrated in the compression damping curves in Figure 3.11. Notice that the characteristic "fish hook" shape of the curve remains. While less "mushy," the smaller hole will be excessively harsh on the square-edged hits. The larger damping hole will be mushier, though it will be better at high speed. This style of damping seems to provide the worst of both worlds—harshness and bottoming.

Note also that orifice-style damping doesn't require round holes. Any fixed orifice will do: square, triangular, oval, and so on.

DAMPING ROD REBOUND STROKE

Now we'll take a look at the flow of oil when the fork rebounds (see Figure 3.12). First the forks extend as the spring pushes on the damping rod. The rebound check valve then closes and chamber B gets smaller, raising its pressure on rebound to the highest level in the fork. There are two ways oil can get

out of chamber B: first through the rebound orifices routed to the inside of the damping rod and, second, between the inner diameter of the check valve and the outer diameter of the damping rod directly into chamber A. Rebound damping is the resistance to this flow.

Chamber A on the other hand, is getting larger on the rebound stroke, and therefore has the lowest pressure. This low pressure in chamber A causes oil to be sucked back in, refilling it.

Just like on the compression stroke, rebound resistance on a damping rod fork is created through orifice damping. Rebound damping, however, is a much simpler job than compression damping. Rebound only has to control the force of the fork spring, whereas compression damping has to deal with whatever forces the road or track dish out. Maximum compression velocities often range from two to six times greater than those during rebound. Thus the limitations of orifice damping are less critical for rebound than for compression.

A major potential problem of a damping rod fork is cavitation (see Figure 3.13). Cavitation is the formation of vapor bubbles in a flowing liquid caused by a decrease in pressure. This occurs specifically in areas where the pressure of the liquid falls below its vapor pressure. This is the same phenomenon as boiling, but in this case it is caused by a decrease in pressure rather than the addition of heat.

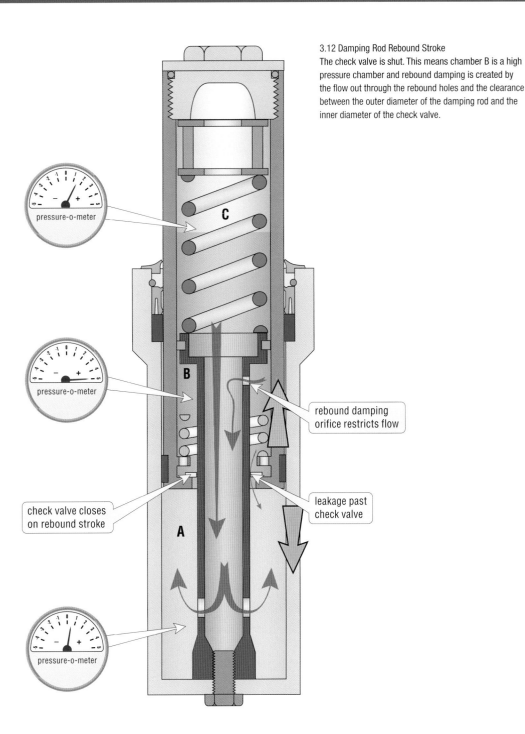

3.12 Damping Rod Rebound Stroke
The check valve is shut. This means chamber B is a high pressure chamber and rebound damping is created by the flow out through the rebound holes and the clearance between the outer diameter of the damping rod and the inner diameter of the check valve.

pressure-o-meter

C

pressure-o-meter

B

rebound damping orifice restricts flow

check valve closes on rebound stroke

leakage past check valve

A

pressure-o-meter

This creates two problems. First, it makes the oil compressible because it contains vapor bubbles or "voids," thereby decreasing the oil's damping characteristics. Second, when the void in the oil rapidly collapses, it produces a shock wave that can damage and pit the surface of the parts (this second issue is much more of a problem in shocks than forks). The potential for cavitation increases at lower pressures and higher temperatures.

On the rebound stroke, chamber A is getting larger and sucking oil back into it. The greater the resistance to flow is at the compression orifices (smaller holes or thicker oil), the

greater the potential for cavitation. Stiffer springs and hotter oil also increase the potential problem.

THE PROGRESSIVE MYTH

This brings us back to the age-old question: "How do you make it firm and plush at the same time?" Most suspension tuners have believed that the solution was to make it more progressive. Perhaps you've noticed the shape of the orifice-style damping curve and thought to yourself: "Wow, that curve is really progressive!"

41

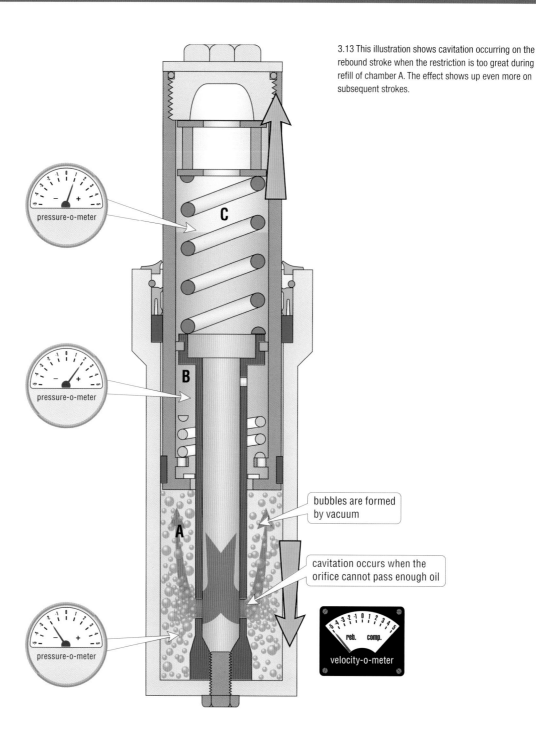

3.13 This illustration shows cavitation occurring on the rebound stroke when the restriction is too great during refill of chamber A. The effect shows up even more on subsequent strokes.

bubbles are formed by vacuum

cavitation occurs when the orifice cannot pass enough oil

In fact, orifice-style damping is the most progressive type of damping there is. But with the shortcomings of orifice-style damping (harshness and bottoming), you can see that more progressive isn't necessarily better.

Consider the compression damping curve labeled "digressive" in Figure 3.14. At low speed it has a lot more compression damping. This will make the action much firmer when hitting the brakes, thereby controlling dive (the front end compressing during braking). It will also help bottoming because on every compression stroke, no matter

what maximum velocity is reached, the velocity begins and ends at zero. This means the damper sees low-speed damping twice per stroke, so any increase in low-speed damping tends to improve bottoming resistance.

Also notice that, at high velocity, the curve doesn't get into the "pain zone." You might think, "Yeah, but it's heading there." In actuality, there is a maximum velocity that the suspension sees in the real world. This maximum velocity is partially dependent on the size and shape of the bumps being hit, the vehicle speed, the mass of the bike, and the suspension setup. The highest velocity I've ever recorded on the ShockClock is 15 m/sec on a "short" supercross landing (the rider hit the face, didn't quite make it).

Granted, that is very fast, but it also has some implications—changes to the damping curve at velocities over 15 m/sec don't have any practical effect even in supercross racing.

GOLD VALVE CARTRIDGE EMULATOR FORK

Fortunately for damping rod fork owners, there is an elegant way to change the shape of the damping curve with the addition of Race Tech Gold Valve Cartridge Emulators. I invented Emulators back in the early 1990s to provide the compression damping curve of a cartridge fork, make it tunable, and offer it at a very reasonable cost.

With the Emulator, low-speed compression has a much better feeling of control while high-speed compression absorbs large and sharp-edged bumps without harshness. This provides the rider with better steering response and causes the bike to feel more planted in the turns, yet more comfortable at the same time.

You can see in Figure 3.15 that the Gold Valve Cartridge Emulator sits on the top of the damping rod and is held in place with the main spring. The Emulator performs two jobs: it provides a digressive compression damping curve that is adjustable, and separates compression from rebound damping so that both can be independently tuned. Let's take a look at how it works.

The Emulator takes over compression damping duties from the damping rod. To do this the damping rod compression holes are enlarged and, depending on the model, increased in number. With larger flow area the restriction at the compression holes becomes negligible. It is certainly still there, but the effect is so small it is no longer significant. Instead, all the compression damping takes place in the Emulator.

With the Emulator installed on top of the damping rod, low-speed damping is controlled by low-speed bleed hole(s) in the valve piston (see Figure 3.15). Oil flows unrestricted from chamber A to the inside of the damping rod, then up toward chamber C. At the lowest velocities there is not enough pressure to open the main valve piston and all the oil goes through the Emulator's low-speed bleed hole.

At higher velocities, particularly when the wheel encounters a square-edged bump or when landing from a jump, the forks must move rapidly. The oil pressure builds in chamber A and beneath the Emulator to a point that lifts the Emulator piston off its seat, allowing the oil to flow into chamber C (see Figure 3.16). The opening pressure is adjustable via the valve's spring preload. Changing the valve spring rate controls the slope of the damping curve once the piston opens—check out the range of adjustment available (Figure 3.17).

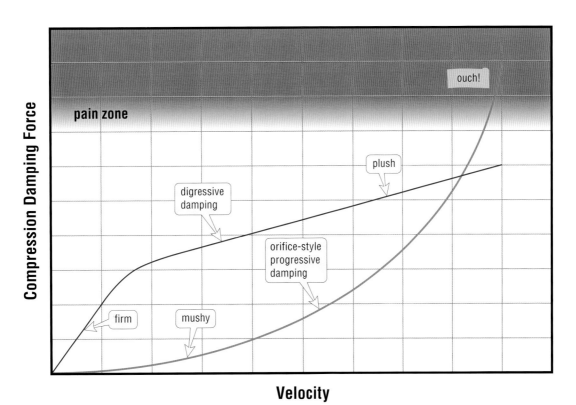

3.14 Many tuners over the years have erroneously believed that the more progressive the compression damping is the better it is. This style of curve actually gives the worst of all worlds—mushy and harsh. A better solution is a digressive curve for most applications.

Here is a closer look at the details of the Emulator (see Figure 3.18). The mid-speed compression damping adjustment is accomplished by changing the valve spring preload that pushes the piston against the Emulator's valve face. By increasing the valve spring preload, more pressure is required for valve opening.

Once installed, making changes is relatively easy. First remove the fork cap and main spring. Use either a long welding rod bent over at the end or a "parts grabber" and lift the Emulator out of the fork tube. Adjust the valve spring preload and reinstall. This can be done on many bikes with the forks still mounted.

Let's look at rebound (see Figure 3.19). Installation of the Emulator does not change rebound damping, therefore, adjustment of rebound damping is made by changing the oil viscosity. Though it may not sound like it, this is still a significant change. In a standard damping rod fork with no Emulator, changing the oil's viscosity will change rebound damping, but at the expense of changing compression damping in a similar way. With an Emulator,

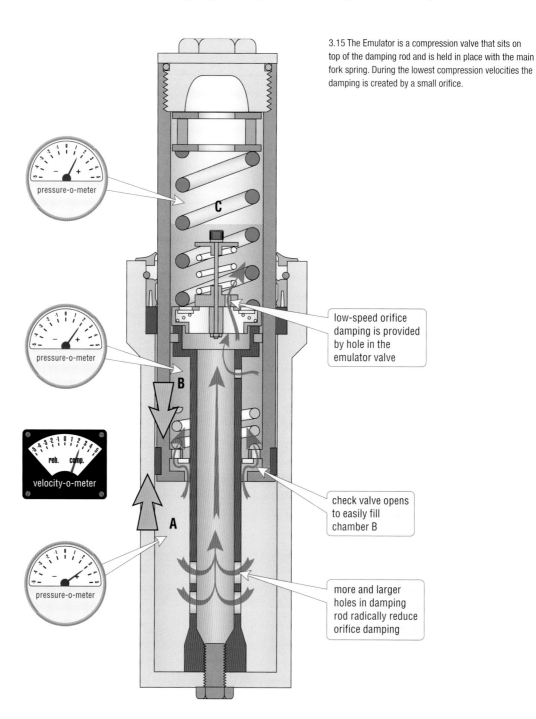

3.15 The Emulator is a compression valve that sits on top of the damping rod and is held in place with the main fork spring. During the lowest compression velocities the damping is created by a small orifice.

pressure-o-meter

pressure-o-meter

reb.   comp.
velocity-o-meter

pressure-o-meter

low-speed orifice damping is provided by hole in the emulator valve

check valve opens to easily fill chamber B

more and larger holes in damping rod radically reduce orifice damping it doesn't matter what weight oil is used to obtain ideal rebound damping because compression damping can be adjusted separately.

So how effective are Emulators? Not only did Jamie James win the AMA National Road Race Championship in 1994 with a factory Yamaha using Emulators, but Lee was part of an endurance team that won the WERA National Endurance Championship in 2001. The team had two identical Suzuki SV650s that were ridden by three riders. The only difference between the two motorcycles was the damping controls in the front forks. One bike used Race Tech Gold Valve Cartridge Emulators on the stock damping rod forks and the other

motorcycle had full cartridge front forks. The lap times were virtually identical between the two setups.

Dirt bikes have had similar results. Back when the Factory Suzuki Team was just making the switch to four-strokes, it campaigned DR350s with both Race Tech cartridges and Emulators. The feedback from the riders was that both were excellent. Many mini bike, vintage, motocross, and road race championships continue to be won with Emulators.

STANDARD CARTRIDGE FORKS
Standard cartridge forks are more sophisticated than damping rod forks. From outward appearances, right-side-up standard

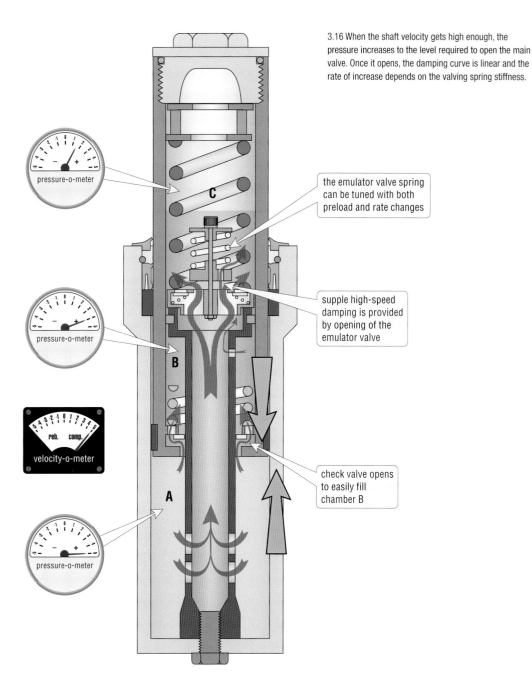

3.16 When the shaft velocity gets high enough, the pressure increases to the level required to open the main valve. Once it opens, the damping curve is linear and the rate of increase depends on the valving spring stiffness.

the emulator valve spring can be tuned with both preload and rate changes

supple high-speed damping is provided by opening of the emulator valve

check valve opens to easily fill chamber B

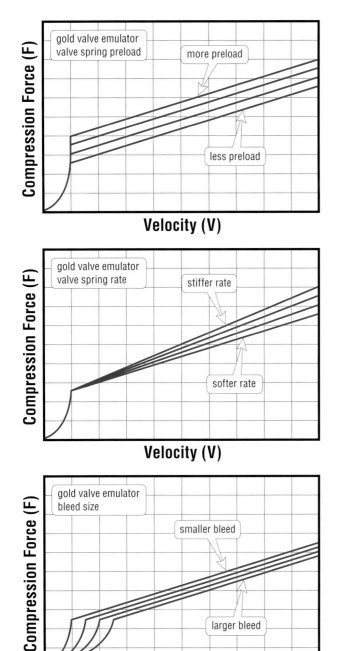

3.17 Emulator adjustments of valve spring preload, valve spring rate, and bleed hole size create tremendous tuning flexibility.

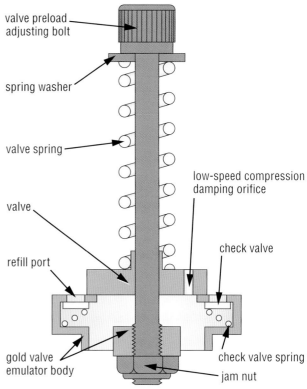

3.18 Emulator Components

cartridge forks look very similar to damping rod forks, but the difference is on the inside.

In standard cartridge forks, the damping is done inside a metal cartridge, hence the name. The cartridge tube is attached to the bottom of the fork leg. The main spring, located inside the fork tube, sits between the top of the cartridge and the fork cap. The drawing shows a small top-out spring that is external to the cartridge.

Inside the cartridge are two valving assemblies—the one for compression is located in the bottom of the cartridge. The valve assembly that governs rebound damping is located on the end of the damping rod at the top. The other end of the damping rod is attached to the fork cap.

Most cartridge forks also have external adjustments for rebound and compression damping. The low-speed rebound adjustment screw is located at the top of the fork cap. The adjustment screw is connected to a long rod that extends down into the cartridge. The end of the rod (or a separate needle) has a taper that acts as a needle valve, controlling the oil flow through the low-speed rebound orifice. When the adjustment screw is turned in (clockwise) the needle is lowered deeper into the hole, restricting the flow of oil and increasing damping. This low-speed adjuster also affects high-speed rebound—as it continues to flow at high speeds—but not to the extent that it affects low-speed rebound.

The low-speed compression adjuster is located at the bottom of the fork leg. (On some models the screw is located on the side of the fork leg.) It works in a similar manner as the rebound adjuster. We'll take a closer look to see how both low- and high-speed damping are accomplished, starting with the compression stroke on a cartridge fork.

Let's say the front wheel encounters a small, round-shaped bump and the fork compresses. Upon compression, the damping rod goes into the cartridge and displaces fluid.

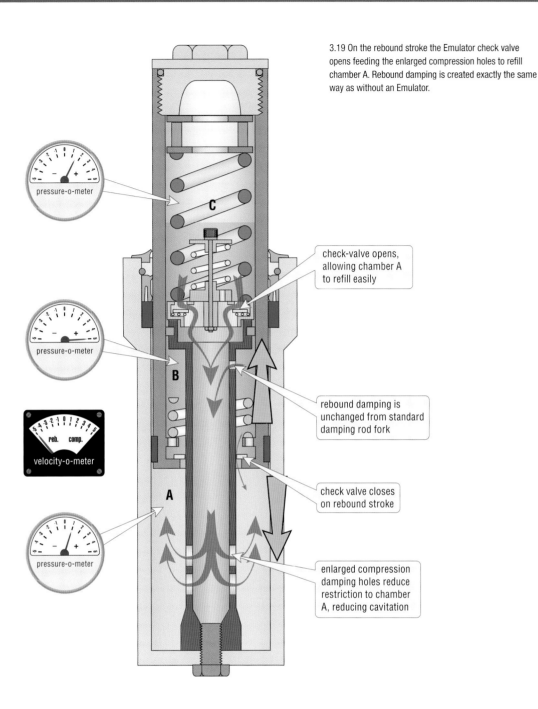

3.19 On the rebound stroke the Emulator check valve opens feeding the enlarged compression holes to refill chamber A. Rebound damping is created exactly the same way as without an Emulator.

check-valve opens, allowing chamber A to refill easily

rebound damping is unchanged from standard damping rod fork

check valve closes on rebound stroke

enlarged compression damping holes reduce restriction to chamber A, reducing cavitation

pressure-o-meter

velocity-o-meter
reb. comp.

C

B

A

This volume of oil (the volume the damping rod displaces) must exit the cartridge. In a standard cartridge fork it is this volume of fluid that controls compression damping.

In Figure 3.21, chamber A is getting smaller, so it has the highest oil pressure. Notice that the rebound check valve is opened as the fork compresses. The check valve creates very little resistance to flow and allows chamber B to fill easily. This means chamber B has only a slightly lower oil pressure than A (notice this is very similar to chambers A and B in a damping rod fork). Chamber C has the lowest pressure.

At very low velocities, all of the flow out of the cartridge will pass through the adjustable low-speed compression orifice. As long as the compression stroke moves slowly enough, the low-speed compression damping circuit in the compression base valve will control all the flow of oil.

Now let's look at high-speed compression. As the shaft velocity increases, so does the resistance to flow through the low-speed adjuster circuit. This causes the pressure in chamber A to increase. At a pressure determined by the stiffness of the shim valving stack, the shims deflect and the port opens. Note that oil still passes through the low-speed compression orifice, but with higher pressure, the bulk of the flow passes through the high-speed damping circuit.

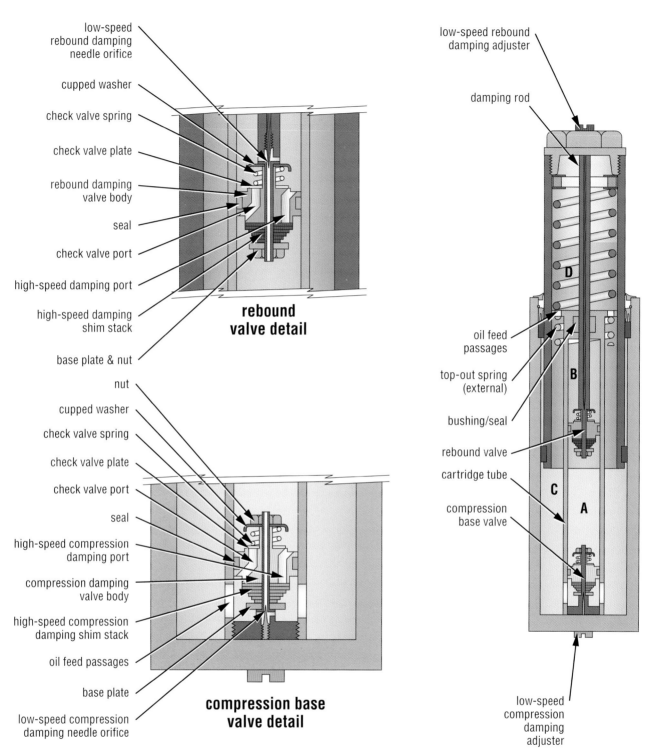

low-speed rebound damping needle orifice

cupped washer

check valve spring

check valve plate

rebound damping valve body

seal

check valve port

high-speed damping port

high-speed damping shim stack

base plate & nut

rebound valve detail

nut

cupped washer

check valve spring

check valve plate

check valve port

seal

high-speed compression damping port

compression damping valve body

high-speed compression damping shim stack

oil feed passages

base plate

low-speed compression damping needle orifice

compression base valve detail

low-speed rebound damping adjuster

damping rod

oil feed passages

top-out spring (external)

bushing/seal

rebound valve

cartridge tube

compression base valve

low-speed compression damping adjuster

3.20 Standard Cartridge Fork Components

In Figure 3.22 you can see that the compression shim stack consists of a series of special small washers. These small washers act like springs: as oil pressure exerts force on the shim stack they deflect, allowing oil to flow past them and out of the cartridge. The individual shims that make up the shim stack can be changed in number, diameter, and thickness to control the amount of damping. (It should be noted that even though the drawing shows oil flow at the right side of the shim stack, actual oil flow takes place around the entire circumference of the valve. It is drawn this way to illustrate two sets of ports, one set flowing in each direction.)

DAMPING

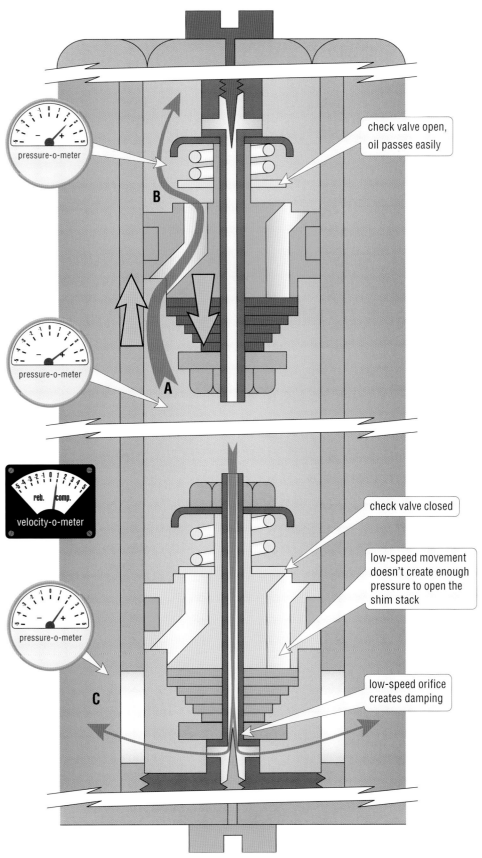

check valve open, oil passes easily

B

pressure-o-meter

A

pressure-o-meter

reb. comp.

velocity-o-meter

check valve closed

low-speed movement doesn't create enough pressure to open the shim stack

pressure-o-meter

C

low-speed orifice creates damping

3.21 Standard Cartridge Fork Low-Speed Compression

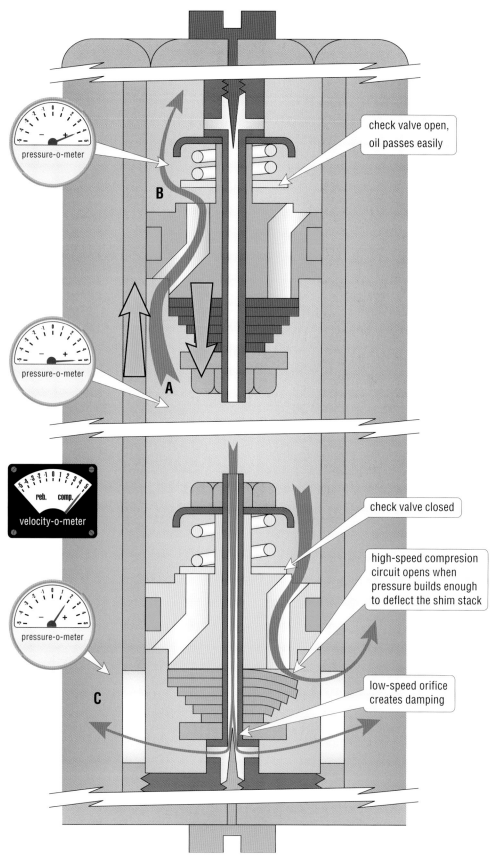

pressure-o-meter

check valve open,
oil passes easily

B

A

velocity-o-meter

reb. comp.

pressure-o-meter

check valve closed

high-speed compresion
circuit opens when
pressure builds enough
to deflect the shim stack

low-speed orifice
creates damping

C

3.22 Standard Cartridge Fork High-Speed Compression

REBOUND DAMPING

Rebound damping on the standard cartridge fork design works in a similar manner to compression damping (see Figure 3.23). As the fork extends, the check valve closes and chamber B gets smaller, making it the highest pressure chamber in the fork. Chamber A is getting bigger and therefore has the lowest pressure.

At low-speed rebound velocities, there is not enough pressure to open the rebound shim stack and all the fluid flows from chamber B into chamber A through the low-speed rebound orifice. During low-speed rebound, the rebound adjuster needle controls the flow of oil.

During high-speed rebound, the pressure in chamber B is high enough to open the rebound shim stack (see Figure 3.24). Oil certainly continues to flow through the low-speed rebound circuit, but the majority of oil will go through the bending shim circuit. Just as with compression damping, the rebound shim stack can be tuned by changing the number, thickness, and diameter of shims.

Let's not forget the process of refilling chamber A. The entire volume of chamber B gets transferred to chamber A, but this is not enough volume to completely refill chamber A—it is deficient by the volume of the damping rod. Fortunately the compression damping valve has a check valve that opens, allowing fluid to pass freely from chamber C back into chamber A.

It is both interesting and important to recognize that the velocity of the rebound stroke is directly related to the amount of travel used. The more travel used, the more energy is stored in the spring and the greater the force is extending the fork. This typically means that low-speed rebound damping will be created on smaller displacements and high-speed will be created when lots of travel is used. The exact velocity will also depend on things like whether the tire is in contact with the ground or the bike is in the air (probably not with a street bike—I hope).

MULTI-STAGE DAMPING

There is a variation on the standard shim stack used in the cartridge fork that produces a more progressive compression damping curve. As you can see in Figure 3.25, the compression shim stack has two shim stacks on top of each other, separated by a smaller diameter washer. At the lowest velocities the shim stack is closed and all the flow goes through the low speed adjuster. As the velocity increases, the low-speed stack (the one closest to the valving piston) opens and oil flows through the compression damping holes—the same as a single-stage shim stack.

In the next drawing (Figure 3.26) the compression stroke is even faster, causing even higher oil pressure in chamber A. With more oil pressure pushing on it, the low-speed shim stack is deflected far enough to make contact with the second (high-speed) shim stack, thereby stiffening up the total stack. With two-stage (or more) shim stacks, the progressiveness

can be tailored. Note that the more stages there are, generally the more progressive the curve will be. This style of stack is common on dirt bikes.

Don't be confused by the terminology. When we refer to a low-speed and high-speed compression stack, you might wonder if the low-speed adjuster and the low-speed stack control the same velocities. Any time there is an open "bleed" hole, it is the lowest speed damping control. The point at which the low-speed stack opens depends on its stiffness.

Keep in mind that the effects of all of these components overlap. The higher the velocity, the less effect the low-speed adjuster has, though it does still flow and have some effect. We will get into further detail about valving stack styles a bit later in this chapter.

CARTRIDGE FORK MID-VALVES

On the compression stroke of a cartridge fork, the job of the check valve on the rebound piston is to allow oil to freely pass from chamber A to chamber B. But what if we put a valving stack in the place of the check valve and call it a mid-valve? What are the possible benefits and limitations?

On the rebound stroke (Figure 3.27) it is easy to see there would be no downside to it. Its job is simply to shut off the flow through those passages, and it would do just that. On the compression stroke there certainly is flow from chamber A to B, but chamber B is getting bigger, so it tends to create a vacuum. If we restrict the flow too much, we could easily cause the fork to cavitate on the compression stroke and cause incomplete filling of chamber A. If, on the other hand, we restrict the flow below the level that causes cavitation, we would be adding compression damping.

What's the difference between adding more damping at the compression piston versus adding it to the mid-valve? Remember that the volume of oil that goes through the compression piston on the compression stroke is exactly the volume displaced by the damping rod. On the compression stroke, the volume of oil that goes from A to B is the area of the inner diameter of the cartridge minus the area of the damping rod times the length of the displacement. This means that a 24mm diameter cartridge with a 12mm diameter damping rod will pass 3 times the volume into chamber B through the mid-valve than out of the cartridge through the compression base valve.

So what is the benefit of the mid-valve? We have been talking about oil as being incompressible, but that is not precisely true. Because there is a slight compressibility of the oil as well as expandability of the cartridge tube, there is a bit of a lag between the damping rod entering the cartridge and the damping being created by oil passing through the compression valve—particularly on very small movements. Because the volume is so much greater through the mid-valve, it doesn't take much valving to create a significant amount of compression damping. The net result of a mid-valve is that the "lag" is reduced.

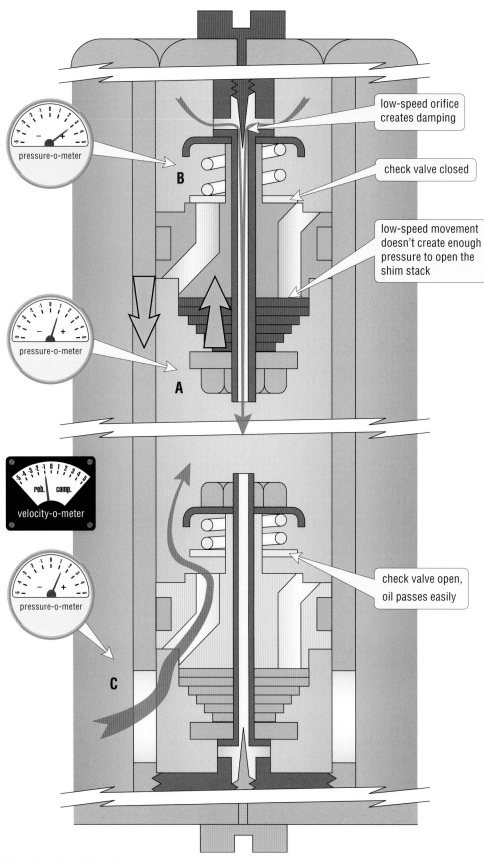

low-speed orifice
creates damping

check valve closed

low-speed movement
doesn't create enough
pressure to open the
shim stack

pressure-o-meter

B

pressure-o-meter

A

reb.   comp.
velocity-o-meter

check valve open,
oil passes easily

pressure-o-meter

C

3.23 Standard Cartridge Fork Low-Speed Rebound

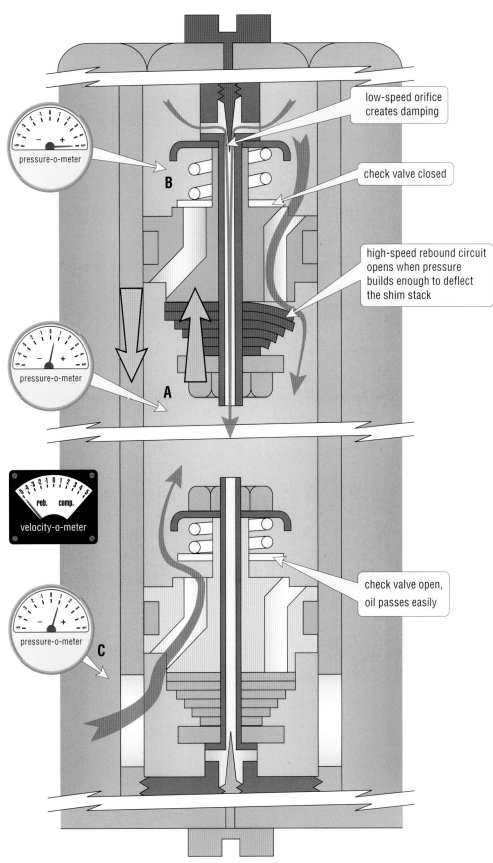

low-speed orifice creates damping

check valve closed

high-speed rebound circuit opens when pressure builds enough to deflect the shim stack

check valve open, oil passes easily

pressure-o-meter

B

pressure-o-meter

A

velocity-o-meter

reb. comp.

pressure-o-meter

C

DAMPING

3.24 Standard Cartridge Fork High-Speed Rebound

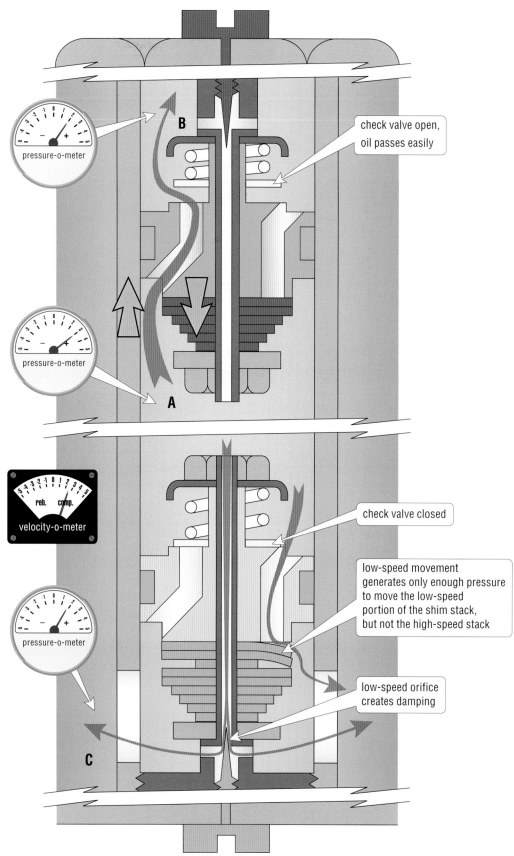

pressure-o-meter

B

check valve open,
oil passes easily

pressure-o-meter

A

velocity-o-meter

reb.   comp.

check valve closed

low-speed movement
generates only enough pressure
to move the low-speed
portion of the shim stack,
but not the high-speed stack

pressure-o-meter

low-speed orifice
creates damping

C

3.25 Standard Cartridge Fork Two-Stage Low-Speed Compression

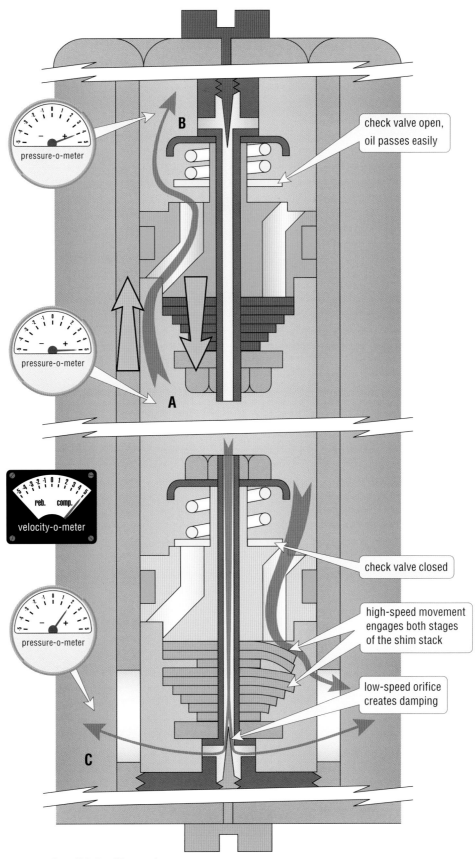

check valve open,
oil passes easily

check valve closed

high-speed movement
engages both stages
of the shim stack

low-speed orifice
creates damping

pressure-o-meter

velocity-o-meter
reb.   comp.

3.26 Standard Cartridge Fork Two-Stage High-Speed Compression

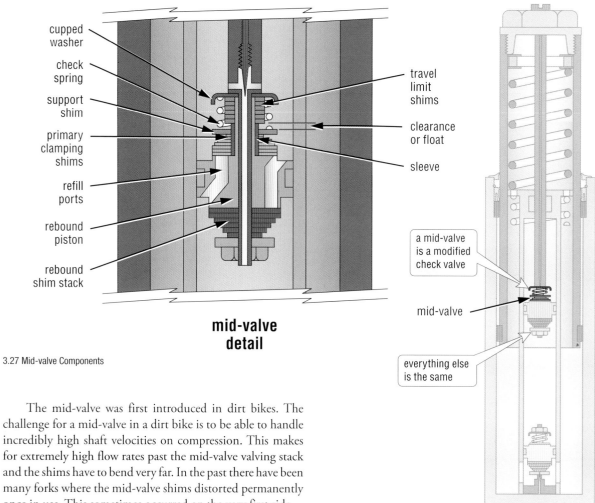

mid-valve
detail

3.27 Mid-valve Components

cupped washer
check spring
support shim
primary clamping shims
refill ports
rebound piston
rebound shim stack

travel limit shims
clearance or float
sleeve

a mid-valve is a modified check valve
mid-valve
everything else is the same

The mid-valve was first introduced in dirt bikes. The challenge for a mid-valve in a dirt bike is to be able to handle incredibly high shaft velocities on compression. This makes for extremely high flow rates past the mid-valve valving stack and the shims have to bend very far. In the past there have been many forks where the mid-valve shims distorted permanently once in use. This sometimes occurred on the very first ride—once bent, they no longer function as a mid-valve. If this happens, why have a mid-valve in the first place?

Though there are potential weaknesses, there are also benefits to be had *if* the mid-valve can be created that doesn't permanently distort and is set up to prevent cavitation.

There are a number of mid-valve designs, but let's look at a very common one. Look at Figure 3.27. This mid-valve consists of a shim stack that slides on a sleeve. This allows the mid-valve stack to displace before it has to bend. There is a secondary shim that supports the bending shims at high deflections, and there is a coil spring to return the stack back to the piston on the change from compression to rebound.

MID-VALVE COMPRESSION STROKE

Refer to Figure 3.28. When the compression stroke begins, the mid-valve immediately displaces a distance we call the "float," "clearance," or "gap." This float is provided because of the immense flow rate from chamber A to B on the compression stroke, particularly on dirt bikes.

As the velocity increases, the shim stack starts to bend. (See Figure 3.29.) It bends until it hits the secondary shim, which helps keep it from permanently distorting. On the

rebound stroke, the entire mid-valve displaces back to the piston face with a little help from the check spring. The rebound stack behaves as normal. (See Figure 3.30.)

In the past I often recommended dismantling the mid-valve and converting it back to a standard check valve as it eliminated the potential problems of permanent distortion and cavitation. Some of the stock designs today have less problems with permanent distortion, and in these cases we may recommend not changing the mid-valve back to a check valve.

In other cases Race Tech offers Rebound Gold Valves that not only have tunable rebound valving stacks but also tunable mid-valves, allowing tremendous flexibility. Race Tech HFR (High Frequency Response) Rebound Gold Valves for pavement utilize a non-displacing mid-valve, so they make the change in direction from compression to rebound very rapidly. The reason we can get away without a displacing mid-valve on these models is that the compression velocities are much lower than on a dirt bike, so the potential for permanent distortion is dramatically reduced.

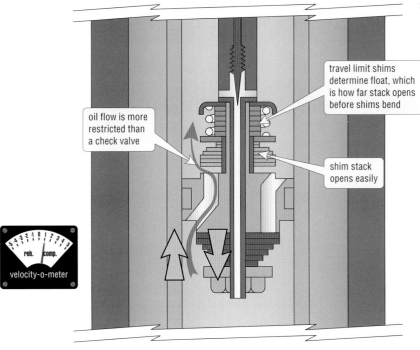

travel limit shims
determine float, which
is how far stack opens
before shims bend

oil flow is more
restricted than
a check valve

shim stack
opens easily

velocity-o-meter
reb. comp.

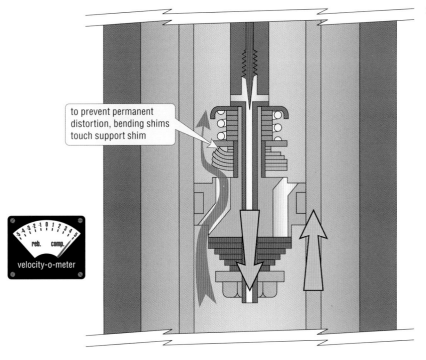

3.29 Mid-valve High-Speed Compression

to prevent permanent
distortion, bending shims
touch support shim

velocity-o-meter
reb. comp.

DAMPING

Bear in mind that cavitation is always a risk—that the more compression damping you create at the mid-valve, the higher the potential for cavitation on the compression stroke. If you're using a mid-valve and you decrease the compression damping on the compression base valve, you increase the chance of cavitation. This is because it is the resistance to the flow through the compression valve (and out of the cartridge) that forces the oil from chamber A to chamber B. You need to seek a balance

between having enough compression valving at the compression base valve and not too much mid-valve valving.

TWIN-CHAMBER AND OTHER PRESSURIZED FORKS AND CAVITATION

With the advent of the mid-valve came an increased potential for cavitation. In the old days before the twin-chamber fork, we used to introduce this subject in the shock absorber section of

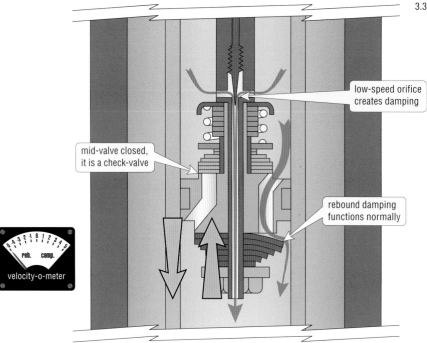

low-speed orifice creates damping

mid-valve closed, it is a check-valve

rebound damping functions normally

velocity-o-meter
reb.   comp.

the Race Tech Technical Edge Suspension Seminars, but this is now a big part of fork design too.

As you may remember, cavitation is the formation of vapor bubbles in a flowing liquid caused by a decrease in pressure. This occurs specifically in an area where the pressure of the liquid falls below its vapor pressure. One way to reduce the tendency toward cavitation is to pressurize the cartridge.

Refer to Figure 3.31 number 1. Here we have a shock shaft attached to a solid piston in a shock body partially filled with oil. There is a hole in the piston and the piston can slide but seals nicely on the body. There is no "top" on the shock, so it is open to atmospheric pressure. Before motion is initiated, the pressure in both chambers A and B are equal at 0.

If we compress the shock *very* slowly, the pressure in chamber B becomes negative (a vacuum) while the pressure above the piston remains atmospheric at 0. (It should be noted that in this example we are using gauge pressures, not absolute pressures. Absolute pressure at standard atmospheric pressure is about 14.7 psi, or 1 atmosphere. Gauge pressure at atmospheric pressure is 0 psi, or 0 atmospheres. 0 psi absolute is an absolute vacuum.) At this very low velocity there is very little cavitation, but with enough resistance there can be some.

Refer to Figure 3.31 number 2. As we increase the shaft velocity, the pressure becomes low enough to create voids or vacuum pockets in the fluid. The faster the shaft is moved, the more cavitation occurs. The smaller the hole—and therefore, the greater the damping effect—the sooner the cavitation happens.

Refer to Figure 3.31 number 3. To remedy the problem, we could put a floating piston on the top of the fluid in chamber

A and put a coil spring with preload against the opposite side of the piston. This way the initial pressure in both chamber A and chamber B not only start off the same before movement, but are at a higher pressure. When movement is initiated, the spring force creates a pressure that helps push the oil through the orifice into chamber B, thus reducing cavitation. If there is enough initial pressure created by the spring, cavitation can be completely eliminated. In reality this can be a difficult solution to assemble, but it is used when the pressures required to eliminate cavitation are fairly low (as in forks).

Refer to Figure 3.31 number 4. On a shock absorber the forces are fairly high, so a more practical solution is the use of a compressed gas instead of a coil spring to create the pressure inside the damping chambers. It is important to note that when the system is at rest, the pressures in all three chambers (A, B, and the nitrogen chamber) are the same. If the nitrogen pressure is high enough to overpower the resistance to flow, cavitation is eliminated. Note that as far as eliminating cavitation is concerned, it doesn't matter whether a piston or a bladder is used in the reservoir.

Let's go back now to the front fork. Look at Figure 3.32. If we want to pressurize the cartridge, we need to make room for a pressure chamber. If we mount the cartridge upside down, we can attach the damping rod to the bottom of the fork. The cartridge tube and compression valve, along with the reservoir piston, are then attached to the fork cap at the top of the forks.

Notice that the shaft that the compression piston is attached to is the same one the reservoir piston slides on. You can see that the reservoir is pressurized with a coil spring.

This illustration is based on a Showa Twin-Chamber. Some detail is omitted, but notice the necked-down part of

DAMPING

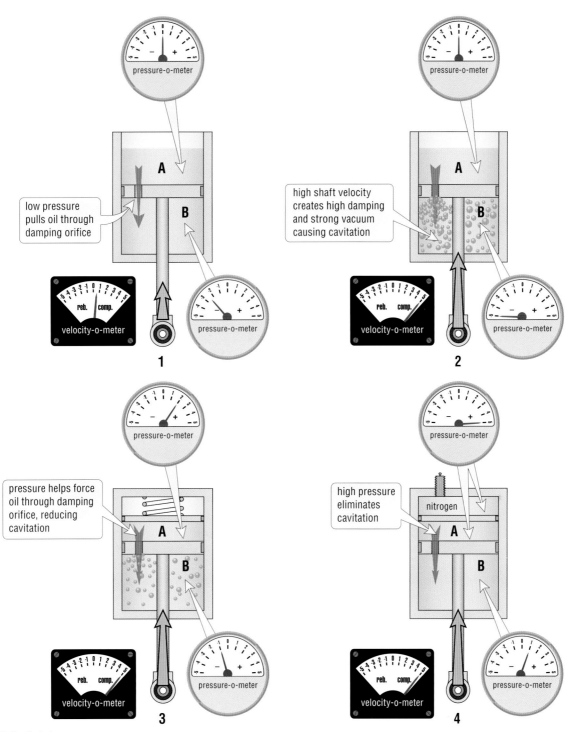

pressure-o-meter

A

low pressure
pulls oil through
damping orifice

B

velocity-o-meter
reb. comp.

pressure-o-meter

1

pressure-o-meter

A

high shaft velocity
creates high damping
and strong vacuum
causing cavitation

B

velocity-o-meter
reb. comp.

pressure-o-meter

2

pressure-o-meter

pressure helps force
oil through damping
orifice, reducing
cavitation

A

B

velocity-o-meter
reb. comp.

pressure-o-meter

3

pressure-o-meter

high pressure
eliminates
cavitation

nitrogen

A

B

velocity-o-meter
reb. comp.

pressure-o-meter

4

3.31 Cavitation Control

DAMPING

the compression damping shaft just below the fork cap—it is marked as "assembly groove." This is Showa's solution for assembly, and we will discuss the details later in the book. Briefly, when the cartridge is initially assembled, it is overfilled with oil. The damping rod is then compressed all the way, displacing the reservoir piston and compressing the pressure spring until it reaches the assembly groove. At this point the reservoir piston shaft seal no longer seals and the reservoir piston stops moving upward. Any excess oil "leaks past." When the shaft is released, the pressure spring extends and the reservoir piston moves down and seals again, trapping the correct amount of oil inside the cartridge.

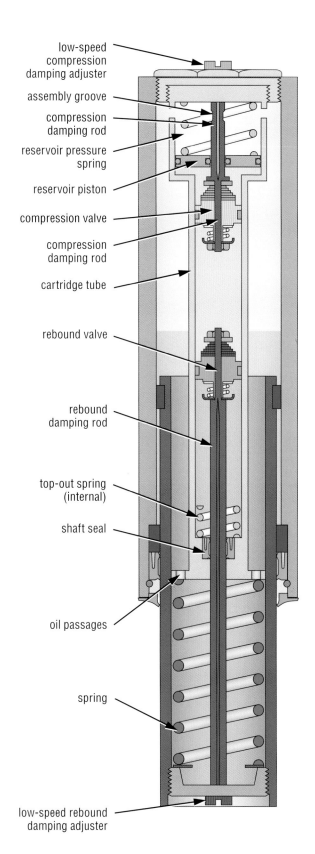

low-speed compression damping adjuster

assembly groove

compression damping rod

reservoir pressure spring

reservoir piston

compression valve

compression damping rod

cartridge tube

rebound valve

rebound damping rod

top-out spring (internal)

shaft seal

oil passages

spring

low-speed rebound damping adjuster

3.32 The Twin-Chamber design inverts the cartridge and adds a spring-pressurized reservoir. The value of a pressurized cartridge is it can eliminate cavitation if there is any.

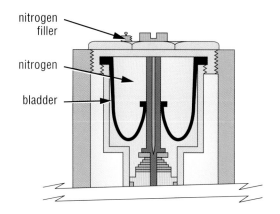

nitrogen filler

nitrogen

bladder

As to the function of the fork, the damping is exactly the same as a standard, non-pressurized cartridge. Oil is forced through the compression valve and moves the reservoir piston because of the displacement of the damping rod into the cartridge. The reservoir provides pressure to eliminate cavitation.

It is interesting to notice that with this pressure-spring design, the pressure in the cartridge starts very low, as the pressure spring preload is very low. The pressure builds as the fork compresses. This means the resistance to cavitation starts very low and improves deeper into the travel. Maximum velocity on most landings from jumps occurs at ⅓ to ½ travel—this is when the potential for cavitation is at its highest. This may be a design limitation but remember, all you need is enough pressure to eliminate cavitation and no more.

Other designs of pressurized cartridges include WP units on some KTMs, which use a bladder with nitrogen instead of a pressure spring. (See Figure 3.32.) The pressure in this design builds with the displacement of the damping rod and the compression ratio of the volume of the reservoir chamber compared to that of the damping rod. This makes it possible for the pressure to remain much more constant compared to using a pressure spring, thus the resistance to cavitation is more consistent through the entire stroke.

Other advantages of pressurized cartridges include the ability to use different viscosities in the inner cartridge and the outer chamber. Increasing the viscosity in the outer chamber makes the hydraulic bottom-out more aggressive, if that's what you need. This can be done instead of replacing the bottom-out "lock" ring with a larger diameter aftermarket ring, eliminating the problem of scoring that these aftermarket rings often have.

There is also a minor advantage with the separation of the inner and outer chamber oil in the event that the outer chamber oil gets contaminated.

There is, of course, a downside to all pressurized forks: added complexity, additional sealing surfaces that increase friction, and the number of places that there can be leaks. Spring replacement is a bit more involved as well. Remember, too, that *if there isn't any cavitation, the major advantage of a pressurized cartridge is minimized*. Also note that cavitation is a much bigger issue on dirt bike forks than it is with street and road race forks because of the high velocities involved.

Remember that the pressure spring in the reservoir does not create damping—rather, it creates pressure to eliminate cavitation and ultimately adds to the main fork spring force slightly. The pressure springs are position sensitive, not velocity sensitive.

Supercross generates higher shaft velocities and more bottoming problems. To deal with it, tuners quite often opt for more mid-valve compression damping. These harsh conditions require stiffer pressure springs in the reservoir, but which ones? The problem in answering that question is that it's hard for the rider to detect cavitation. Typically the rider may feel it bottom or perhaps feel a looseness due to the decrease in rebound damping, but in testing, those symptoms are really hard to pin on cavitation. Most shock dynos cannot even come close to creating the velocities required to induce cavitation, so they won't be able to detect it either. The rule of thumb is: higher compression velocities and more mid-valve damping require stiffer pressure springs or more reservoir pressure. (See www.racetech.com for recommendations.)

OTHER FORK DESIGNS

The 2009 model year saw many new cartridge styles introduced into the sportbike market. Suzuki and Kawasaki introduced the BPF "Big Piston" forks with 39 and 37mm pistons, while Yamaha brought out 30mm cartridges with compression only in one leg and rebound only in the other.

If the notion of an "imbalance" created with compression in one leg and rebound in the other seems to pose a problem, you can stop worrying—unless the front axle flexes appreciably, both fork legs are going up and down at the same time. In fact, in the 1980s Marzocchi had a series of dirt bike forks that had only one fork spring: rebound damping was in that leg and compression was in the other leg. Though they were never considered the best-performing forks, the bikes they were fitted to showed no evidence of turning left better than right (or vice versa), nor did they exhibit any unusual binding.

These new designs have shifted from rod displacement to piston displacement. This means that, instead of the damping rod volume displacing the fluid to create compression damping, they are more like a shock where the entire volume swept by the piston (cartridge inner diameter times travel used) is being used to make damping. In theory this provides the same advantage as the mid-valve does in dealing with the "compressibility" of the oil and expandability of the cartridge tube.

The downside, in my opinion, is that the damping pistons are *way too restrictive*. The volume of oil going through the piston on a 39mm BPF Showa is ten and a half times that which a 12mm diameter damping rod pushes in a conventional cartridge. This means there is a big tendency for the piston orifices themselves to create significant harshness.

But, to be fair, everything has upsides and downsides. The most important consideration is whether or not a tuner can make the forks perform, and the answer to that question is usually yes. The degree of performance you can wring out of these designs depends on knowledge of the problem and skill in testing and troubleshooting on the part of both the test rider and the tuner. This is why Gold Valve Kits for these forks have radically increased flow areas.

SHOCK DESIGN

It may come as a surprise, but the study of shock absorber design won't be particularly difficult by this point in the book. If you understand the previous concepts presented, shocks are easy. There are six major shock designs we are going to look at, starting with twin-tube shocks.

Twin-Tube Shocks

This type of shock is the most popular style on the planet by a long shot (see Figure 3.33). If you look closely, you can see it looks very similar to a standard cartridge fork, with the shock shaft the equivalent of the damping rod. On the end of the shock shaft is a rebound piston with a check valve on the top side. There is a "base valve" (compression valve) at the bottom of the cartridge with a check valve on the top side. Outside the cartridge is a compressible air space to deal with the displacement of the shock shaft. These shocks must be mounted in the orientation shown and cannot be inverted.

There are subtle variations, like the addition of a Freon bag inside the outer chamber instead of letting the air contact the oil directly. Contrary to what you might think, the use of Freon as a gas has nothing to do with cooling the shock. This variation had limited improvement.

There are also designs that feature a floating piston ring that seals on the outer diameter of the cartridge tube and the inner diameter of the shock body, allowing the shock to be pressurized through an opening in the seal head. This is done in an effort to control cavitation and allows the shock to be mounted in any direction.

Emulsion Shocks

Emulsion shocks are single-tube shocks that have no reservoir and are not quite full of oil because they require an air space to deal with the displacement of the shock shaft. They must be mounted in the orientation shown, with the body up and the shock shaft down. The compression valving stack is on the bottom of the piston while the rebound stack is on the other side.

These shocks are generally pressurized to raise the temperature and lower the pressure at which cavitation occurs within the suspension fluid itself. As you might imagine, the potential for cavitation and foaming is real—the idea behind the design is that once it "foams up," it will become consistent. Emulsion shocks can actually work quite well but are not considered to be a high-performance design.

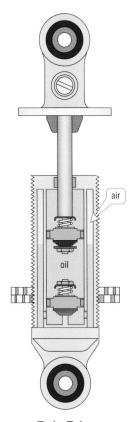

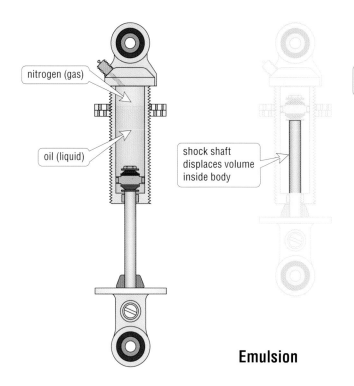

nitrogen (gas)

oil (liquid)

air

oil

shock shaft displaces volume inside body

nitrogen compresses

Emulsion

Twin-Tube

3.33 (Above) The twin-tube design looks very similar to a standard cartridge fork. The shock shaft has a rebound piston attached. The bottom of the cart has a compression base valve and there is an air space on the outside of the damping tube.

3.34 (Top right) This illustration shows the effect of shock shaft displacement. The solid shock shaft displaces oil volume in the shock body as it compresses. Because oil is incompressible, there must be a compressible space inside the shock for the entire stroke or it will not compress.

3.35 (Bottom right) All of these designs are related to the original DeCarbon mono-tube design and are considered to be high performance.

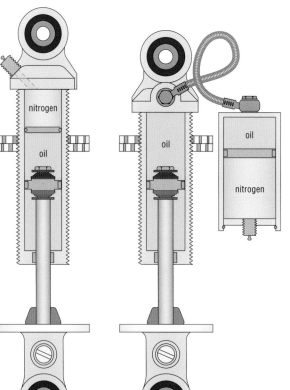

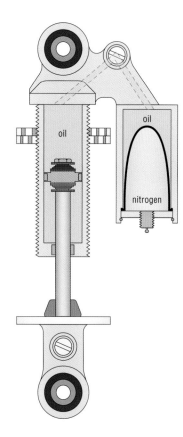

nitrogen

oil

oil

oil

nitrogen

oil

nitrogen

DeCarbon Internal Floating Piston

Remote Piston Reservoir

Integral Bladder Reservoir

DeCarbon Reservoir Shocks

If we were to separate the oil from the nitrogen with a floating piston in the main shock body, we would have a basic DeCarbon reservoir shock. I group remote reservoirs, bladders, and diaphragm reservoirs into this group. All are high-performance designs.

When the French scientist Dr. Christian Bourcier DeCarbon invented this design, he used a floating reservoir piston in the main shock body, but all the styles mentioned are variations of this theme. Externally DeCarbon's original design looks like an emulsion shock, but internally it's quite different.

By pressurizing the nitrogen space, we can reduce or eliminate cavitation. Remember that the amount of nitrogen pressure required is directly related to the amount of compression damping required—this was discussed in the pressurized fork section. Nitrogen is used in this design because it's dry, inexpensive, inert, and easily acquired in high-pressure bottles, but it is not the only gas that can be used.

One of the problems with the original DeCarbon design for many motorcycle applications was that, because the floating piston was in the main shock tube, the shock was considerably longer than a twin-tube or emulsion shock. A solution to this was attaching a remote reservoir with a hose. Now this idea has evolved into an integral reservoir built into the body. The integral design not only simplified the design, but it has the added benefit of a very short heat path to the added surface area of the reservoir body keeping the oil cooler. That being said, if the shock doesn't fade appreciably with temperature (the shock loses damping when it gets hot), this advantage is unimportant.

Shock Adjusters

Rebound adjusters can be used in all the shock designs mentioned. The adjusters generally position a tapered needle in an orifice and are low-speed adjusters. There are two mechanisms for moving the adjuster needle. The first type uses a knob threaded onto the eyelet that moves a crosspin resting against the adjusting needle rod. The second type uses a screw with a tapered tip that pushes the rod directly. (See Figure 3.37 for details.)

Another rebound adjuster design has four positions—this type has a barrel inside the shock shaft with four different size holes in it. One of these holes is aligned with an outlet port to determine which one flows.

When the reservoir is attached outside the main shock tube, we have the opportunity to add external compression adjusters. The volume that the shock shaft displaces flows into the reservoir and—while this may not be a lot of fluid—is enough to influence the shock's behavior with an adjuster. Increasing the shaft diameter increases the volume of flow to the reservoir, making the adjuster more effective.

There are many adjuster designs: a simple one is shown in Figure 3.37. The low-speed adjuster is the one on the right

and is just a simple tapered needle in an orifice. The high speed adjuster on the left is a coil spring on a valve plate: using the adjuster alters the spring preload. On rebound the refill check valve opens and allows the oil to return to the main shock body.

Most production compression adjusters are fairly ineffective, so much so that when doing blind testing, most riders cannot tell much difference with any of the settings. These findings have been backed up with dyno testing. The advantage of ineffective adjusters is that the user can't mess it up—on the other hand, they can't improve things much either.

There are no general statements that can be made about which brands of adjusters are more effective, but this is where good testing or dyno work comes in. One of the design considerations of Race Tech G3-S Custom Series Shocks was to have a significant range of external compression adjustment. We were able to achieve an impressive range of 33 percent.

Through-Shaft Shocks

A simple version of a through-shaft design is a linear steering damper, with compression valving on one side of the piston and rebound on the other. The shock is completely filled with oil. Generally speaking, there is no compressible air space required because the shock shaft volume going in is equal to the volume going out. However, it is preferable to have a compressible space to allow for expansion of the oil with temperature. This basic design is used in Race Tech Caddies Softail Shocks.

Solid-Piston Shocks

Solid-piston shocks can be linear or rotary vane style. The linear version shown uses a solid piston in a twin-tube design. Passages or hoses are attached to the inner and outer tube and a valving block can be built into the shock body or attached with hoses and remotely mounted. This basic design is used by Öhlins in its TTX Series shocks (see Figure 3.39).

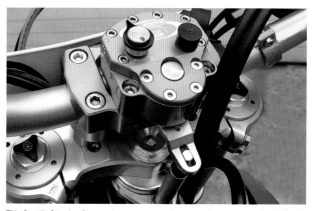

This Scott's Steering Damper is a rotary vane damper that does an excellent job of controlling headshake. Even if headshake is not a problem, the damper allows the rider to relax quite a bit more.

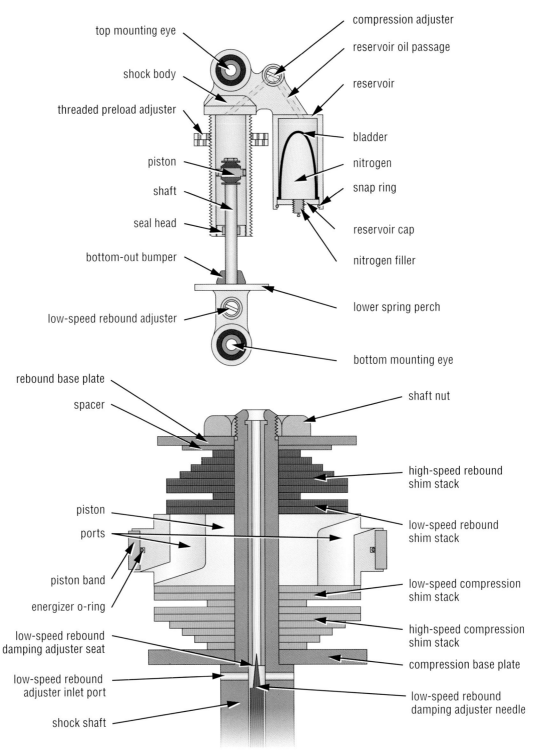

top mounting eye

shock body

threaded preload adjuster

piston

shaft

seal head

bottom-out bumper

low-speed rebound adjuster

compression adjuster

reservoir oil passage

reservoir

bladder

nitrogen

snap ring

reservoir cap

nitrogen filler

lower spring perch

bottom mounting eye

rebound base plate

spacer

shaft nut

piston

ports

piston band

energizer o-ring

low-speed rebound
damping adjuster seat

low-speed rebound
adjuster inlet port

shock shaft

high-speed rebound
shim stack

low-speed rebound
shim stack

low-speed compression
shim stack

high-speed compression
shim stack

compression base plate

low-speed rebound
damping adjuster needle

3.36 Shock Valving Components

The TL1000S Suzuki introduced in 1997 uses a rotary vane style damper attached to the swingarm with links and heim joints. The spring is attached separately on a unit that looks like a shock but isn't. The valving consists of two assemblies that look very much like cartridge fork valves, with one controlling compression and the other rebound—in fact, we fit Fork Gold Valve Kits to these when we revalve them.

The TL dampers suffer from high friction and a tendency for the attachment heim joints to get sloppy, but they can be made to work very well with internal polishing, anodizing, and care of the

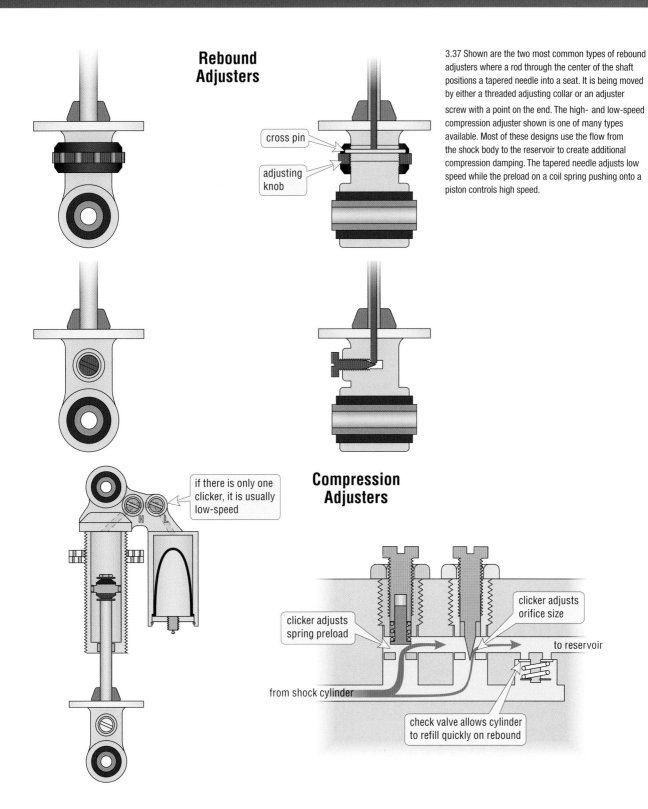

Rebound Adjusters

cross pin

adjusting knob

3.37 Shown are the two most common types of rebound adjusters where a rod through the center of the shaft positions a tapered needle into a seat. It is being moved by either a threaded adjusting collar or an adjuster screw with a point on the end. The high- and low-speed compression adjuster shown is one of many types available. Most of these designs use the flow from the shock body to the reservoir to create additional compression damping. The tapered needle adjusts low speed while the preload on a coil spring pushing onto a piston controls high speed.

if there is only one clicker, it is usually low-speed

Compression Adjusters

clicker adjusts spring preload

clicker adjusts orifice size

to reservoir

from shock cylinder

check valve allows cylinder to refill quickly on rebound

heim joints. Their big downfall was a lack of understanding by tuners, who removed the stock damper and easily (and perhaps too eagerly) replaced the spring unit with a complete standard shock. It is notable because it was, as far as I know, the first production version of a solid-piston shock design.

Another version of the rotary vane design is a Scott's Steering Damper. These are not suspension units technically, but they do dramatically affect handling, and they are a damper. There are pavement and dirt versions, and they have both high- and low-speed damping adjustment and perform very well.

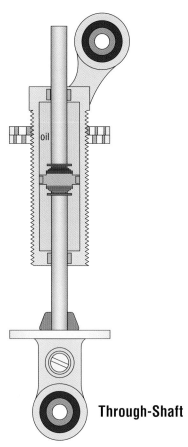

Through-Shaft

3.38 Through-shaft shocks don't require a reservoir as the shaft volume entering is the same that is leaving. Reservoirs are only added to compensate for the expansion of the fluid with temperature.

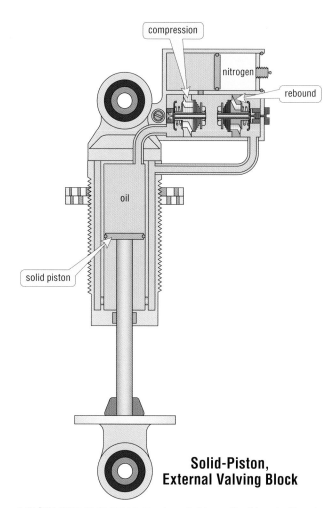

**Solid-Piston,
External Valving Block**

3.39 Solid-piston shocks come in many forms. In this case the oil is pushed through a valving block to create damping. The reservoir is attached between the valving pistons where the pressure is lowest. This allows a lower required pressure.

POSITION-SENSITIVE DAMPING SYSTEMS

In the Race Tech Technical Edge Suspension Seminars, we delve into linkages and leverage ratios in quite a bit of detail. Linkages (and, in fact, all shock mountings) have a leverage ratio curve. The leverage ratio, as we define it, is basically the travel of the wheel divided by the travel of the shock. With a linkage, the opportunity to vary the leverage ratio through the stroke becomes quite significant.

This allows the suspension to be plush on the little bumps and stiff on the big ones. This is, obviously, of particular significance for dirt bikes. Without a linkage, the ability to change the leverage throughout the travel becomes quite limited. Through testing on dirt vehicles of any type, we've found that a progression of 25 to 32 percent is a good range of change between 50 and 250mm travel.

Without a linkage, it is difficult to get more than about 12 percent. This means setups without linkages—including ATVs and automotive A-arms—benefit not only from progressive spring setups but also position-sensitive damping.

You might recall that I said damping is sensitive to velocity, not position. This is precisely true. It is, however, possible to make the damping change throughout the position of the stroke as well.

There are a number of ways to do this. Öhlins uses two different size pistons attached to the shock shaft with the piston on the end of the shaft going into a "cup" in the bottom of the shock body at the end of the shock stroke. In the automotive off-road world, King Shocks have external bypass tubes located at different heights along the shock body. The WP PDS (Position Sensitive Damping System) also uses two pistons similar to Öhlins, but both pistons are the same size. WP's design is by far the most popular in the motorcycle world, particularly because they come as original equipment on KTM motorcycles. KTM removed the shock linkage and mounted the shock directly from the swingarm to the frame in 1998. This introduced the need to make both the spring rate and the damping change with position.

Referring to Figure 3.40, you can see there is also a metering needle attached to the bottom of the shock body. There are two phases: the first is before the needle enters the shock shaft, and the second is after the needle has entered. In the initial movements before the needle enters, the oil

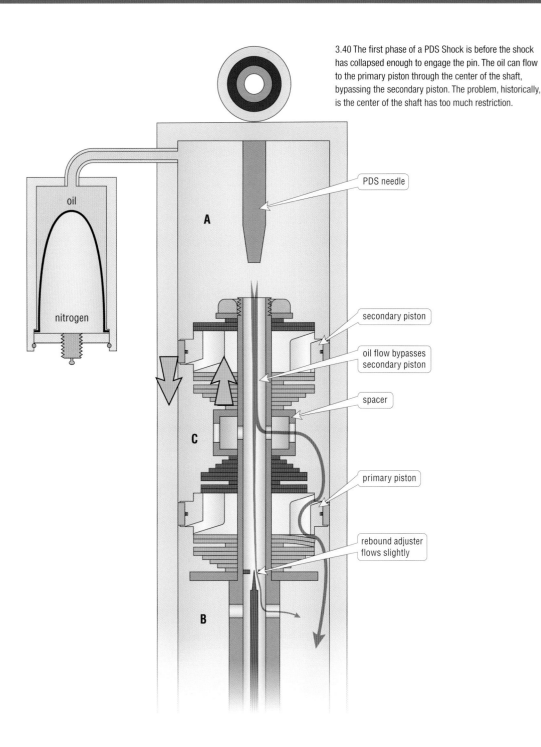

3.40 The first phase of a PDS Shock is before the shock has collapsed enough to engage the pin. The oil can flow to the primary piston through the center of the shaft, bypassing the secondary piston. The problem, historically, is the center of the shaft has too much restriction.

oil

nitrogen

A

B

C

PDS needle

secondary piston

oil flow bypasses secondary piston

spacer

primary piston

rebound adjuster flows slightly

flow goes from chamber A through the center of the shaft, bypasses the "secondary" piston, goes out through ports in the shaft and spacing sleeve, and goes through the "primary" piston compression circuits.

Once the shock compresses enough to engage the metering needle, the oil in chamber A can no longer bypass the secondary piston, so it is forced through it. The damping created by the secondary piston is added to the damping created by the primary piston because the same volume of oil still flows through the primary piston.

From my perspective, the major flaw in this system is the restriction in flow area to the primary piston through the center of the shaft. I did a series of tests with the PDS in 1999 and initially, no matter what I did with the valving on the primary piston, it was always harsh on square-edged bumps. Then I removed the secondary piston entirely. The rider's feedback was that it was much plusher on braking, acceleration, and small, single, square-edged bumps. The standard metering needle was not engaged in this area! All that needed to be tested then was to put the secondary piston back on and remove the metering needle entirely—it was harsh again. Over the years WP has increased the bore size in the center of the shaft, and this has helped.

Terry Hay of Shock Treatment (Race Tech's Australian distributor) invented a novel solution that has had worldwide success. One of the problems with the stock metering needle was it was very short and, if it were any longer, the needle would hit the rebound seat and start destroying things.

Terry made a metering needle that was much longer than stock and telescoped into itself. This made the progression more consistent. But what about the restriction in flow rate? He simply surrendered to the fact that the bore of the shaft would be restrictive and forced the secondary piston to flow on high speed hits throughout the entire stroke. This required a significant decrease in compression damping on the secondary piston. In my opinion (and yes, I am biased), Terry's Telescopic PDS Needle along with Race Tech's P Series Progressive Shock Springs and a Gold Valve combine to significantly improve the KTM suspension performance.

DAMPING

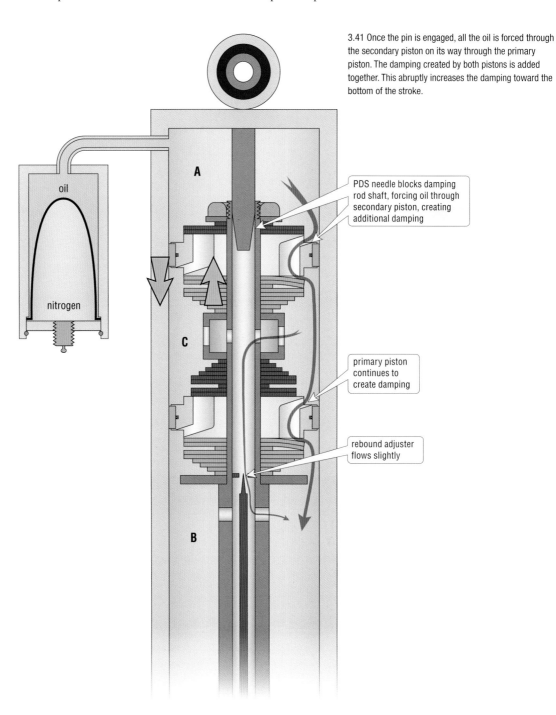

3.41 Once the pin is engaged, all the oil is forced through the secondary piston on its way through the primary piston. The damping created by both pistons is added together. This abruptly increases the damping toward the bottom of the stroke.

oil

nitrogen

A

C

B

PDS needle blocks damping rod shaft, forcing oil through secondary piston, creating additional damping

primary piston continues to create damping

rebound adjuster flows slightly

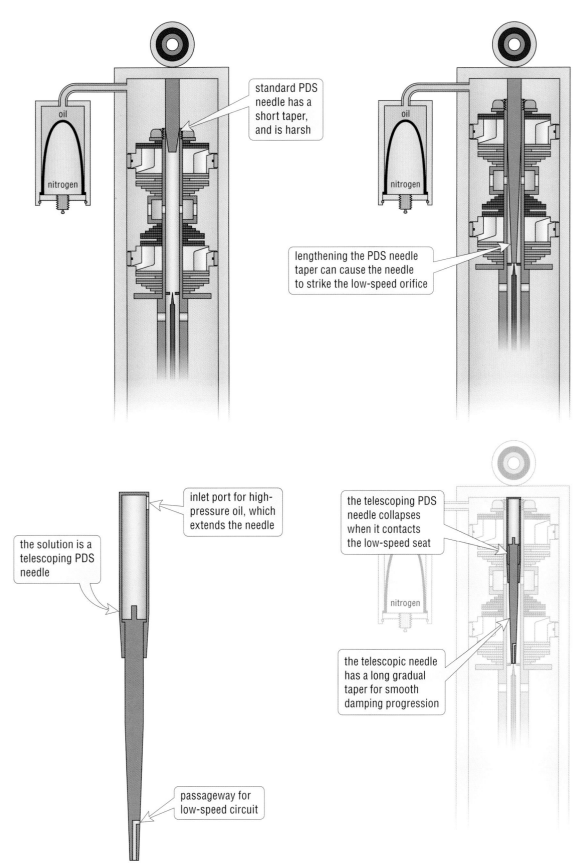

standard PDS needle has a short taper, and is harsh

lengthening the PDS needle taper can cause the needle to strike the low-speed orifice

oil

nitrogen

oil

nitrogen

inlet port for high-pressure oil, which extends the needle

the solution is a telescoping PDS needle

the telescoping PDS needle collapses when it contacts the low-speed seat

nitrogen

the telescopic needle has a long gradual taper for smooth damping progression

passageway for low-speed circuit

3.42 The Telescopic Needle creates a gradual progression over a longer stroke eliminating the abruptness and harshness. This is enhanced with revalving.

FADE

Fade is a decrease in damping during use. It is usually caused by one of three things. First is the loss of viscosity when the oil heats up. (Losing viscosity means that the oil thins out.) This can be because the viscosity index of the oil is low (poor quality oil) or because the oil's viscosity index has broken down with wear (poor quality viscosity-index-improver additives). This decreases damping, particularly in the low-speed range. Remember that, on the energy level, a shock converts kinetic energy into heat, so the shock heats up when in use. Front forks generally heat up much less than rear shocks because there are two fork legs instead of one shock, giving the front forks much more surface area in comparison to the shock. They are also up front hanging out in the breeze cooling off, while the shock is often stuffed in and hidden from the wind. On some models the shock is extremely close to the exhaust pipe, which doesn't help matters either. Fade can also be caused by the oil becoming more compressible as it heats up.

Another cause of fade is mechanical blowby. This can happen when different materials expand differently as they heat up. If the shock body is made of aluminum and the piston is made of steel, the aluminum body expands faster than the steel piston as the shock heats up.

This is not a problem if the sealing design on the piston can handle the difference in expansion. A poor sealing design, however, can leak. If the oil is going around the piston and not through it, the damping decreases and the rider experiences fade.

A common culprit is the energizer O-ring underneath the piston band. On KYB and Showa shocks, particularly on older models (pre-2000), the energizer O-ring can wear off and form a flat spot, lessening the preload on the piston band—sometimes to nothing. This problem is hidden because the stock piston band is endless (full-circle hoop) and doesn't expose the condition of the O-ring. Measure the installed outer diameter of the piston band and make sure it is larger than the inner diameter of the bore.

Another source of fade is cavitation, an issue we have discussed in quite a bit of detail already. If the shock loses pressure for any reason, it will show up as a decrease in damping both on compression and rebound.

I remember when a rider came up to me and told me he had fixed the harshness problem on his stock shock. He told me he let some of the nitrogen pressure out and now it's great. I asked him how much, and he told me he only let out a little—he just pressed the valve core and it went "pssssssst." That might be almost all of the pressure, for all I know. Now, I want to be clear, I'm not suggesting that this is a solution for harshness. I'm presenting it to describe the effect of cavitation. Any time the compressibility of the oil increases, as with cavitation, the damping decreases. To be clear: this was not a viable solution to the harshness problem.

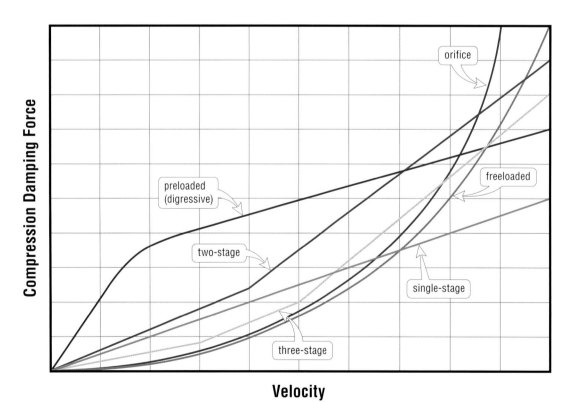

3.43 Damping curves come in many shapes and styles. The orifice curve is of the classic velocity squared variety. Tapered or straight stacks provide a linear curve. Two-stage stacks increase the rate of change in damping when the low-speed shims touch the high-speed stack. Preloaded stacks are digressive. Freeloaded stacks start open therefore begin quite similar to orifice, however as the velocity increases, the shims bend, and the damping is less than it would be if the orifice were fixed.

DAMPING

VALVING STYLES

We are going to look at a number of valving styles as seen in Figure 3.43. The major question is: how progressive do you want it? The short answer—progressive enough but not too progressive. Perhaps not the answer you wanted to hear, but this is what we do when we go testing. We are re-shaping the damping curve. More progressive is not necessarily better nor is being too linear or digressive. The trick is to find the right shape curve for the specific application. Keep in mind that damping is sensitive to velocity, so the shape of the bump is as big a deal as the size. Small square-edge bumps can cause quite high velocities, and rounded bumps hit at very high vehicle speeds can do the same.

Orifice Style Valving

We've looked at orifice-style damping and its drawbacks. The fact that it is related to the shaft velocity squared means that when the velocity is doubled, the damping increases by four. The result is a suspension setup that feels both mushy and harsh. As we discussed before, both the Emulator and cartridge forks were invented to eliminate this type of damping.

Single-Stage Valving

Referring to Figure 3.44 the first type of bending shim style valving stack we'll look at is a single-stage, flat piston, and no preload, tapered stack. Most modern valving systems use some kind of bending shim valving stack on a valve piston. This type of valving is inherently linear, meaning that if you double the velocity, the force increases by a consistent percentage. By changing the stiffness of the valving stack, the rate of increase is tuned.

It may seem confusing at first glance but notice that these illustrations only show the left half of the stack and don't show anything on the top side of the piston.

Additive Damping

Imagine for a moment that we remove the shim stack from the piston entirely and decrease the feed port size. What do

**single-stage
flat piston
no preload
tapered stack**

clamping shim

3.44 This is a very common valving style for road race and street bikes.

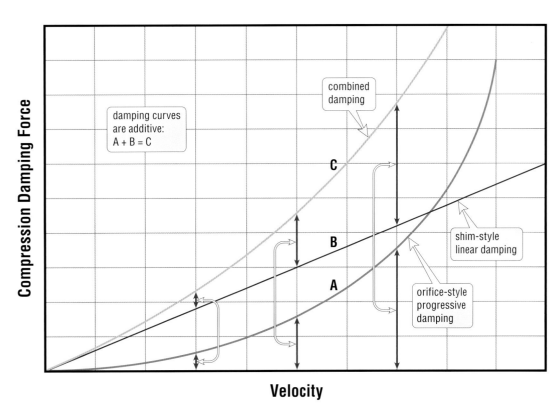

3.45 This shows how damping is additive for a typical piston and valving stack. In this case, curve A is created by the piston orifices alone and is proportional to the velocity squared. Curve B is the linear damping created by the single stage shim stack alone. Curve C is the total of both the piston and the shim stack combined.

we have? We have orifice-style damping. We've just turned a cartridge fork into a damping rod fork. The point here is that just because it is a cartridge doesn't mean the valving works well. There are, in fact, models that have come from the factory with this scenario.

Next, let's replace the shim stack. As mentioned, shim stacks are inherently linear, so if we install a shim stack on this restricted, small-port piston, the damping of the shim stack is added to the damping of the piston. See Figure 3.45.

To figure out if a change to a damping system adds to or decreases from the existing damping, the key question to answer is, "Does the same amount of oil flow through that circuit?"

Let's say we added a compression adjuster to a shock and it functions on the volume of oil that goes into the reservoir—in this case it doesn't affect the volume of oil going through the compression valving. The compression adjuster therefore adds to the overall damping. The addition of a mid-valve on a fork doesn't change the volume of oil going through the fork compression base valve and, once again, is additive.

On the other hand, on a cartridge fork, the low-speed compression adjuster bleed circuit is separate from the main compression piston shim stack. Backing out the adjuster and increasing the bleed size increases the flow through this adjuster circuit. The increase in flow through the adjuster circuit comes at the expense of the flow through the main piston shim stack circuit, meaning that the overall damping is decreased.

Gold Valves

We introduced the digressive concept when we introduced Emulators. How does this concept apply to cartridge forks or shocks? When the piston ports are overly restrictive (too small) the damping created by the piston alone may already be too harsh on high-speed hits. To make matters worse, the shim stack adds more damping on top of that. This may work ok at low speeds, but on high-speed hits it's way too stiff.

I invented Gold Valves in the very early 1990s and, at the time of this publishing, we have over 60 unique valve designs with many different port configurations. In general Gold Valves increase the flow area. This increase has a very similar effect to that found in damping rod forks when we drill out the stock compression damping holes when installing an Emulator. The compression holes on the damping rod serve the same function as the compression damping piston ports. Gold Valves put the damping control onto the shim stack, allowing a much greater range of tuning flexibility, including the ability to dramatically reduce harshness.

Two-Stage Valving

We have already looked at two-stage valving in the cartridge fork section. Two-stage valving (Figure 3.46) is commonly used in dirt bikes where a large range of demands are placed on the suspension. One thing that makes dirt bikes more challenging is that they commonly encounter bumps much greater in size than their suspension travel. Landing off jumps can generate very high velocities as well. Dirt bike forks on a normal motocross track quite commonly see 7 m/s velocity with an average rider. They also have to deal with "normal" lower-speed situations like brake dive going into turns. Two-stage valving is a good setup to handle this range of obstacles.

The smallest-diameter shim—the one farthest away from the piston—is called the clamping shim. Its diameter is the most critical part of the valving stack because all the other "working" shims bend on it. On a two-stage stack there is a small-diameter shim that separates the low-speed stack from the high-speed stack. This small-diameter shim is called the crossover shim, and both its diameter and thickness are important. Using a larger diameter will stiffen up the low-speed while a thicker crossover will delay the stiffening support of the high-speed stack, making it softer.

A good rule of thumb is that the crossover diameter should be larger than or equal to the diameter of the clamping shim. This helps maintain the crossover gap.

On dirt bike shock compression stacks, it is not uncommon to use three-stage valving stacks. Note that generally the more stages there are the more progressive the curve will be. The overall suspension stiffness, however, still depends on the stiffness of the specific stack. In other words, a three-stage stack could end up either stiffer or softer, or more or less progressive, than a two-stage stack, depending on the exact shim sizes. How many

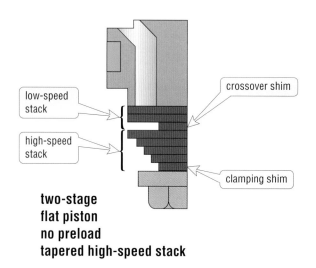

low-speed stack

crossover shim

high-speed stack

clamping shim

**two-stage
flat piston
no preload
tapered high-speed stack**

3.46 This valving style is commonly seen in dirt bikes where the velocity range is much higher than for street bikes. Landing off jumps as well as rocks and roots can cause particularly high shaft velocities.

stages work best is determined solely by testing. That being said, dirt bikes generally use more stages than pavement bikes.

Preloaded Stacks

There are situations where additional low-speed damping is desired but without the addition of more high-speed damping. Supermoto is an excellent application for this type of damping—it requires pitch control because of its long travel and heavy braking. This means controlling the front-to-back movement experienced during braking and acceleration. If, with a non-preloaded stack, the stiffness of the stack was increased enough to control the pitch (a relatively low-speed phenomenon), the ride over square-edged bumps would be quite harsh.

Refer to Figure 3.47 to see that preloading can be accomplished a number of ways. The first illustration shows the use of a flat piston with a "hoop shim." This is a large inner-diameter shim. The "nesting shim" is thinner and fits inside the hoop shim. The difference in thickness of the hoop and nesting shims provide preload for the rest of the working shims. By varying the thickness of the nesting shim as well as the stiffness of the rest of the working shims, the shape of the damping curve can be controlled nicely.

Another method of preloading is "stepping" the face of the piston to create a "recessed" piston. The step is like a pocket in the piston face. If the step is .2mm deep and the shim stack is bolted directly onto it, the preload will be .2mm.

Instead of stepping the face of the piston, a taper can be machined as well. This will produce similar results as the two previous methods.

Race Tech's G2-R Gold Valves provide a more advanced version of preloading, thanks to the addition of restrictor stacks. (See Figure 3.48.) The G2-R starts with a stepped piston with large ports, and then the restrictor stack goes against the piston face to control preload. In fact, the preload can be reduced to zero or even "freeloaded."

The restrictor stack can also be changed in diameter to incrementally restrict the piston port size. If you're thinking that I've been saying "bigger is better" through the course of this book, you're right—but there are also times when this isn't the case. In supercross, for instance, one of the key requirements is bottoming resistance,

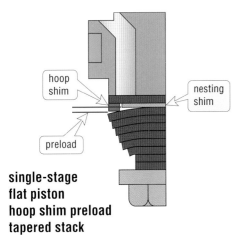

**single-stage
flat piston
hoop shim preload
tapered stack**

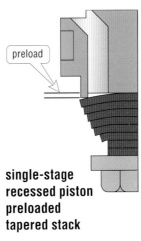

3.47 (Left) Two methods to create preload are shown. The first is through the use of a large inner-diameter "hoop" shim. The "nesting" shim fits into the hoop shim inner diameter and is thinner. The difference between the thicknesses is the preload. The second method steps the piston face itself. A variation of this is an actual taper on the piston face.

**single-stage
recessed piston
preloaded
tapered stack**

3.48 (Below) The G2-R Valve is extremely flexible. It can be preloaded, freeloaded, restricted incrementally. This adds some complexity but offers the highest degree of tunability.

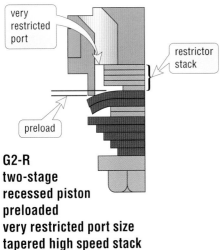

**G2-R
two-stage
recessed piston
preloaded
very restricted port size
tapered high speed stack**

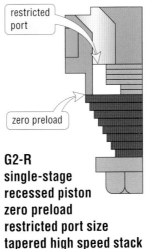

**G2-R
single-stage
recessed piston
zero preload
restricted port size
tapered high speed stack**

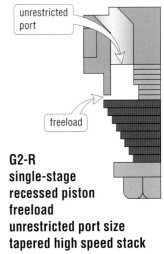

**G2-R
single-stage
recessed piston
freeload
unrestricted port size
tapered high speed stack**

because supercross landings are typically the highest velocities recorded in all of motorcycledom. The key point is, when shaping a damping curve you want to create the *best* progression, not the most and not the least. In general I like to use just enough compression damping and progression to do the job (resist bottoming, control dive, and so on) and no more.

Freeloaded Stacks

A freeloaded stack is one that starts with a small-diameter shim against the piston face. This shim does not cover the feed ports in the piston and therefore presents an open orifice to the oncoming flow. It is the most progressive style of damping outside of a fixed orifice.

This style of stack has been tried a number of times over the years (including by myself for quite an extensive period). In my experience, it never works. It exhibits the same drawbacks as orifice-style damping, namely, it's mushy and harsh. It also has the added challenge of sealing the piston off on the rebound stroke.

Straight versus Tapered Stacks

One question that comes up commonly in the Race Tech Suspension Seminars is, "Why use a tapered stack instead of a straight one?" It is a widely held belief that the tapered stack is more progressive than the straight one. This is not true in the deflection (velocity) range these stacks actually see. They are both linear stacks, meaning that once they open, they increase stiffness at a constant slope.

Many tuners mistakenly add thicker or more shims "deeper" in the stack in an attempt to create a more progressive high-speed response. This attempt is futile as this is not how these stacks work: they are linear. Increasing the stiffness deeper into the stack or higher in the stack makes the entire stack stiffer.

So why tapered stacks? Simple—this helps prevent the permanent distortion of the shims (Figure 3.50). On a straight stack all the shims open the same amount and they all bend on the clamping shim, so the stress is concentrated at the bending point. With a tapered stack the working shims bend at multiple points (on each preceding shim), spreading out the stress. Tapered stacks also have more clearance to open before they hit the base plate (thick washer).

Thin Shims versus Thick Shims

Have you ever wondered why shock manufacturers use large numbers of thin shims against the piston face instead of a smaller number of thicker shims? There is more than one way to create the desired stiffness of a valving stack, after all. Sometimes fifteen .15mm thick shims are used instead of a lesser number of thicker shims—why?

No, it's not progressiveness, or that they had a bunch of extras lying around. The answer is permanent distortion. If you stack up a thin shim and a thick one made out of identical materials, clamp them in a vise in the middle and start bending both of them at the same time, you will notice that the thicker shim permanently distorts before the thinner one.

The reason is that as the shims are bending, the molecules on the top are being stretched while the ones on the bottom are being compressed (see Figure 3.51). In the middle is a "neutral axis" where there is no stress. The further away from the neutral axis, the more stress on the molecules. The molecules furthest from the neutral axis are working the hardest. This means that a thicker shim, with molecules further away from the neutral axis, will distort with less deflection.

So where are the thinner shims used? Typically they are found in the low-speed stack of a two-stage stack. They are used in that context because the shims in the low-speed stack have to bend further than the high-speed stack by the thickness of the crossover.

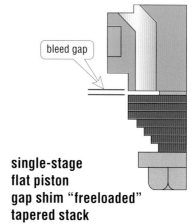

single-stage flat piston gap shim "freeloaded" tapered stack

3.49 A "freeloaded stack" has clearance between the first working shim and the piston. I have never seen this work. It is similar to orifice style damping.

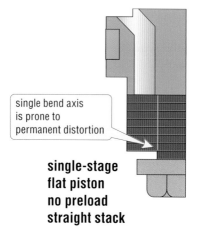

single-stage flat piston no preload straight stack

3.50 Contrary to popular belief the tapered stack is not progressive. Its advantage is that it has multiple bending axes that assist in smoothing the abrupt bend of a straight stack thereby resisting permanent distortion (creasing). It also provides more clearance from the base plate.

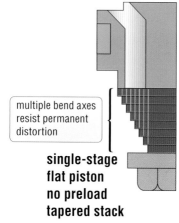

single-stage flat piston no preload tapered stack

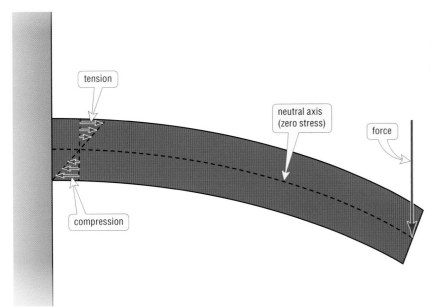

3.51 When a beam attached to a wall is loaded, it bends. The material on the top surface are being stretched apart while the material on the bottom is being compressed. There is an axis right in the middle that has no stress at all called the neutral axis. The further away the material is from the neutral axis, the more it is stressed.

So the next question is how does the stiffness vary with thickness? The stiffness is proportional to the thickness cubed, but keep in mind this is only valid for shims of the same diameter and material. Refer to the chart below for guidance.

What this means is it takes eight .10mm thick shims to equal the stiffness of one .20mm thick shim. This can come in quite handy when comparing valving stack stiffness, or if you find a valving stack with shims that are permanently distorted. If they are distorted and the rider liked it when it was just revalved, you can calculate another stack with the equivalent stiffness of the original stack but made out of thinner shims and, quite possibly, eliminate the problem.

Rebound Separator Valves

One of the problems with a standard low-speed rebound adjuster is that it flows in both directions. When it is set perfectly for rebound, it can be way too mushy on compression and, in certain conditions, bottom easily. When it is nice

and firm on compression, it is way too slow on rebound, causing packing and loss of traction. The solution is to create asymmetric (different in each direction) damping.

This can be done in many ways. I first observed it on '81 Honda CR250s and 480s with Showa shocks. Showa changed the location of the asymmetric valve to the inside of the shock shaft shortly thereafter. Öhlins has had a valve attached to the end of their shock shafts for a number of years as well.

In 2004, Terry Hay (yes, the same Aussie with the PDS Telescopic Needle) created a version of this concept that could be incorporated on a stock shock. He called it a Rebound Separator Valve (RSV). It was built into a replacement shock shaft nut. See Figure 3.52.

Here's how it works. Starting on the rebound stroke there is a check valve that opens up causing the rebound to function normally, with the tapered adjuster needle controlling the flow. On compression the check valve shuts and the adjustable rebound circuit is fed with a bleed hole specifically sized for the application thereby giving it more low-speed compression damping. The modification improves traction and feel as well as bottoming resistance. Race Tech has utilized Rebound Separator Valves with impressive feedback in all genres.

Other Valving Styles

There are a number of other styles of valving systems. Among these are ball bearings covering piston ports that are preloaded by coil springs. These springs can be varied in both rate and length to create the desired damping curve. This system has been employed by Works Performance Shocks for years with great commercial success.

Emulators use coil springs preloading a valve piston. As mentioned previously, the valve spring stiffness, preload, and

Shim Stiffness to Thickness Coefficient for a fixed OD

$\mu \propto t^3$

μ — Stiffness Coefficient

$\propto$ — is proportional to

t — Thickness of Shim

t	t^3	μ
0.10	0.001	1
0.15	0.0034	3.4
0.20	0.008	8
0.25	0.0156	15.6
0.30	0.027	27

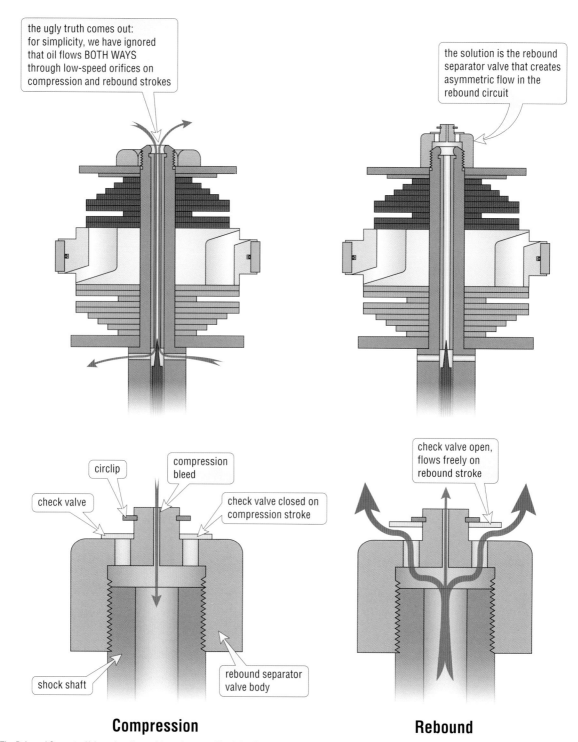

Compression

Rebound

3.52 The Rebound Separator Valve solves the problem of an open bleed that flows in both directions. The RSV creates asymmetric flow using a check valve.

bleed size can be changed to control the shape of the damping curve quite nicely.

There are leaf spring systems and even systems that change the oil viscosity with a magnetic field. There are also systems that use only electro-magnetism and no fluid. These have potential for regenerative features by capturing the energy and recharging batteries. These last two methods seem promising as we move forward into programmable valving systems.

The lesson here is that I don't care how you create the damping curve; all I care about is what the curve is. If ball bearings and coil springs work, then they work. There are many, many ways to create a damping curve.

Chapter 4
Friction

Friction is the resistance that one object encounters when sliding over another. The amount of friction is dependent on the materials that are in contact with each other, the normal force, and whether there is movement or not. Friction turns kinetic energy into heat.

It is my opinion that friction is the first area that should be addressed before any other suspension tuning or setup is done. Measure static sag and the "stiction zone" to get clues as to the severity of the problem and work to minimize friction before moving on to springs and damping.

The main thing to remember about friction is: "friction … bad".

STATIC FRICTION
Stiction, or static friction, refers to the friction present when there is no movement between the surfaces. Static friction is dependent on two things. The first factor is the coefficient of friction μ, which is dependent on materials, temperature, surface finish, and so on. The second factor is the force perpendicular to the surfaces at the contact point, referred to as the "normal force" [F_{normal}]. The formula is $F_{friction} = μ \times F_{normal}$.

You may have reacted to the fact that the surface area in contact is not in the formula. In most cases friction is completely independent of surface area. There are exceptions to this; most significant is rubber on the road, possibly because the material squishes into surface irregularities.

There is almost always a layer of "stuff" between the two surfaces, and it has a big effect on friction. The stuff can be composed of many things: oil, grease, moisture, oxides, etc. If there's a thin layer of grease on the surfaces, it can cut friction tenfold in comparison to completely clean. If the stuff is

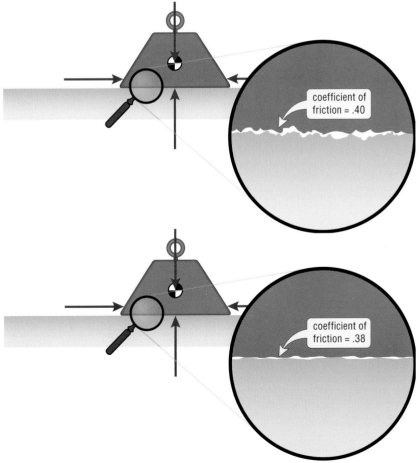

4.1 Surface roughness has an effect on friction but not as much as you might think. It is believed that this has something to do with the number of contact points even on a "smooth" surface.

coefficient of friction = .40

coefficient of friction = .38

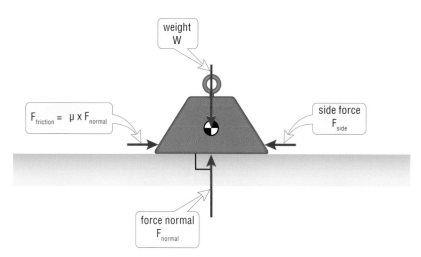

weight
W

$F_{friction} = \mu \times F_{normal}$

side force
F_{side}

force normal
F_{normal}

4.2 In this example the block is resting statically on a horizontal surface. The normal force is equal to the weight of the block. When a side load is applied there is an equal frictional resisting force created. As the side load is increased so does the frictional force up to a maximum value of the coefficient of friction times the normal force. At this value it breaks loose and goes into dynamic friction, which is typically slightly less than the maximum static value.

completely removed, friction forces can be huge, and the two surfaces can seize together completely.

Just to be clear, the frictional force does not exist until the side load is applied. The more the side load, the greater the friction, until the maximum frictional force has been exceeded and you get movement.

If we have a block sitting on a horizontal surface, the weight is pushing down vertically. In this case the normal force is equal to the weight. If we apply a side load parallel to the surface [F_{side}], this load will cause the block to move if it is greater than the maximum available frictional force.

No movement if: $F_{side} < F_{friction\ max}$
Movement if: $F_{side} > F_{friction\ max}$

With this drawing we introduce the concept of vectors. The vectors are the arrows representing the forces. Vectors have both magnitude and direction—the size of the force (magnitude) is represented by the length of the arrow (double the force = double the length of the arrow).

One of the great things about vectors is that we can add them together or break them apart. This allows us to solve complicated things easily. The rule is that if we have two vectors and we want to see what their combined effect is, we simply place the tail of the second vector on the tip of the first vector. The combined effect of both vectors is represented by a new vector starting at the tail of the first vector and ending at the tip of the second. This is called the resultant vector.

This technique can be done with any number of vectors added to each other. It is often used for breaking forces apart into perpendicular components, as we will do in a moment.

Now, let's go back to our example. If the block is on an incline (see Figure 4.4) and we have no other external forces, the normal force is not equal to the weight. The normal force is the component of force pushing perpendicular to the surface. In the graphic you can see the weight is still vertical, but we have broken it up into two parts and replaced it with two forces. The first is the component pushing the block down the hill ($F_{down\ the\ hill}$), and the second is the component pushing it into the hill ($F_{perpendicular\ to\ the\ hill}$).

addition of vectors

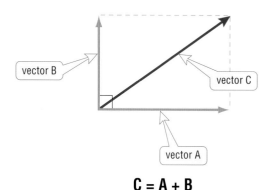

resultant vector C

vector B

vector A

A + B = C

breaking vectors apart

vector B

vector C

vector A

C = A + B

4.3 Forces can be represented by vectors that have both magnitude and direction. Vectors can be added together or broken apart into any direction that would help our analysis.

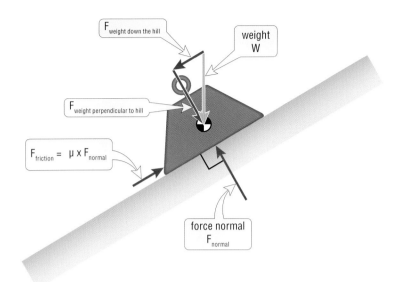

The normal force is equal to the component of the force pushing it into the hill (note that it is less than the weight). The same calculations regarding movement still apply. In this case the side load that could cause movement is the component of the weight parallel to the surface ($F_{weight\ down\ the\ hill}$).

Fork Dynamics

Let's look at what happens in a telescopic front fork when the wheel hits a bump. Upon contact, the force is directed radially from the point of contact to the axle. (See Figure 4.5.)

We can now break this force into two components: one that compresses the fork and one that tries to bend it in half. The component that tries to bend it in half increases the normal force on the fork bushings and therefore increases friction that inhibits movement. The contact actually does bend the tubes, particularly where it has the most leverage—right below the triple clamp. Keep in mind that this bending is temporary, as the tube springs back when the load is removed. With upside-down forks, this means the inner (upper) bushing must go through a kink just below the triple clamp. This can cause severe binding and excessive wear on the inside of the outer tube.

On severe hits, particularly on dirt bikes, the frictional force can be greater than the damping and the spring forces combined. If you are testing to eliminate a harsh fork action, look at friction first. Pay particular attention to the sliding surface on the inside of the outer fork tube. If the hard anodizing is worn through, this may be the source of your harshness. If you don't take care of it, you'll never get the performance you are looking for. We'll explain more on hard anodizing in a moment.

FORK SLIDING BUSHINGS

In the beginning fork sliders were made of aluminum and contacted the hard-chromed fork tubes directly. This configuration didn't wear well nor was it very slippery. Next bronze bushings were introduced, and these problems were improved somewhat. Modern fork bushings are made of steel, coated with bronze, and then coated with Teflon® (DuPont's version of polytetrafluoroethylene or PTFE)—more on Teflon in a moment. These provide a dramatic improvement in both friction and wear. The bronze layer is a built-in safety designed to provide an adequate surface when the Teflon wears through. The biggest reason they need to be replaced is they get imbedded with metal shavings and other contaminants. Other causes of damage are: disassembly, dented sliders, and rarely, pure wear.

DYNAMIC FRICTION

Once the static friction between two components is overcome and they begin to slide, we enter the world of dynamic friction. Let's look at an example of static versus dynamic friction. You are on an icy street and there is a little old lady in a '62 Cadillac right next to you. Of course you want to impress her, so when the light turns green, you nail the throttle. The little old lady pulls away from you like you are standing still. This is because you broke static friction and lost traction by going into dynamic friction.

So which is greater—static or dynamic friction? All things being equal, static friction is greater. "Hooked up" is greater than "broken loose." And in general greater slip velocity will decrease the friction slightly. This is the reason that when you push on your forks, it is harder to start your fork tubes compressing than to keep them compressing. The exceptions to this general rule are again tires, especially certain compounds, where a little slip can actually create more friction than hooked up but only a little.

Some people think that if you want to go fast on an off-road motorcycle, higher revs and throwing a lot of dirt are the way to go. This is often not the case. For example,

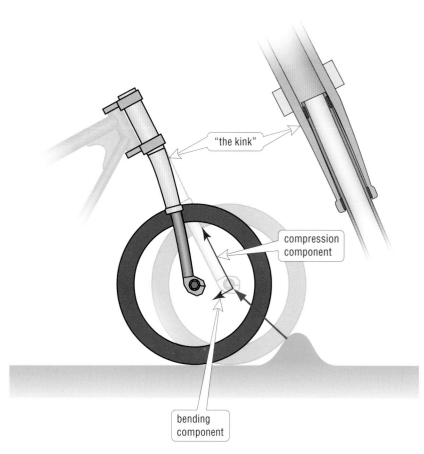

4.5 When a front wheel hits a bump with the brake off, the force goes radially to the front axle at an angle as shown. This force can be broken up into components: first is a component that tends to compress the fork and second a force that tries to bend it in half. The fork bends mostly just below the triple clamp where there is the most leverage. This creates a temporary "kink" that the upper fork bushing has a hard time getting through, causing binding and excessive wear.

"the kink"

compression component

bending component

FRICTION

Jean Michele Bayle, at the 1996 U.S.G.P. at Glen Helen, won the race with a flat front tire. He hauled around the corners and only threw up a tiny roost. Everyone chasing him was throwing up roost that was literally knocking spectators over. JMB pulled away a second a lap with a flat front tire, and he looked like he was out for a Sunday ride.

We're often fooled in motocross because we've got knobby tires digging into the dirt. Most road racers know that when they are just barely spinning is actually when they have the *most* traction. When they're spinning a lot, they're not going as fast as they could (and it's pretty hard on tires too).

This is very noticeable in racing shifter karts. Lee attended Yamaha's press introduction for its on- and off-road racing teams in 2002, and everyone tried their hands at go-kart racing. It was fascinating to watch the pro supercrossers powersliding through the turns but always being one to three seconds a lap slower than the factory kart racers. The kart pros knew that too much sliding—though very cool looking—always cost more time than keeping the tires hooked up and propelling them forward.

COATINGS

Hard anodizing is a coating that is applied to aluminum and is quite different than color anodizing. Hard anodizing makes the surface dramatically harder, more durable, and more slippery. It is commonly used on aluminum fork sliders and shock bodies and is fairly inexpensive.

The quality of the hard anodizing can be quite varied. The less expensive methods can wear out fairly easily. Once the coating is gone, the soft aluminum is exposed and the fork has much greater friction.

Let's go back to the upside-down forks with the kink in them. With the forks disassembled, inspect the condition of the anodizing on the inside of the outer fork tubes. Take an inspection mirror and a flashlight or a bore scope and inspect for wear right where the lower triple clamp would be. Using an inspection mirror is a must: if you don't use an inspection mirror and just look down the tube, you will likely see only reflections and you'll miss the wear. If the anodizing is worn through but they're not too bad, the tubes can be stripped, hard anodized again, and polished.

Exotic coatings like titanium nitride and DLC (Diamond Like Carbon) can further decrease friction. Titanium nitride is not used much anymore because DLC is slipperier and more durable. These coatings can get pretty expensive (DLC for a pair of tubes is in the $600–$800 range), but if you are looking for the edge, go for it.

An important tip on DLC coatings is that the newer the forks are the better. This is because the fork tubes have to be unscrewed from the fork bottoms, coated, and screwed back on. If you've got old fork bottoms, you can gall and destroy a perfectly good set of fork bottoms by taking them apart. The older they are the more chance of damage.

Teflon has been used in many forms with good success. This dry film lubricant can reduce friction dramatically. Teflon can be further combined with other friction reducers like molybdenum disulfide (moly). It can be combined with other materials to bond it to surfaces. Ni-Tef (nickel Teflon) is another coating with good results. The challenge of all Teflon-based coatings is that they have a tendency to wear out with use. Both Teflon and moly have been added to suspension fluids with limited success over the years. One problem is that they have a tendency to settle to the bottom of the fork when not in use, just like non-stick cookware at home.

POLISHING

Surface roughness has an effect on friction, though it is smaller than most people might think. Doubling the surface roughness might cause only a few percent change in friction. This doesn't mean surface roughness doesn't matter—it does, and efforts to reduce friction can really pay off.

This is particularly true on older right-side-up damping rod forks; both the outer slider and the inside of the chrome tube are eligible. At Race Tech we have a small-bore engine hone (not a ball hone) that we wrap with 500-grit sandpaper and run with a drill motor to polish.

Polishing the inside of a cartridge tube is pretty simple. Get a ⅜-inch (10mm) steel rod at your local hardware store. Take a hacksaw and cut an axial slot in the end of the rod. Next prepare strips of cloth about 25mm (1 inch) wide. Put one of them in the slot and wrap up enough layers so that when you stick it into the tube it has some compression on it. Put the rod in a hand drill. Wet the cloth and apply some automotive polishing compound. Polish until you see the finish you're looking for.

SURFACE TREATMENT

There are surface treatments available today that are considered to be "best kept secrets" by many race teams. They go way beyond simple polishing. My favorite is from a company called WPC Treatment. WPC is not a coating, it is a treatment that enhances the surface to reduce friction and strengthen parts. It is widely used on engine parts, including pistons, cranks, gearboxes, and all parts of the drivetrain. We use it in suspension components, particularly forks where friction can be a large part of the total force.

The WPC process fires ultra-fine particles toward the surface of a product at very high speeds. The resulting thermal discharge permanently changes the surface, strengthening structure and creating a harder more durable part. Materials like Teflon can often be added and subsequently imbedded in the surface for further friction reduction. I use this treatment in the engines of my record-setting Bonneville land-speed racing motorcycles with great success.

As I mentioned earlier, the main thing to know about friction is: friction … *bad*! As far as suspension components are concerned, the less friction you have on sliding surfaces, the better the suspension works. Look for any clues to excessive friction (check the stiction zone in the springs chapter) and do your best to eliminate the cause. Most of this chapter has been discussing front telescopic forks, as they have much greater problems with friction than the rear, but attention to the free operation of the linkage, swingarm, and shock can pay large dividends in performance as well. See the troubleshooting sections on sticky forks and sticky shocks for more ideas for friction reduction.

It is interesting to note that there have been times we have removed a lot of friction from a set of forks and as a result, they started to bottom. As you might guess, the solution was not to add the friction back in! We added stiffer springs, more compression damping, higher oil level, and so on until the bottoming was eliminated and the ride was dramatically better.

Materials and lubricants affect both static and dynamic friction to different degrees. I highly recommend using the finest suspension fluids available as they can make a significant reduction in friction for a nominal cost.

At the time of this writing, I have not seen aftermarket fork seals that outperform the original equipment. They are either stickier or they leak—or both—but some are pretty close to OEM in performance. Also you should pre-lube your seals with a high-end seal grease like Ultra Slick Grease. In a pinch you can use fork fluid, but the seal grease lasts longer.

It is my opinion that friction reduction is an area that will dramatically improve in the coming years. Remember—reduce friction first, then go to springs, then damping.

FRICTION

Chapter 5
Geometry

When we as riders talk about handling, what we're really talking about is a feeling that comes from a combination of chassis geometry, chassis rigidity, engine characteristics (power, width of powerband, and flywheel inertia), mass distribution (center of gravity both horizontally and vertically), mass centralization, tire characteristics, ergonomics (handlebar, seat, and footpeg location), and suspension. These quantities interact and overlap. It can get very confusing, however, because a change in flywheel inertia, for instance, can feel very similar

to a change in compression damping. To understand this a little better, let's take a closer look at a major component—chassis geometry.

Geometry refers to the physical relationships of the chassis components. Some of the many factors are the wheelbase, wheel diameter, rake (steering head angle), fork offset, swingarm angle, countershaft location, sprocket sizes, center of gravity location, and so on. From these we can calculate both front and rear trail, anti-squat angle, and anti-squat percentage.

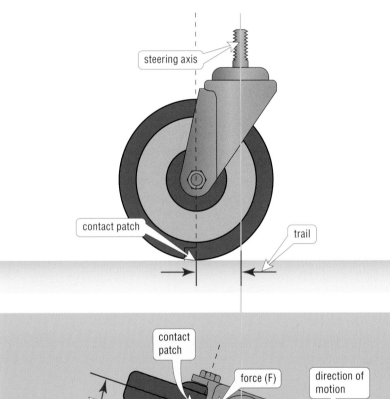

5.1 A caster has a vertical pivoting axis. This means the amount the wheel follows behind the axis is a direct measurement of trail. This trail creates a self-correcting torque when the wheel is out of alignment.

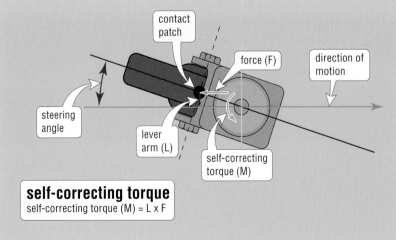

It is worth repeating that geometry and suspension setup are interdependent. In other words, they work together as one affects the other.

TRAIL

The big daddy of all geometry numbers is front-end trail. Ground trail is the distance from the center of the tire contact patch to the point where the steering axis intersects with the ground. It is measured along the ground. In other words, it is the amount the contact patch "trails" the steering axis.

Let's look at a caster on a grocery shopping cart as in Figure 5.1. In this case the rotating axis is vertical and the rearward offset is a direct measurement of trail. If the wheel gets out of line, there is a torque that self-centers the wheel. Ground trail on a suspended front end is most commonly measured with the suspension fully extended.

With a telescopic front end mounted at an angle, it becomes a bit more complicated (Figure 5.2). The fact that the steering axis is at an angle creates trail even with no offset. Rake, also known as caster angle, is defined as the angle of the steering axis from vertical. Offset is the distance perpendicular to the steering axis the front axle leads the steering axis. Testing has shown that with typical rake angles of 23 to 28 degrees or more, zero offset actually creates too much trail. Forward offset (from now on simply called offset) is added in the triple clamps and front axle to decrease the trail (Figure 5.3).

The more trail a bike has, the greater the self-centering effect of the front wheel. This gives the bike more stability, but it's harder to turn the bars. Within a usable range, more trail generally provides more grip (traction) when cornering. Most people have this concept backwards, thinking more

offset means a longer wheelbase and therefore more stability. While the wheelbase does grow with increased offset, the trail actually decreases and therefore stability decreases.

If the rake is increased, so is the ground trail (Figure 5.4). Conversely, if the rake is decreased, the ground trail is decreased. This decrease in rake and trail also occurs dynamically (when the bike is being ridden) whenever the front end dives, such as during braking.

All that is necessary to calculate ground trail is three things: rake, wheel diameter, and total offset (triple clamp offset + axle offset). There is a free spreadsheet trail calculator on www.racetech.com in the Seminar Student Downloads section. Keep in mind that when any of these parameters are changed, it affects other geometry numbers. For example, changing the front wheel diameter will change both rake and trail as well as the center of gravity, swingarm angle, and rear anti-squat, among other things.

If you start measuring wheel diameters, you will find that tires with the exact same size markings will be different diameters, sometimes dramatically so. This means changing tires, particularly changing brands of tires, can have a significant effect on handling.

It should be noted that, as of this printing, most supermoto bikes have *terrible* ground trail numbers. This requires the rider to "back it in." When I first measured Micky Dymond's KTM back in 2006 and saw ground trail numbers of 92mm, I immediately started making triple clamps to correct it. He went on to win the National Championship and the Pikes Peak Hill Climb. Next we worked with Darryl Atkins and Benny Carlson on the works Aprilia Team with similar results. An improvement of one to one and one-half seconds per lap

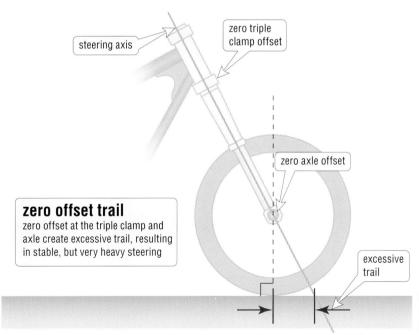

steering axis

zero triple clamp offset

zero axle offset

zero offset trail
zero offset at the triple clamp and axle create excessive trail, resulting in stable, but very heavy steering

excessive trail

5.2 If the wheel is placed right on the steering axis with no offset and a positive rake is added, it creates too much trail.

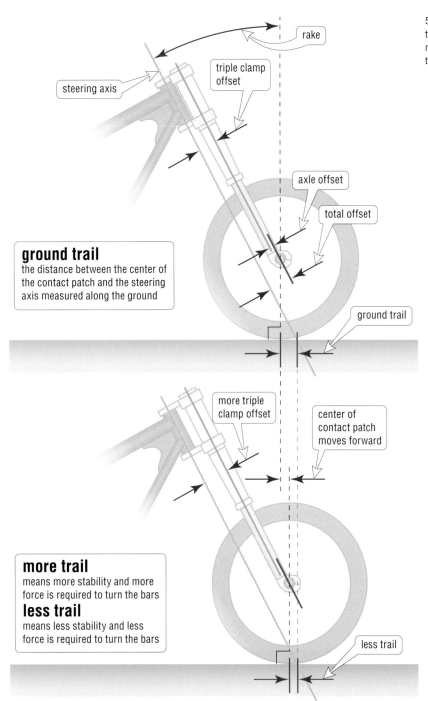

rake

steering axis

triple clamp offset

axle offset

total offset

ground trail
the distance between the center of the contact patch and the steering axis measured along the ground

ground trail

more triple clamp offset

center of contact patch moves forward

more trail
means more stability and more force is required to turn the bars
less trail
means less stability and less force is required to turn the bars

less trail

5.3 Trail (or ground trail) is the distance the center of the front wheel contact patch trails the steering axis measured along the ground. An increase in offset moves the contact patch forward, decreasing trail.

on a 45-second lap time track is not uncommon, even for riders of this caliber! Riders of lesser skill quite often see three to four seconds per lap. This is a very big deal.

REAL TRAIL

We have been talking about ground trail. But there is a better way to measure trail—real trail (Figure 5.5).

Trail is a measurement of the length of the lever arm that provides the self-centering torque on the front wheel. Torque is simply a rotational force around an axis. Torque = force × lever arm length (the perpendicular distance the force is applied from the rotating axis). The key word here is *perpendicular*. Ground trail is measured along the ground, not perpendicular to the steering axis. Real trail, on the other hand, is the distance from the steering axis to the center of the tire contact patch measured perpendicular to the steering axis. This is a much better method. That being said, ground trail can be valuable as a comparison method if wheel diameter

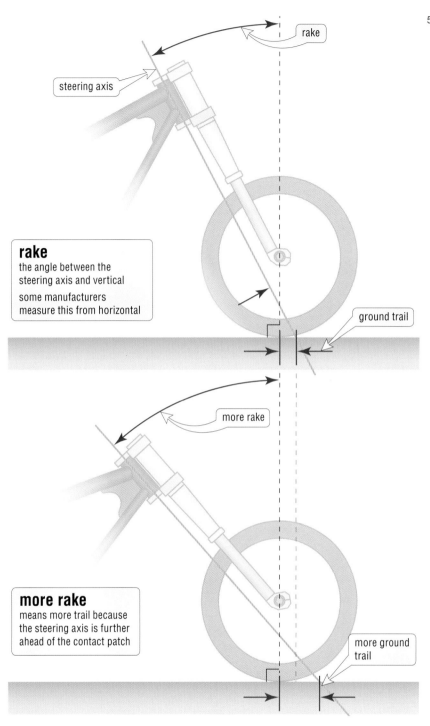

rake
the angle between the steering axis and vertical

some manufacturers measure this from horizontal

steering axis

rake

ground trail

more rake
means more trail because the steering axis is further ahead of the contact patch

more rake

more ground trail

GEOMETRY

and rake are held constant. This concept of real trail was first introduced to me by Tony Foale, a highly respected frame designer, author, and engineer. He also does an in-depth analysis of anti-squat (covered briefly later on in this chapter) in his book *Motorcycle Handling and Chassis Design*.

Trail is most commonly measured with the suspension fully extended, but when the motorcycle is being ridden, trail is constantly changing. This is due to both the movement of the suspension components and the changing terrain. For example, when a dirt bike is being ridden in sand at slow speed, the wheel is pushing sand in front of it (Figure 5.6). The effect is that the center of the tire contact patch is moved forward and the trail is dramatically decreased. In fact, it can easily produce negative trail, which is dynamically unstable. This explains why you feel so uncoordinated at slow speeds in sand (yes, it's really the bike, not you). Once the bike gets up

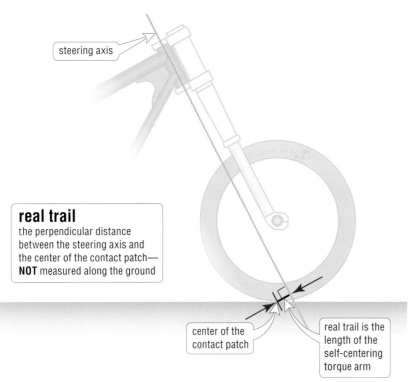

steering axis

real trail
the perpendicular distance between the steering axis and the center of the contact patch—**NOT** measured along the ground

center of the contact patch

real trail is the length of the self-centering torque arm

GEOMETRY

to speed it gets "on top" of the sand, the contact patch moves backward, and everything feels stable again.

If we look at a supercross rider in a washboard whoop section (whoops that are close together), you can imagine it is important to get "on top" of the whoops. If the rider slows down enough and lets the front wheel drop down into the bumps, the tire contact patch moves forward and the trail goes negative (Figure 5.7).

With this in mind, you can understand the importance of hitting the bump straight on, with the wheel square to the bump—if you don't, look out! It is a tough technique to learn or teach, but the faster the rider goes, the easier it gets. A word of caution here: the answer is *not*, "Just pin it, Billy!" If you've seen a top rider like James Stewart go through a washboard whoop section, you've seen this in action.

Something else to keep in mind is that suspension setup has a huge effect on trail when riding. If two identical bikes are set with the same initial (extended) trail and one has a softer set of fork springs or even less preload, it will have less rake and trail when in use (dynamically). This is because the forks will compress more—particularly when getting on the brakes going into turns.

REAR WHEEL TRAIL

Rear wheel trail is the perpendicular distance from the steering axis to the center of the rear wheel contact patch. In the past most people have referred to wheelbase alone, again measured along the ground or more commonly from the centers of the front and rear axles. The longer the rear wheel trail the

slower the rear end "comes around," giving more straight-line stability at the expense of turning slower.

ANTI-SQUAT

On the rear, swingarm angle and chain forces combine to cause stiffening or softening of the effective rear spring rate during acceleration or deceleration. This effective stiffening is called anti-squat as it "holds up" the rear end of the motorcycle during acceleration, keeping it from squatting. It is a transient (temporary) effect linked to acceleration, and the effect increases with greater acceleration. The complete analysis can get quite involved, so in the scope of this book we will provide a simplified overview.

To begin let's look at how a motorcycle is driven forward. Power is applied to the ground at the rear tire. The rear tire is connected to the chassis through the rear axle and the chain. Forward drive is transmitted to the chassis by the rear axle directly in a straight line to the swingarm pivot (not in a straight horizontal line). The swingarm pivot is the point at which this force is applied, meaning that the angle of the swingarm where it is attached to the frame determines the direction of this force.

Now we need to step back and look at a little physics. When we apply a force to a body, the body reacts based on the mass of the body, the point of application, and the size and direction of the force in relation to the body's center of gravity. If the force is applied in direct line with the CG (center of gravity) there will be no rotational force (torque) applied (Figure 5.8). If the force line does not go directly through the

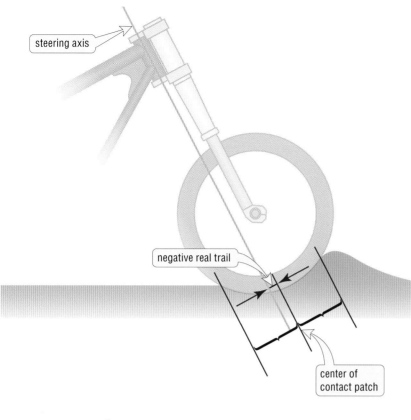

steering axis

5.6 When going slowly in sand, the sand gets pushed up ahead of the wheel. The center of the contact patch moves forward. This decreases trail to the point of becoming negative and unstable.

negative real trail

center of contact patch

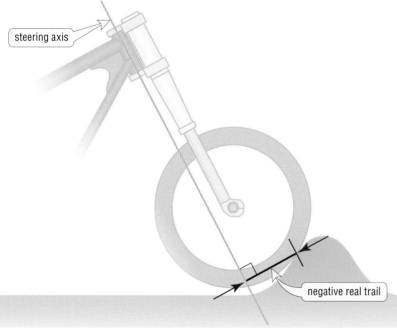

steering axis

5.7 Letting the front wheel drop into supercross whoops causes the contact patch to move forward, decreasing trail, quite often to negative.

negative real trail

GEOMETRY

CG, a rotating torque is generated (Figure 5.9). In addition, the force can be applied anywhere along the force line, and the body will react exactly the same way.

Imagine we hold the sprung mass of the motorcycle and rider at the CG. If the swingarm slope is positive (the countershaft is above the rear axle), the swingarm force will tend to lift the sprung mass. If this line of force does not go through the CG, it will also create torque.

Now let's add the chain (Figure 5.10). It can only pull on the countershaft sprocket. If the chain slopes down from

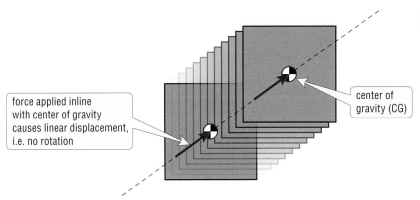

force applied inline with center of gravity causes linear displacement, i.e. no rotation

center of gravity (CG)

the countershaft sprocket to the rear sprocket, it will tend to pull the sprung CG down, making it softer. If not aligned with the CG, it will rotate the sprung mass as well. All this constantly changes, of course, as the rear suspension moves.

With some mathematical analysis we can figure out the effect of each of these components on the chassis independently, but what a pain!

Fortunately there is a simpler way to analyze the rear end anti-squat graphically (refer to Figure 5.11). Force vectors on rigid bodies are sliding vectors. This means we can apply both these forces anywhere along their lines of action. This means if we can locate the intersection point of the swingarm axis and the chain axis, we can apply both of these forces there. This intersection point is called the instantaneous force center (IFC). To be clear, it is the point at which we can combine the two forces and represent them with one force (resultant force) that has the same effect on the chassis as the two individual forces.

Now let's reattach the rear wheel to the motorcycle. We know the force comes in via the rear tire's contact patch with

force applied offset to the center of gravity displaces AND rotates due to torque (M) = (F x L)

lever (L)

force (F)

5.9 When a force is applied in a line that does not go through the CG, the body not only displaces, it also rotates.

the ground and goes through the IFC. This gives us two points to draw the line.

The angle of this force line from the center of the contact patch through the IFC from horizontal is called the anti-squat angle. It is the exact same angle we would have calculated as the resultant force of the chain and swingarm had we not done a graphical analysis. This makes the analysis much simpler because we know that the resultant horizontal component of the force is the driving force at the rear tire contact patch. If we also know the angle, we can calculate the vertical component with trigonometry ($F_{vert} = F_{driving} \times \cos$ [anti-squat angle]). We know the point of application is the IFC, so the rest of the analysis practically does itself (just kidding).

Referring to Figure 5.12, you can see the anti-squat angle changes with swingarm angle. If the line of force through the IFC goes through the combined CG, it will not create a rotating torque, but the vertical component will tend to lift the motorcycle. If the line passes below the combined CG, not only will it lift the motorcycle, effectively making the suspension stiffer, it will also create a torque that rotates the chassis backward (counterclockwise viewed from the right), loading the rear suspension. This torque is counterclockwise, so it will tend to compress the rear suspension, effectively making it softer.

To clarify, this torque counteracts some of the lift. As long as the anti-squat angle is positive, it will still lift the motorcycle but not as much as if it were going through the CG. In this case the combined lifting and rotation tend to cancel each other somewhat—as long as the lifting is greater (the anti-squat angle is positive), there is still a net anti-squat effect. Notice that as the suspension compresses further, the anti-squat angle gets smaller. As long as the anti-squat angle is still positive, the net forces will continue to hold up the motorcycle during acceleration, though to a lesser degree.

Here's when we need to make some assumptions so this doesn't get hairy (is it too late?). Let's assume 50/50 weight distribution. Let's also assume the height of the combined CG (center of gravity) of the sprung mass of the bike and rider is half the wheelbase. These assumptions are pretty close to reality for many motorcycles and will help simplify the calculations.

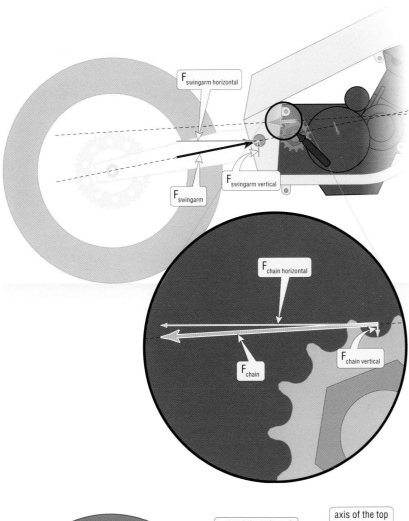

5.10 When the motorcycle accelerates, the sprung mass is being pushed by the swingarm and at the same time pulled back by the chain. Both these forces can be broken into vertical and horizontal components. The sum of the horizontal forces is the force of acceleration.

$F_{swingarm\ horizontal}$

$F_{swingarm\ vertical}$

$F_{swingarm}$

$F_{chain\ horizontal}$

$F_{chain\ vertical}$

F_{chain}

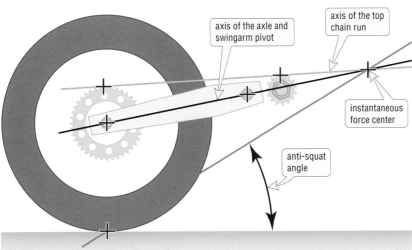

axis of the axle and swingarm pivot

axis of the top chain run

instantaneous force center

anti-squat angle

5.11 The instantaneous force center or IFC is located where the axes of the swingarm and the chain intersect. The anti-squat angle goes from the center of the rear contact patch and goes through the IFC. The greater the angle, the greater the anti-squat.

What we need to figure out is how large the forces are, realizing that they vary dependent on how hard the bike accelerates. A modern 1000cc sportbike has enough power and tires are good enough to accelerate at 1g—the acceleration of gravity. Yes, I realize gravity is a vertical acceleration and

this is a horizontal acceleration, but this will help simplify things as well.

Recall Newton's Second Law of Motion, $F = ma$ or force equals mass times acceleration. The mass being accelerated is the combined sprung mass of the bike and the rider.

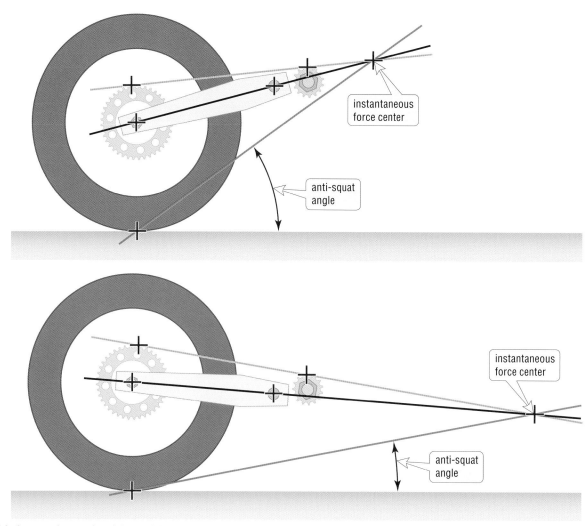

5.12 As the suspension goes through the travel, the amount of anti-squat decreases.

When the bike is at rest this combined sprung mass is being accelerated by gravity vertically downward. In order to accelerate horizontally, this same mass must have a horizontal force applied.

Because we located the CG at 50 percent of the wheelbase both horizontally and vertically, this means when we accelerate at 1g, the front wheel will just barely lift off the ground. See Figure 5.15. Here's why: when the bike accelerates, it wants to rotate counterclockwise around the rear tire contact patch, tending to cause a wheelie. In other words there is a torque or moment (force × lever arm) around the contact patch equal to the force due to horizontal acceleration times the height of the CG. On the other hand the clockwise torque that tends to keep it on the ground is equal to the weight (suspended mass times acceleration of gravity which is vertical) times half the wheelbase.

Because the height of the CG is equal to half the wheelbase, the lever arms are the same length. And because the vertical acceleration of gravity is equal to the 1g horizontal acceleration we have chosen, both of these torques are equal. If we accelerated

any harder, the front end would lift off the ground and wheelie over. This is because the horizontal force would become greater than the weight thereby increasing the counterclockwise torque to an amount greater than the clockwise torque.

When the front wheel lifts, the rear suspension must hold up all the weight of the bike and rider instead of just half. If we want the suspension to be independent of this load transfer, the anti-squat force from the swingarm and chain must be equal to the added vertical load. This means the upward vertical component must equal half the horizontal force due to the acceleration of the bike.

If the anti-squat line goes through the CG of the sprung mass of the bike and rider, the upward anti-squat force will equal the horizontal driving force. This is twice as much as we need to isolate the anti-squat force. We call this the 200-percent anti-squat line. To make a 100-percent anti-squat line, we must draw a line with half the slope (not half the angle). This will give us half the vertical force, which is exactly what we need for the rear suspension to move freely without lifting or squatting.

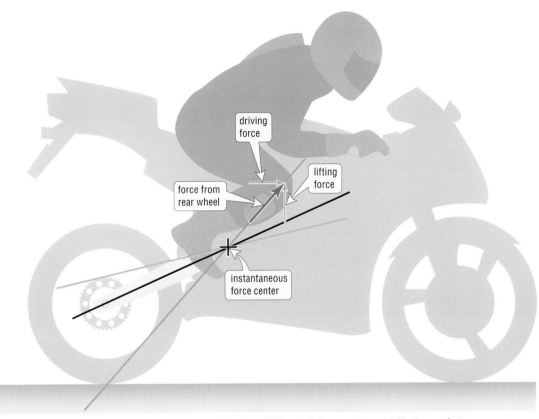

5.13 If the anti-squat line goes through the CG, it will lift as much as it pushes forward. This undesirable scenario is avoided by the manufacturers.

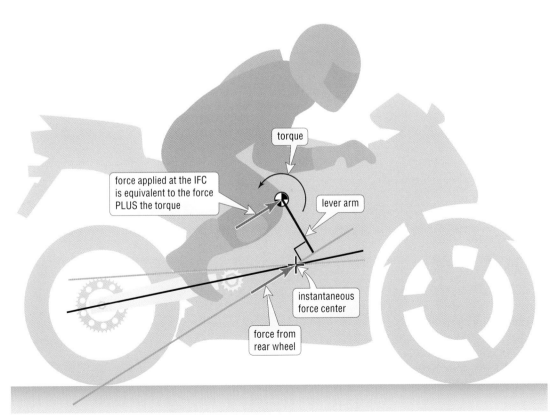

5.14 When the anti-squat angle is below the CG, the vertical lifting component decreases.

To graph this we draw a vertical line through the front axle. The 200-percent anti-squat line will intersect this line at twice the height of the CG. The 100-percent anti-squat line will intersect it at the height of the CG and a 0-percent anti-squat line intersects it at the ground. See Figure 5.16.

As you can imagine, the anti-squat angle and percentage changes constantly as the suspension moves and as the rider sits, stands, hangs off, or tucks. The more suspension travel, the more the change. So the next question is: what anti-squat is best? If there is way too much anti-squat (200 percent or so), the

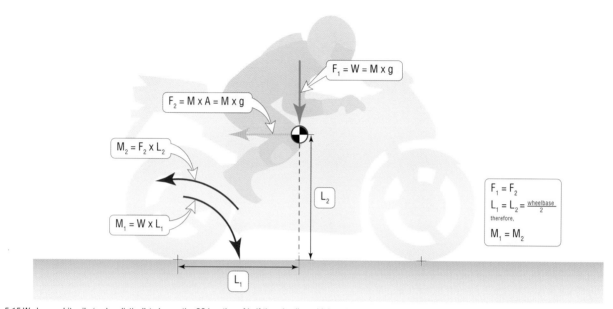

$$F_1 = W = M \times g$$

$$F_2 = M \times A = M \times g$$

$$M_2 = F_2 \times L_2$$

$$M_1 = W \times L_1$$

$$L_2$$

$$F_1 = F_2$$
$$L_1 = L_2 = \frac{wheelbase}{2}$$
therefore,
$$M_1 = M_2$$

$$L_1$$

5.15 We have arbitrarily (and realistically) chosen the CG location of half the wheelbase high and in the middle of the wheelbase. If we accelerate at 1g, the front wheel will just begin to lift off the ground transfering all the front wheel load onto the rear suspension. To separate the driving forces from the suspension we need to support this extra load with anti-squat force.

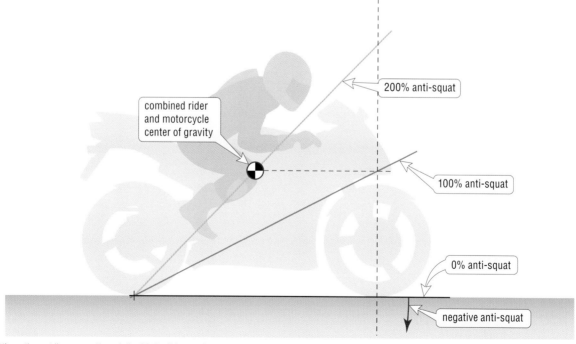

200% anti-squat

combined rider and motorcycle center of gravity

100% anti-squat

0% anti-squat

negative anti-squat

5.16 If the anti-squat line passes through the CG, it will have twice as much anti-squat as we need so we call this 200-percent anti-squat. The 100-percent line would have half the slope. For the 50/50 weight distribution scenario we have chosen, the 100-percent line would intersect a vertical line coming up from the front axle at the CG height.

GEOMETRY

92

suspension can actually top out under acceleration. If it does, it no longer has the ability to follow the ground, and the result is a loss of traction and a stiff ride. On a dirt bike the ability to stiffen the rear suspension with the throttle has a couple benefits. The first is when landing a jump, and the second is getting lift on the takeoff of jumps for clearing doubles, and other big obstacles. In order for this to occur with any significance, the anti-squat must be 100 percent or more.

The downside to anti-squat above 100 percent on a dirt bike comes when accelerating over small square-edge bumps, particularly when exiting a turn. This anti-squat dynamic can add considerably to the harsh feeling that these types of bumps naturally create.

When anti-squat is less than zero, the forces tend to pull the wheel off the ground. This situation is rare for street bikes as swingarm angles rarely go past horizontal, but it is not that uncommon for dirt bikes because they have lots of travel.

When the anti-squat percentage is less than 100 but above zero the sprung mass is not fully supported and the rear end will squat some. The lower the percentage, the more it will squat during acceleration. This squatting action creates counterclockwise rotational momentum and will use up more travel leaving less travel available to handle the bumps.

Remember that the anti-squat percentage is more important with bikes that can accelerate harder, specifically the bikes with higher "power-to-the-ground-to-weight-ratio" like liter road race bikes. There is a distinct advantage to anti-squat percentages slightly above 100 percent: when the throttle is opened on a liter sportbike, the momentary push against the ground can actually increase traction. Too hard a push, however, causes the CG to move upward, pulling the tire away from the ground and ultimately decreasing traction moments thereafter. This means that both too little and particularly too much anti-squat can decrease traction.

The critical areas for anti-squat are acceleration during cornering, when accelerating from a dead stop, accelerating out of turns on a dirt bike, and on jumps and whoop sections.

When a manufacturer designs a bike, it attempts to minimize the change in anti-squat throughout the suspension travel. This is the reason countershaft sprockets are so close to the swingarm pivot. On the tuning end, we need to know what things change anti-squat and which way we need to go.

GEOMETRY MEASUREMENT

There is an old saying that says you can never get where you want to go until you know where you are. This maxim holds true for tuning as well: you can't achieve the results you're after until you have an accurate assessment of your starting point.

In our opinion, the most sophisticated system for chassis measurement out today is GMD Computrack (www.gmdcomputrack.com). It is a precise optical device that not only measures geometry but also alignment, including twists and offsets. It is used by many factories for their race teams as well as for research and development.

The GMD Computrack Network specializes in measuring, straightening, and optimizing (setting up the geometry) of all types of motorcycles. This is a really good place to start, as a tape measure and protractor just don't cut it when it's time to tune. If you use the complete services offered by the GMD Computrack network, it will use its sizeable database of knowledge to get you where you want to go.

Do not get thrown off if a tuner uses ground trail and swingarm angle only. Keep in mind that, when comparing apples to apples, these are valid tuning parameters. However, when comparing different machines, they do lose some of their validity.

GEOMETRY TUNING

If you want to tune on your own, it is still vital to know your starting point and make known, incremental changes. Also bear in mind that it is impossible to change one thing without affecting other aspects of the suspension or geometry. A suspension setup change can have a very similar result to a geometry change. The results obtained by changing the fork preload could be very similar to those you get by altering the front end ride height (repositioning the tubes up or down in the triple clamps).

To Increase Front End Trail

* Adjustable fork bottoms—move the axle back
* Triple clamp offset (adjustable or fixed)—decrease offset (move the fork tubes back), 2mm increments
* Larger front tire outer diameter
* Raise the front end by sliding the fork tubes down in the triple clamps or increasing fork spring preload (less front end sag) (increases rake), 5mm increments
* Lower the rear end with shock length, rear wheel outer diameter, or running more rear sag (increases rake) 5mm increments

To Increase Rear Anti-Squat

* Raise the rear end (increase the swingarm angle) with adjustable rear shocks or frame ride height adjusters, or lengthen the shock internally
* Smaller countershaft sprocket—note that this can also affect the swingarm length
* Larger rear sprocket—note that this can also affect the swingarm length
* Raise swingarm pivot in the frame on models with available inserts (2006–09 GSX-R1000, etc.)
* Shorten effective swingarm length by shortening the chain or with gearing and the chain adjuster
* Lower the CG by getting in a tuck
* Move CG forward by sitting further forward on seat
* Raise the front end ride height (not preferred as this has more effect on rake and trail)
* Smaller rear tire outer diameter—though this generally makes only a very, very small difference

A few things to keep in mind: First, more is not necessarily better. Second, when in doubt consult with the pros. Third, just because everyone else is doing it doesn't mean it's the best. Fourth, just because everyone else is doing it doesn't mean it's wrong. See the troubleshooting chapter for guidance.

WEIGHT BIAS

Weight bias refers to the amount of force on each of the tires either laden (rider on board) or unladen, normally displayed as a front-to-rear percentage or ratio. For example, 48/52 would mean 48 percent on the front and 52 percent on the rear. The amount of traction available is directly related to the amount of force between the tires and the ground. (See the Traction Control appendix.)

Most modern sportbikes have a slight front end weight bias, 51 or 52 percent. When a 74kg (162 lb) rider is put on board, it becomes very close to 50/50. Most modern dirt bikes have slightly less front end weight bias, 48 to 50 percent. When the rider is put on board (standing on the pegs), the shift is also rearward so that front end bias dips to 44 to 46 percent with a 74kg rider. This means that, for both sport and motocross bikes, more of the rider's weight is on the rear wheel—heavier riders will automatically have a more rearward weight bias than lighter ones.

The most effective way to shift the weight bias is with rear axle position. The further the axle is moved back, the more load is shifted to the front. Moving the rider position is also effective. On a road race bike a few layers of padding on the back of the seat/rear tail section can shift the rider forward significantly. On a dirt bike the rider has much more room to move about, and the habit of choosing a seating location has a huge effect on potential lap times. Most riders, particularly as they get older, have a habit of sitting too far back. A stepped seat can help remind a rider to sit forward.

Many things have been said about methods of "weighting the front end." Lowering the front is probably the most common and, while it is true that a change does occur, the change is miniscule. I know, I know, you've tried it and it works! You can feel more force on your palms. I would invite you to use an accurate scale or load cell and check out the actual difference yourself. Another common step taken is lowering the bars: again, the difference is slight. The reason you feel it more is your upper body is rotated forward and you are supporting more of the weight on your hands. Granted, there is a tiny change, but you haven't significantly shifted your weight forward.

Awareness of the effect of weight bias can be part of a successful setup, and understanding what changes are effective can save a lot of time.

SOMETIMES VELCRO *IS* THE ANSWER

In 1996 I participated in the 54th running of the famous 24 Hours of Montjuich endurance road race at the Circuit de Catalunya in Spain. Our team, which was made up entirely of motorcycle journalists, had four riders ranging from 5 feet, 5 inches to 6 feet, 3 inches. This created both an ergonomic and weight distribution problem as there was no seat setup that worked for all of us. Our effective but not-so-elegant solution was to add adjustable foam layers connected with hook-and-loop fasteners and secured with duct tape. This allowed quick changes to compensate for my short T-Rex arms as well as the orangutan arms of my German teammate. When the checkered flag fell, our team finished 7th overall and 2nd in our class of 750 Supersport, just ahead of 250GP front-runner Carlos Cardus' team on a factory Ducati superbike. Viva la Velcro! — *Lee Parks*

Chapter 6
Troubleshooting and Testing

In this section of the book we have compiled a list of common problems riders have with their suspension. These may be encountered on the dirt, street, or track. To help understand the issues we have included diagrams that symbolize our best effort to replicate three-dimensional movement in two-dimensional space. There are three parts to the troubleshooting section: first is a quick pictorial overview of ideal suspension versus real-world expectations given current technology, second a simple description of what happens at the extremes of possible suspension setup, and third the common problems associated with forks and shocks on bikes.

When going through possible solutions, they are listed in order of easiest or more likely and go toward less likely. For example it might list an external adjuster change before an internal valving change. It's a lot easier to change an adjuster than revalve internally though the internal change might be far more likely.

The Testing Procedure section (page 106) is presented after the Troubleshooting Scenarios. It is perhaps the most important part of this book. If you have a good testing procedure, you will be able to come up with good settings even as your depth of knowledge grows.

Use the illustrations and information as a guide to fine-tuning your suspension and make sure to use the Testing Form on page 251 to keep track of your results. Using this guide will reduce the guesswork of achieving a perfect ride and help make suspension troubleshooting easier and fun.

DAMPING EXTREMES

1. ***Too Much Rebound Damping (Packing)***
   The suspension is held down in the stroke because it cannot rebound fast enough and each bump causes additional compression. The ride becomes harsh because too much force is needed to initiate more movement. This also causes a loss of traction because of tire deflection.

2. ***Too Little Rebound Damping (Pogoing)***
   In this scenario the suspension does not control the stored-up spring energy, which causes a pogo stick–like effect. The uncontrolled vertical movement can take the wheel off the ground and cause a loss of traction.

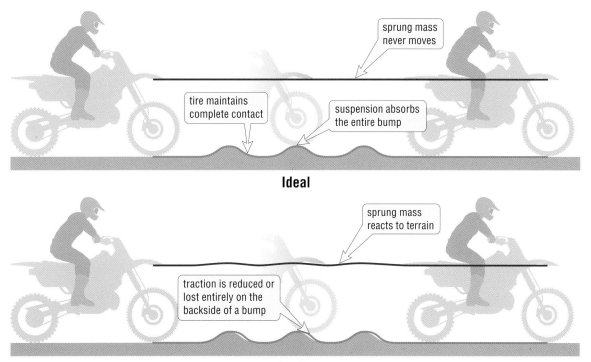

The ideal ride has perfect wheel contact on both the front and the back of the bump while the sprung mass maintains a perfectly level path. The best real, world suspension isn't quite there, but this is the goal.

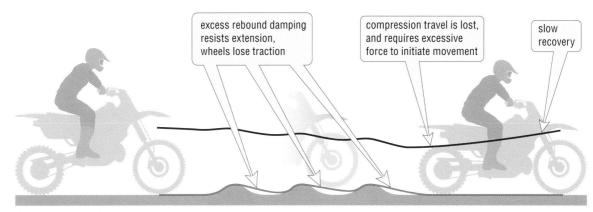

Extreme 1: Too much rebound damping

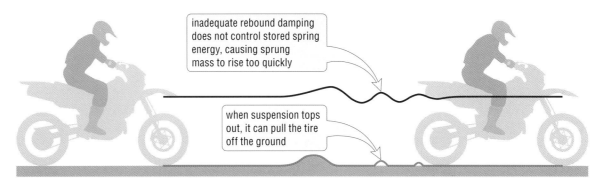

Extreme 2: Too little rebound damping

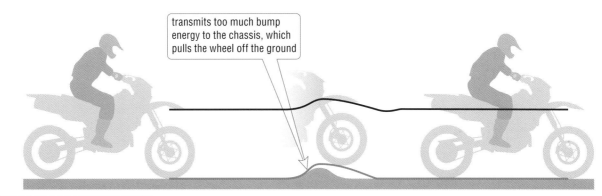

Extreme 3: Too much compression damping

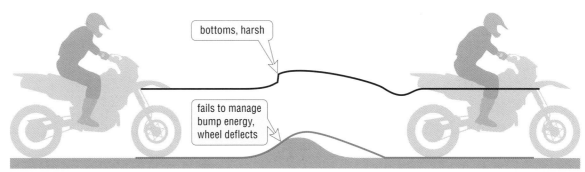

Extreme 4: Too little compression damping

3. *Too Much Compression Damping (Harshness)*
Here the suspension causes the wheel to deflect off the bump on impact because there is too much resistance to movement. This makes for a very harsh ride.

4. *Too Little Compression Damping (Bottoming)*
The wheel moves past the crest of the bump during compression and is not able to follow the backside of the bump, causing a loss of traction. It feels mushy and can bottom easily.

TROUBLESHOOTING SCENARIOS
Forks

1. *Bottoms—Too Soft, Mushy*
Ask questions:
   1. What kind of conditions? (G-outs, landing on jumps, face of jumps, etc.) We are determining whether the velocity is low or high.
   2. Does it feel good otherwise? (If yes, go to A)
   3. Does it feel too soft everywhere? (If yes, skip A, go to B and C)
   A. Oil level low—raise oil level—affects mostly the last ⅓ of travel
   B. Not enough low-speed compression damping
   C. Not enough high-speed compression damping

D. Spring rate too soft
E. Not enough preload
F. Dirt in valving, broken valve, bent shim, burr on the piston/shim
G. Cartridge rod bushing worn out (typical problem with pre-1996 KYB)
H. Compression valve O-ring broken, especially if just rebuilt
I. Cartridge rod not attached to cap—broken or unscrewed—oops

2. *Too Stiff—Deflects, Harsh, Nervous, Twitchy*
Ask question: Everywhere or just on square edges? (Just square-edged: see B and C)
   A. Too much compression damping adjustment— high-speed and/or low-speed
   B. Too much compression damping internally— change high-speed first, then low-speed
   C. Spring rate too stiff
   D. Too much low-speed rebound damping—packing
   E. Oil level too high
   F. See #9 (sticky forks)

3. *Poor Traction*
   A. Poor tire type/compound
   B. Too much tire pressure

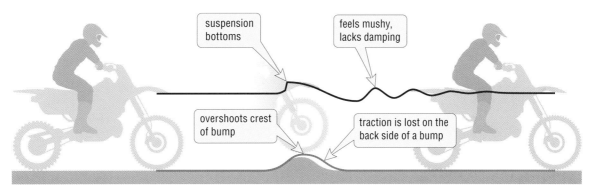

Front 1: Front bottoms, mushy

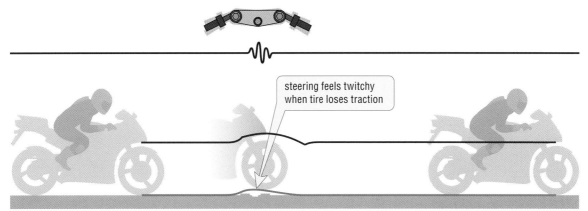

Front 2: Front too stiff

C. Tire pressure way too low
D. Too much low-speed rebound damping
E. Too much low-speed compression damping
F. Not enough low-speed rebound damping
G. Not enough low-speed compression damping
H. Not enough weight on the front end
  1. Swingarm too short
  2. Rear axle moved up too far
  3. Seat too far back
  4. Bars too high or too far back
I. See #5 (pushes, not enough trail)

4. ***Doesn't Turn***

Note: This may be the most misunderstood and misdiagnosed fork symptom. It is quite often more a geometry issue than a suspension issue though these overlap. Ninety-nine percent of the time the tuner/rider drops the front end (raises the fork tubes in the triple clamps) in an attempt to cure this. His thinking is typically one of two things: either he's trying to "weight the front end" or he is trying to decrease trail. Does dropping the front end weight the front end? Yes, but not so much as you'd notice it. This is a common misconception. As to decreasing the trail—the reason you'd want to decrease trail is because it is too difficult to turn the bars. If there is a lack of traction, you'd want to go the other way—increase the trail. Along with an increase in trail generally comes an increase in traction (grip). So, begin by asking the question:
Do the bars turn easily or is it hard to turn the bars?
If it is easy to turn the bars start with #3 (poor traction), then #5 (pushes)
If it is hard to turn the bars go to #6 (excessive force required)

A. Tire profiles too flat or too wide, rim too wide
B. Riding Position—not enough weight on the front end
  1. Seat too low
  2. Bars too high
C. Riding Style (not everything is the bike!)
  1. Rider doesn't understand the concept of countersteering
  2. Not weighting the front end
  3. Elbow down riding style—wrong for dirt
  4. Elbow up riding style—wrong for pavement
  5. Sitting too far back, not weighting the front end—wrong for dirt and pavement
  6. Rider centerline to outside of bike centerline—wrong for pavement
  7. Steering with both arms—wrong for pavement (steering should be done with inside arm only)
  8. Not looking through turn
  9. Riding two-up—passenger not leaning with the bike
  10. Riding two-up—not enough weight on the front, too much on the rear
  11. Luggage added to the rear
D. Wheelbase too long

5. ***Pushes*** *(easy to turn the bars but the bike doesn't turn, low traction),* ***Steering Feels Loose, Power Steering*** *(flat track term),* ***Chatters When Entering a Turn, Runs Wide Mid-Corner and Exit, Tucks*** *(turns too quickly—this is not enough trail but not as severe as Pushing)*
Note: this is usually a chassis geometry problem—not enough trail

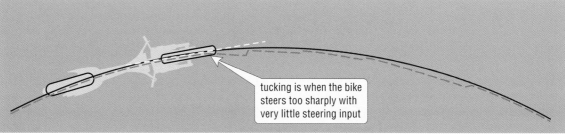

tucking is when the bike steers too sharply with very little steering input

Front 5.1: Front tucks

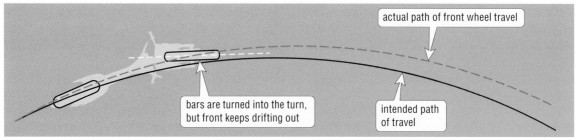

actual path of front wheel travel

bars are turned into the turn, but front keeps drifting out

intended path of travel

Front 5.2: Front pushes

A. Front end rides too low in comparison to the rear
B. Raise the front end (slide fork tubes down in triple clamps)
C. Lower the rear end
D. Fork spring rate too soft
E. Not enough fork spring preload
F. Low-speed rebound too high, causing packing
G. Not enough low-speed compression damping
H. Increase low-speed compression damping adjustment or valving stack stiffness
I. Go to a single-stage valving stack instead of two-stage—dirt
J. Anything that makes the rear higher than the front

6. **Takes excessive force to turn the bars, plenty of traction, doesn't complete the turn**
   Note: this is a chassis geometry problem—too much trail
   A. Front end rides high dynamically in comparison to the rear
   B. Lower the front end (slide the fork tubes up in the triple clamps)
   C. Too much fork spring preload
   D. Spring rate too stiff
   E. Rear ride height too low
   F. Air pump—replace fork seals
   G. Anything that makes the rear lower than the front
   H. Too much low-speed compression damping
   I. Bars too narrow, uncomfortable bend
   J. See #9 (sticky forks)

7. **Dives under Braking—(steady state)**
   A. With telescopic forks it should! Linkage-type front ends may not dive or may even rise.
   B. On braking, the total dive is controlled by spring forces only (rate, preload and air slightly), not damping.
   C. Fork angle too flat (choppered), too much rake
   D. Fork springs too soft
   Note: Damping affects the rate of dive and "overshoot" but does not affect the front ride height after any appreciable length of time.
   E. Too much rear ride height
      1. Ride height adjuster too high
      2. Rear preload excessive

8. **Feels Loose**
   A. Not enough low-speed rebound damping
   B. Not enough high-speed rebound damping—big bumps only
   C. Not enough compression damping
   D. Spring rate too soft
   E. Steering bearings loose or worn
   F. Swingarm pivot or linkage bearings loose or worn
   G. Tire pressure too low or way too high
   H. Fork flex, chassis flex, swingarm flex
   I. Worn-out fluid
   J. Damping rod bushings worn out (pre-1996 KYB cartridge type forks)
   K. Worn-out rebound piston ring—very rare

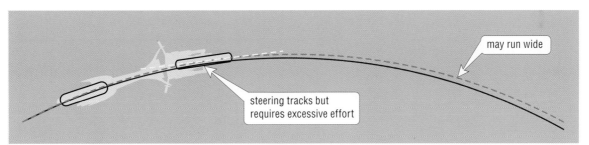

may run wide

steering tracks but requires excessive effort

Front 6: Front high effort to turn the bars

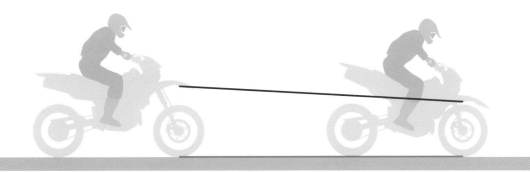

Front 7: Front excessive dive

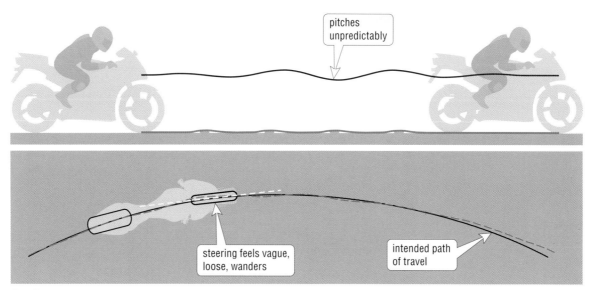

Front 8: Front feels vague

9. **Sticky Forks**
    A. Misaligned fork tubes when viewed from the front (splayed out or wedged in)—axle clamp not centered (most common)
    B. Triple clamps bent
    C. Bent fork tubes
    D. Bent axle
    E. Dented sliders
    F. Upside-down forks with poor bushing design
    G. Outer tube anodizing worn through
    H. Air pump—replace seals, particularly at the lower triple clamp
    I. Seals not broken in or poor design (aftermarket)
    J. Seals not lubricated
    K. Poor quality oil
    L. Poorly designed fork brace or fork brace adjustment—right side up forks
    M. Triple clamp too tight—USD (upside-down) forks

    N. Misaligned fork tube height
    O. Forks not broken in—(twin-chamber)
    P. Bushings damaged from dent or worn out
    Q. Metal imbedded in bushings
        1. Preload washers not located properly—USD forks
        2. Aluminum preload washers
        3. Steel spring spacer directly on aluminum cap
        4. Bottom-out system needs chamfering— pre-1995 KYB cartridge forks
        5. Fork caps "shedding" on installation—burr on thread
    R. Cartridge rod bushing too tight
    S. Spring guide rubbing on inner diameter of spring/ incorrect manufacturing or guide growing from soaking in solvent—USD forks
    T. Fork spring outer diameter too large—spring outer diameter grows during compression and can bind on inner diameter of fork tube

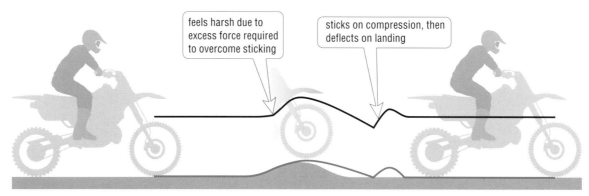

Front 9: Front sticky forks

10. *Headshakes—(fast side-to-side movement of the bars)*
  A. Chassis not straight—twisted or offset
  B. Misalignment of wheels—chain adjuster marks are off
  C. Fork flex, chassis flex, swingarm flex
  D. Worn-out or loose steering bearing or binding dragging
  E. Not enough trail—not enough self-centering effect
  F. Too much trail—returns past center then re-corrects the other way quickly
  G. Oil level too high (street)—headshakes during braking
  H. Bottom-out mechanism too long or too abrupt (street)—headshakes during heavy braking
  I. Not enough low-speed rebound damping
  J. Too much rebound damping
  K. Too much high-speed compression damping—deflects on bumps
  L. Tire pressure too high or too low
  M. Poor tire compound or type
  N. Tire not mounted properly on rim, bent rim, or cord not straight
  O. Wheel out of balance—bent rim
  P. Brake rotor bent—headshakes during braking
  Q. Fork mounted fairing not aerodynamically balanced
  R. Any type of aerodynamic imbalance
  S. Anything that makes the front end lower than the rear decreases trail
  T. Too much steering swing inertia
  U. See #9 (sticky forks)
  V. Additional solutions
    1. Steering damper—Scott's Performance has an excellent damper
    2. Tighten steering bearings so that they drag slightly—poor man's steering damper

11. *Chatters (Patters)—(up and down wheel movement)*
  Note: This can be a vibrations/harmonics problem where the excitation (input) frequency matches the natural frequency of the suspended system. It is often confused with, and can cause, headshake.
  A. See #5 (pushes, not enough trail)
  B. Not enough rebound damping
  C. Not enough compression damping
  D. Change spring rates stiffer or softer to change natural frequency—start with stiffer
  E. Too much compression damping
  F. Too much rebound damping
  G. Tire pressure—too much or too little
  H. Tire design

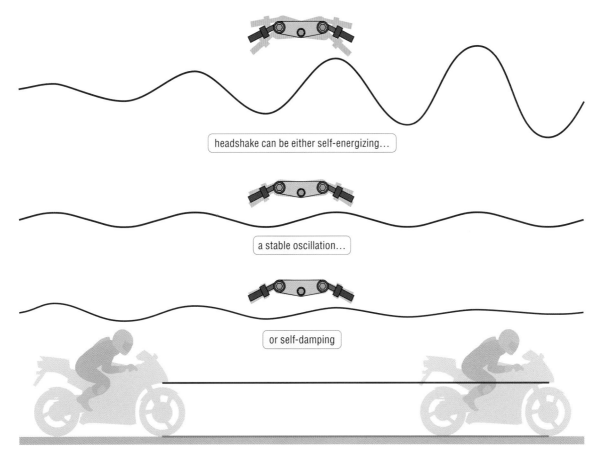

headshake can be either self-energizing…

a stable oscillation…

or self-damping

Front 10: Front headshake

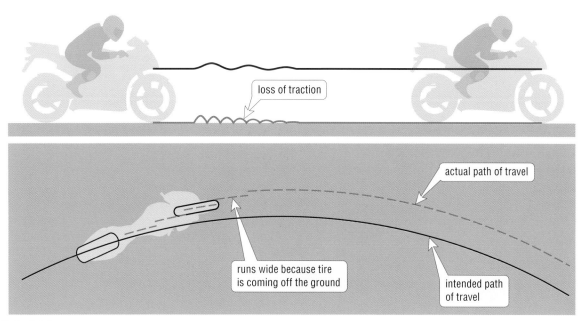

Front 11: Front chatter

I.   Chassis/swingarm flex

J.   Preload change—changes center of pressure height

K.   See #9 (sticky forks)

12. ***Bounces off the Ground on Jump Landings***

    A.   Bottoms severely, loads the frame, and recoils (see #1, bottoms)

    B.   Not enough high-speed rebound damping

    C.   Not enough low-speed rebound damping

13. ***Deflects on Square-Edged Bumps, Roots, Rocks, Expansion Joints, Square Holes, "Botts' Dots"***

    A.   Too much high-speed compression damping— either valving stack or piston orifice restriction

    B.   Spring rate too stiff

C.   Too much preload

D.   Too much low-speed compression damping

E.   Too much low-speed rebound damping

F.   Way too soft and bottoms severely

G.   See #9 (sticky forks)

14. ***Leaky Seals***

    A.   Old seals

    B.   Nicks in tube

    C.   Worn bushings

    D.   Bent tube

    E.   Improper installation

    F.   Fork tube too smooth

    G.   Excessive brake dust (sintered metallic pads)

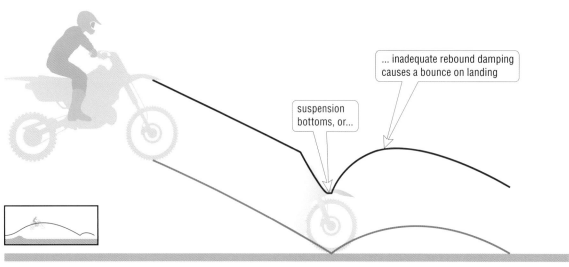

Front 12: Front bounces on landings

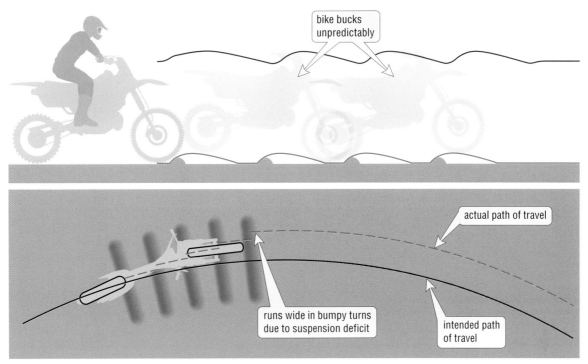

Front 13: Front deflects on bumps

15. *Front Tire Wear—Road Race*
  A. Tire edge tear
    1. Improper tire pressure
    2. See #5—chassis geometry issue, not enough trail
  B. Tire center wear
    1. Too much tire pressure
    2. Front end chatter
    3. Tire out of balance
    4. Excessively stiff forks
    5. Improperly adjusted steering bearings
    6. Not enough turns on your way to work or exhibition of speed—too much drag racing on the way to the pub.

Shocks
1. *Kicks*
Note: This is the most commonly misdiagnosed symptom on a dirt bike. This symptom is usually diagnosed as not enough rebound damping, however it is usually caused by one of two things: 1) it's way too stiff or 2) it's way too soft.
Kicks #1—Too Stiff
    1. Too much high-speed compression damping
    2. Spring rate too stiff
    3. Way too much low-speed compression damping
    4. Too much rebound damping (not too little)
    5. Linkage bearings bad, tight, dry
    6. Too high tire pressure
    7. Way too much preload
    8. See #8 (sticky shock)

Kicks #2—Too Soft
    Severe Bottoming (see #2, bottoms)

2. *Bottoms*
  A. Not enough low-speed compression damping
  B. Not enough high-speed compression damping (landing on jumps)
  C. Spring rate too soft
  D. Too much static sag
  E. Worn piston ring O-ring, piston ring, or body
  F. Suspension fluid worn out or poor quality (fades when shock heats up due to low viscosity index)
  G. Shaft seal blown
  H. Not enough nitrogen pressure, cavitation
  I. Blown bladder (usually caused by blown shaft seal)
  J. Bent or distorted valving shims

3. *Swaps—Dirt*
  Ask questions:
    1. Does it feel harsh/deflect? Too Stiff
    2. Does it bottom out easily? Too Soft
    3. One bump or into a series of whoops? If it is on a series of whoops, it could be a rebound problem. Too much rebound damping (packing especially on a series of whoops) or too little high-speed rebound damping (uncontrolled rebound on a series of whoops).
  A. Too much high-speed compression damping—deflecting, not bottoming
  B. Not enough low-speed rebound damping—loose

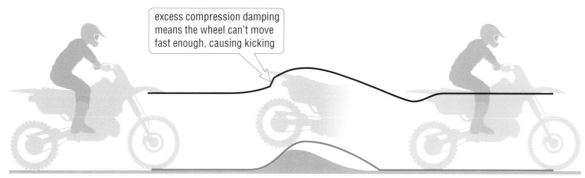

Rear 1: Rear kicks

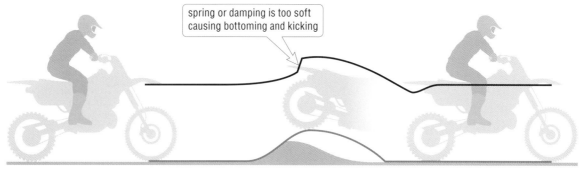

Rear 2: Rear bottoms

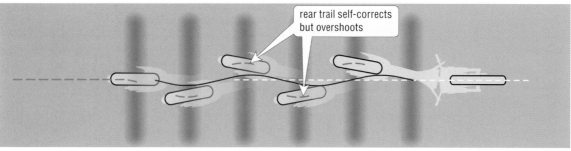

Rear 3: Rear swaps

C. Not enough high-speed rebound damping—loose on whoop section
D. Spring rate too stiff—deflects
E. Spring rate too soft—mushy/bottoms
F. Bottoming severely
G. See #8 (sticky shock)

4. *Feels Loose/Shock Pumps*
A. Not enough low-speed rebound damping
B. Not enough high-speed rebound damping
C. Not enough low-speed compression damping
D. Spring rate too soft
E. Too little preload

5. *Poor Traction*
A. Too much low-speed rebound damping (main cause)

B. Too much low-speed compression damping
C. Not enough low-speed rebound damping (much too little)
D. Not enough low-speed compression damping
E. Too much tire pressure
F. Poor tire type/compound
G. Tire worn out
H. Shock heim bearings worn out (loose)
I. Linkage bearings worn out (loose)
J. Spring rate too stiff
K. Not enough swingarm angle—not enough anti-squat
L. Too much swingarm angle—too much anti-squat
M. Too much preload
N. Too much rear ride height (adjuster too high)
O. See #8 (sticky shock)

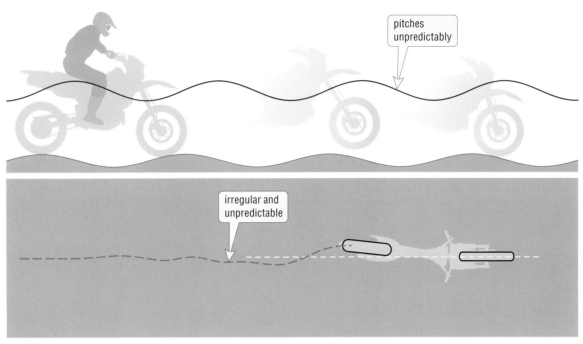

Rear 4: Rear feels loose

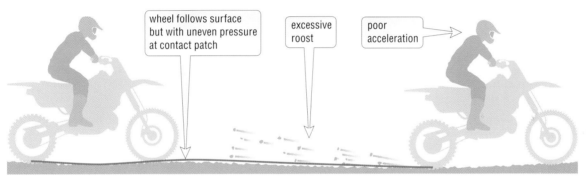

Rear 5: Rear poor traction

6. **Squats on Acceleration**
   A. Too little swingarm angle—not enough anti-squat
   B. Spring too soft
   C. Not enough preload (too much static sag)
   D. Countershaft sprocket too big—not enough anti-squat
   E. Rear sprocket too small—not enough anti-squat
   F. Compression damping too soft—changes rate of squat, not final amount of squat

7. **Not Tracking**
   A. Too much low-speed rebound damping—poor traction
   B. Too much high-speed compression damping—deflecting on square-edged bumps
   C. Too much low-speed compression damping—skating, poor traction
   D. Misaligned chassis

   E. See Forks #9 (sticky forks) and Shock #8 (sticky shock, front and rear)

8. **Sticky Shock**
   A. Linkage not maintained
   B. Swingarm bearings not maintained
   C. Shock eyelet bearings not lubed
   D. Floating brake rod or backing plate not lubed—common on vintage bikes with floating rear brake
   E. Missing or improper bearing spacers
   F. Bent shock shaft—usually caused by mounting bolt or clevis installed backwards

9. **Blown Shock Bladder**
   A. Oil leak—shaft seal blown—caused by nicked or pitted shaft, hard-chrome worn through, old or worn-out seal
   B. Improperly rebuilt shock recently finished with way too little oil

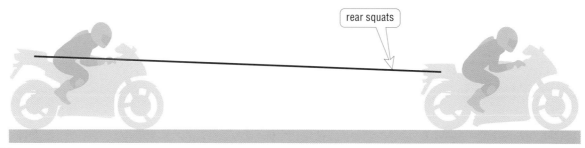

Rear 6: Rear squats

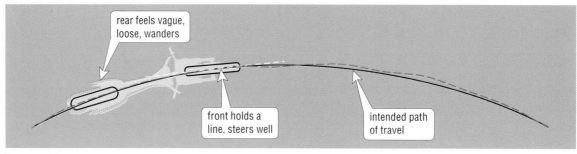

Rear 7: Rear not tracking

TESTING PROCEDURE

Because of the number of variables involved in suspension setup and the unique preferences of each rider, there is no one perfect setup for everyone. This is part of why testing is so critical. If you follow this procedure exactly and always use the testing log sheet in the appendix, you can make significant improvements in your bike's suspension.

Use this procedure on both practice and race days. The more detailed you are, the easier it will be to predict future needs when you switch locales. Remember that proper suspension setup is best achieved with a great rider/tuner team. The better your rapport and communication, the more effective you will be. If you are in the unfortunate situation of having to be both rider and tuner, go through the same process and do your best to keep an open mind.

Here is a key question: when making a change does the rider feel the change or the percentage change? In other words if you make a .5 kg/mm spring rate change is that a lot or a little? The correct answer to this question is vital for proper suspension tuning whether it is spring, damping, or for that matter, friction. The answer is the rider feels the percentage change, not the change itself. If the original spring rate was 5kg/mm then a .5 change would be 10 percent—this is noticeable. If the original spring rate was 15kg/mm a .5 change would only be about a 3 percent change, which may not be noticeable at all. Studies have shown that the smallest change most humans can feel is 10 percent. I have found that some riders can feel as small as a 5 percent change. The point is you need to make a big enough change for riders to be able to tell. Too small a percentage change is worthless and confusing.

There is an old rule of thumb that says that with proper setup you should bottom once a lap. I disagree strongly. Let's say your bike is set up perfectly for your local motocross track and now you go to another track that's significantly smoother. The rule would have you softening the suspension to the point of being mushy, perhaps even uncontrollable, with big pitch changes fore and aft. On the other hand some riders prefer a setup where the rear bottoms gently somewhat regularly—5 to 10 times a lap. The key word here is *gently*. Normally I like to give the rider some cushion and not let it go metal to metal ever.

As far as road racing is concerned, it is quite common to use up most of the fork travel during braking, but I suggest you should never bottom out metal to metal and *never* remove the bottom-out device. If you do there is no room for error, with the possibility of losing the front end. The rear, on the other hand, barely moves in relationship to the front. A properly set up rear end will not come close to using all the travel on most tracks.

1. Before leaving for the track, record the initial settings on the testing log.
2. Start with spring rates from the Race Tech website's product or Digital Valving Search. Check and set static sag, free sag, and check your stiction zone. Remove excess friction before doing any testing.
3. On the way to the track, or before, if possible, go over the testing procedure with the rider.
4. It is often helpful to use last year's bike for comparison.

5. Once at the track have the rider do at least two 10-minute warm-up sessions without caring about suspension action. Have fun and get loose.

6. For dirt riding wait until the track is worthy of testing. If the track is not very rough, it doesn't make sense to test. If the rider wants to ride while the track is still smooth that's OK, just don't make any suspension decisions.

7. Once the track is ready ask the rider to do two or three laps, focusing on using the exact same lines every time and concentrating on the suspension action. Instruct the rider to ride cautiously, at 90 percent, not 100 percent. *(Road racers should use tire warmers.)*

8. Record the rider's initial feedback about what the bike is doing on the testing log. Ask him to decide which end of the bike is worse and start working on that end.

9. Make one change at a time. This a universal testing rule that most tuners know—and most tuners break.

10. Do *not* tell the rider what changes you are making. If you do, you can rest assured that it will affect the results.

11. Make big external changes first. Try to bracket the problem with external adjusters, but bear in mind that some adjusters don't make much difference (particularly most original equipment shock compression adjusters).

12. Record all changes and comments on the testing log in the appendix. You do not have to record all the settings at this point, just the changes. Lap times can be helpful for fine tuning, but do not rely on lap times, as too many factors affect them, including traffic and track conditions. Both MX and road race tracks can change dramatically during the day, including wind conditions and track temperature. Be aware of rider's energy level.

13. Have the rider test for two to three laps with each change, and no more. Any longer than this and the rider will start to make things up.

14. Watch the bike on the track, taking note of the relative movement of the wheel and the chassis. The wheel should move up and down fairly quickly and the chassis should stay fairly even. You may take the side panels off on dirt bikes to see suspension action better. On dirt bikes look for excessive roost: lots of roost can equal a lack of traction. Listen to the engine particularly as the rider goes over bumps. A more even rpm usually means less deflection.

15. When the rider comes in, ask, "How was it?" Let him know it might be better in one area and worse in another. Let him know the change might not be big enough to tell. Avoid "leading questions" that might prompt an inaccurate response.

16. If you would like to use a checklist to prompt the rider, you can use something like this for dirt:
    How was it on:
    - Bottoming?
    - Square-edge bumps?
    - Plushness?
    - Traction?
    - Tracking straight?
    - Feeling of control?

17. Get feedback on the *symptoms*, not the cause. If the rider tells you what it is doing and then tells you the cause, politely ask him why he thinks it needs that change. What is it doing? Where?

18. If the rider couldn't tell, go back to the previous setting. (Sometimes the problem is very obvious when you go back to the previous setting.)

19. Do your best to figure out the shaft velocity at which the problem occurs. Is it high-speed or low-speed? When making valving changes, change that part of the damping curve. (A ShockClock or other data acquisition system can be helpful here.)

20. Double check the rider's feedback by using an earlier setting to see if the feedback is consistent. Don't tell the rider what you are doing.

21. On the last test of the day, use the original settings (from the beginning of the day) to double check your work. This one takes courage.

Note: Take everything with a grain of salt. Don't believe your eyes or your ears. Be willing to be wrong. Have fun!

Chapter 7
Tools and Equipment for Suspension Service

There is an old saying: the tools make the mechanic. While this is not entirely correct, there is something to this concept. Without the proper tools, equipment, workspace, and so on, even the best suspension technicians will be limited in the quality and swiftness of their work. Using the proper tools is essential to success for suspension jobs, ensuring that the job gets done correctly and without any undue damage to the motorcycle or components being serviced. If you plan on being a professional suspension service technician or tuner, having the proper tools will be critical for profitability.

The starting point is your workspace, whether it is your garage floor, a trailer/truck for mobile operations, or a full-on workshop. You will need a well-lit, properly-ventilated, clean area with a floor that can support full-size motorcycles and/or ATVs on stands or lifts with room left over to store units in progress. No matter what you do, there will be occasions when you will be waiting on parts.

Set up your work area with shelving to store parts, jobs in progress, and so forth. You will need cabinets for chemical storage, an oil disposal drum, parts washing machine, air compressor/air lines, drill press, and, of course, a sturdy work bench built to the correct height for you to work comfortably. As you will be working with oil and chemicals, a metal or laminate bench top is strongly recommended.

These items can be sourced locally from hardware and tool stores for the most part. You can also build or purchase large pieces such as benches, cabinets, and so on based upon your budget, needs, and the level of professionalism you wish to convey.

Now that your work area is prepared, you will need to disassemble some vehicles. Street and dirt motorcycles will require special stands; ATVs are a little easier to deal with as they are more stable. If you will be working primarily on ATVs, you don't need much in the way of special stands. If, however,

This K&L scissor jack (shown with optional post adapters) is useful for heavier, flat bottom vehicles like ATVs and many street bikes.

This front stand lifts the bike by the steering stem, allowing the forks to be serviced.

This hydraulic lift is a bit quicker and more stable than the scissor jack shown, but it takes up a little more floor space.

you would like to be able to have both front and rear shocks off the unit at once, some sort of a stand will be required.

Dirt bikes are relatively easy to work with as they are fairly lightweight. There are a variety of stands on the market that work well, or you could build something basic on your own fairly easily. Make sure your dirt bike stand will carry the bike high enough and well-balanced enough to remove the front and rear suspension simultaneously.

Street bikes are a little more challenging. They are heavier and often have easily damaged painted body panels in the way. A front wheel chock such as the Condor Pit Stop from Lee Parks Design is indispensable for setting sag as well as for steadying the bike while working on it. Supporting the rear end is fairly straightforward, with a number of options such as stands from Pit Bull, K&L, and others. A center jack can be used in conjunction to raise the front end—the K&L MC450 is the industry standard. An option for lifting only the front end for fork removal is a front end stand.

Our favorite stand for suspension service is the K&L MC360 lift, which hangs the bike with both wheels off the ground for front and rear service and allows the bike to be

This Park Tool Vise was originally made for working on bicycles but can be used on forks as well. A bench-mount base is available for a bit more stability.

moved around on wheels even when it is half taken apart. Sport and touring bike owners tend to be very concerned about scratches and other damage—one dropped Ducati or Gold Wing can burn up the profits of several suspension jobs, not to mention the cost in customer relations. Using quality equipment will help keep the bike upright, off the floor, and easy to work on, as well as conveying a high level of professionalism.

Now that you have removed the suspension components from the bike, it's time to get to work improving their performance. Good quality basic hand tools such as sockets, wrenches, and screwdrivers are of course required. Cheap imported tools can round off or leave ugly marks on fasteners that many owners simply won't tolerate. Six-point sockets and wrenches will help ensure easy removal without broken tools—it can take surprising effort to crack loose a factory-installed fastener the first time. (And don't forget that torque wrench for reassembly.)

Higher quality ratchets will have finer ratcheting action, making it easier to work in tight places. Anodized fork caps made of soft aluminum may require large, special wrenches with unique sizes or shapes to remove them without damage, like those in the Race Tech TFCW line. A special spring compressor (such as the TFSC series) may be required for street bike forks, and almost always for shock absorbers (TSSC series). These are very critical tools: damage from flying components—or, worse yet, personal injury—can result from improper spring removal or installation. Like our moms used to say, "It's all fun and games until someone loses an eye!"

You will want a quality bench vise to hold components and special vise jaws designed for suspension work. Race Tech TMVJ 065 vise jaws fit directly into Craftsman, brand vises (and others). They are aluminum and have a V-cut that holds rounded components securely, plus they include special pins to facilitate TFSH shaft holding tools. When working with suspension components, you are constantly holding, loosening, or tightening various shafts, from fork cartridges to shock shafts—holding them securely without damage is essential.

Never use vise grips on a suspension shaft, damping rod, or similar, as they will create damage that ruins seals and bushings. This can result in lost damping and fluid leaks, not to mention expensive component replacement. There are also freestanding and bench-mounted stands that will hold a fork or shock from Park Tool. These stands can be used as a workstation, as they allow the components to be rotated, inverted, and so on while they are clamped in the holder. These units are not as sturdy as a bench vise, but they are a bit more versatile.

The cartridge forks found on many street bikes, mini bikes, and older MX models may require a TFCH-series cartridge holding tool. This tool keeps the cartridge from spinning during disassembly and reassembly. This style of fork may also need a TFBT-series bleeding tool for bleeding the cartridge upon assembly. The tool attaches to the rebound

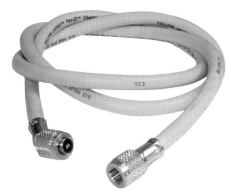

Nitrogen hose: This high-pressure hose works between the TSNR 01 Nitrogen Regulator and TSNG 02 Nitrogen Gauge. Finger-tight fittings are quick and easy.

A nitrogen regulator provides output pressure to 300 psi.

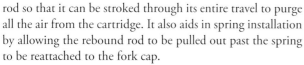

A shock nitrogen charging tool easily reaches hard-to-get-to recessed valve stems without an extension. Valve core plunger is located on the top for easy use.

Series Seal drivers: Split design for both conventional and upside-down forks.

rod so that it can be stroked through its entire travel to purge all the air from the cartridge. It also aids in spring installation by allowing the rebound rod to be pulled out past the spring to be reattached to the fork cap.

Most forks should have the fork oil set by level rather than volume for accuracy. Remember that fork oil level sets the air space in the fork (the secondary spring effect), and is an excellent tuning variable. The TFOL 02 Fork Oil Tool is in a class by itself. There are other models on the market that are less expensive, but they seem to require three hands to operate. Twin-chamber forks require the use of a Graduated Cylinder (TFGC 500) to measure the volume as there is no practical way to use a Fork Oil Level Tool. Of course, you must have an assortment of fork seal drivers like those in the TFSD series. A good seal driver will be of a split design, so it will work on inverted forks. It should also be hefty in order to drive the seal properly, and concentric to ensure an accurate fit at the seal and into the seal cavity.

Part cleaning is a critical part of suspension work. In the old days solvent was the way to go, but today with new laws to protect both us and the environment, and new technology, things have changed. Ultrasonic wash stations are top of the line. They do an amazing job on some nasty parts. There are also "vaporless" parts washers that clean themselves with a

Pro oil level tool: Collapsible tube to set oil level. Easy, two-handed use!

push of a button over night. Hot soapy water-blast cabinets do a great job on muddy parts as well. Safety-Kleen has a full assortment for your selection.

Shock service will require a nitrogen charging station consisting of a nitrogen bottle (available from your local welding supply house) equipped with a regulator such as the TSNR 01, TSNH 48 hose, TSNG 02 gauge, and a TSNN 01 needle. If you plan on servicing KTM products with WP Suspension, a TSNC 02 charging tool will save you hundreds over the OEM tool.

Nitrogen needle: Designed for gas-charged shocks with self-sealing-type rubber valves.

A reservoir cap removal tool screws onto the Schrader valve to facilitate removal of the bladder cap.

A shock clip tool removes shock retaining clips.

A WP nitrogen charging tool clamps onto the reservoir of all WP shocks with a reservoir.

Series Seal head setting tool: allows easy removal and installation of most shock seal head assemblies.

Other shock-servicing musts are a reservoir cap puller such as the TSCT 01. This tool will pull out the reservoir cap without damaging the unit or abusing your fingers. Shock seal head circlip removal frustration can be avoided with a TSCP 01 clip tool. Installing seal heads can be a headache as they want to cock sideways—the TSSS series makes this task much easier by quickly and evenly driving in the seal head.

If you will be servicing KTM/WP-brand shocks, a TSPS-series needle pin tool is needed to extract and replace the metering pin and/or telescopic needle. Some brands of shocks have a dust cap that is threaded—these will require TMPS-series pin spanners in order to remove the cap without damaging it. Öhlins shocks and forks will require myriad special tools that vary with the application. Öhlins tools are available through select Öhlins distributors.

After you have completed your suspension work, it will be necessary to dial in the preload, set the sag, and adjust the clickers. A Race Tech Sag Master TSSM 01 will make short work of sag setting and the TSPA 01 Shock Preload Adjusting Tool will aid in reaching preload collars. For adjusting clickers buried underneath handlebars, the TFCA 01 is invaluable.

Don't forget to record all your settings. Provide a copy of these settings to your customer while saving one for your records to refer to later as needed.

If you are going to be testing on a regular basis, you may wish to consider investing in the ShockClock. It will provide you with data, details, and information that even the best test rider cannot convey, in addition to quantifying or disputing the rider's feedback. It is one of the most efficient, affordable data acquisition tools available.

This overview will get you started by providing the essentials needed. There are many more tools you may need or want to own as time goes on based on your business as well as the types of jobs you encounter. You can never have too many tools, only too few! Build your toolbox as your budget, work, and needs dictate. Take care of your tools by keeping them organized, clean, away from hammers as much as possible, and especially away from friends who want to borrow and not return them.

See the complete listing of suspension tools at racetech.com and refer back to this chapter as you go through the service department section of the book. The beginning of each process includes a list of the tools needed to complete each job.

Sag Master: Used to measure static "race" sag. Sag is read directly—no more subtracting!

Pin Spanners have a unique design with a reverse taper on the hardened pins. This helps them dig in so that they don't pop out during use.

T Series Shock metering needle pin spanners can be used to remove the compression needle from the shock body on KTM WP PDS shocks.

This fork spring compressor for road bikes can be used in the field as well as in the shop.

A shock preload adjusting tool can be used aggressively on preload adjusting collars without damaging them.

Chapter 8
Suspension Service Department

TOOLS, TIME, AND SKILL REQUIREMENTS

Suspension service jobs vary in their degree of difficulty as well as their tool and skill requirements. Special tools will be needed often, so you will want to be prepared ahead of time—this will ensure you don't have to stop in the middle of your work to find these items. Always have access to a quality service manual for procedures, wear specifications, torque values, and details specific to the model you are working on. This section is designed to be a general guide for each major type of suspension system used on today's (and yesterday's) motorcycles, but it cannot cover the nuances of each specific fork and shock ever made.

The photos included with each how-to project will help you to be prepared and know in general what to expect as you begin the service/installation job. Time and difficulty will vary based upon the model of motorcycle combined with your personal mechanical aptitude—the ratings provided are intended only as a guideline. Remember that quality tools make a significant difference, so don't skimp, as it could cost you in the long run. Special tool requirements are to be expected, so plan ahead. If you are going to be removing and replacing suspension components from the bike, make sure you have the appropriate stands to support the bike while you work.

You will also need expendables such as spray chemicals and proper waste oil storage and disposal capability. Always wear safety glasses and have a first aid kit readily available. Be mindful of the environment while you are working.

Skill Levels (indicated by number of wrenches)

- **#1 Basic:** Minimal special skills or tools required. A service manual for the bike, this book, and product installation instructions will be needed, combined with basic mechanical skills and background.
- **#2 Intermediate:** Some special skills and tools will be required. A service manual for the bike, this book, and product installation instructions will be needed. You will also need to be comfortable working with new or unfamiliar procedures without intimidation. Assistance may be required on your first attempt.
- **#3 Advanced:** Special skills, procedures, and tools will be required. Training and/or assistance from an experienced individual is recommended on at least the first attempt. There is greater potential for personal injury, so use caution when working.

Time Commitments

- **A Level:** Minimal time required: 2 to 3 hours with experience, 3 to 6 hours first attempt.
- **B Level:** Moderate time required: 4 to 5 hours with experience, 5 to 8 hours first attempt.
- **C Level:** Major time required: 5 to 6 hours with experience, 6 to 9 hours first attempt.

Tools

Basic hand tools; digital calipers, tape measure, 8–19mm combination wrenches, 6–14mm ¼" drive sockets/ratchet, 10–19mm ⅜" drive sockets/ratchet, 22/24/27mm ½" drive sockets/ratchet, 4–10mm Allen sockets, long 6/8/10mm Allen sockets, 17/19/22/24 combination Allen socket, small/medium/large straight slot screwdrivers, #2/3 Phillips-head screwdrivers, pliers, snap ring pliers, side cutters, file, hammer, punch, impact wrench, tubing cutter

Special Tools

See Tools Section of each project introduction for details.

Equipment

Bike stands/jacks, etc. *(see tools section for details)*

Expendables

Spray solvent (brake/contact cleaner, etc), spray oil (WD-40, Bel Ray 6–1, or similar), grease, suspension oils in assorted viscosities, thread locker (high strength Loctite), spray polish, shop towels, sandpaper assortment (280-400 grit), plate glass, shop roll (500 grit), steel wool, Scotchbrite pads, waste oil/chemical storage.

PROJECT 1
Damping Rod Forks

 Skill Level:

 Tools: Basic Tools, Fork Seal Driver (TFSD series), Oil Level Setting Tool (TFOL 02), Damping Rod Holder Tool (OEM), Bike Stand/Jack

 Time: A

Damping rod forks are used on late model as well as vintage street and dirt bikes. This is the simplest fork design, requiring a minimum of special tools and skills. Damper rod forks are conventional style (shiny tube on top), are easy to work on, and can be improved dramatically with Gold Valve Cartridge Emulators. Generally the biggest challenge with this style of fork can be removing the bottom bolt—an impact wrench is a must. Some models will require snap ring pliers to remove the seal retaining circlip, and vintage models may require some damping rod machining when Emulators are installed.

Service Tip: If the bottom bolt spins around but won't come out, try pulling the chrome tube out hard while running the impact wrench. You can also try putting the fork main spring back in and pushing against the chrome tube, otherwise you will have to obtain a damping rod holding tool or make one yourself.

Disassembly

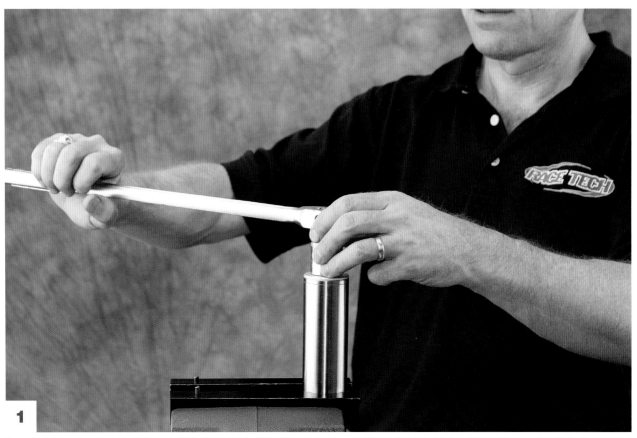

1

Clamp the fork tube in a vise with soft jaws specifically designed to hold fork tubes. Loosen the cap with a socket and ratchet, making sure to press down during the last few threads to prevent stripping or uncontrolled release. *Note: some models like Honda GLs have extreme amounts of preload, which can be dangerous released without control.*

SUSPENSION SERVICE DEPARTMENT

114

If the fork cap is stuck, it is often helpful to shock the thread. Hammer on the fork cap with a properly sized socket to help break the thread loose. If you use this method, be aware you can damage both the socket as well as marring the cap. Make certain you are wearing safety glasses before considering this option. In many cases you can put a few sheets of paper or a rag between the socket and the cap to protect it. *Note: the socket doesn't have to fit the hex.*

To measure the amount of preload on damping rod forks, rest the fork cap on the end of the spacer or spring and measure from the top of the fork tube to the sealing lip (the surface that would contact the fork tube when tightened) on the cap. This is a direct measurement of preload unless the thread on the cap is hitting the thread on the fork tube.

Remove the parts from the fork tube. In this case we remove a washer, spacer, another washer, and the fork spring.

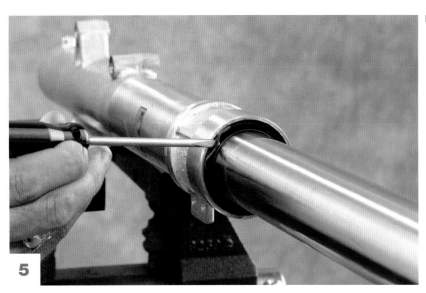

Remove the seal clip with a clip tool or small screwdriver.

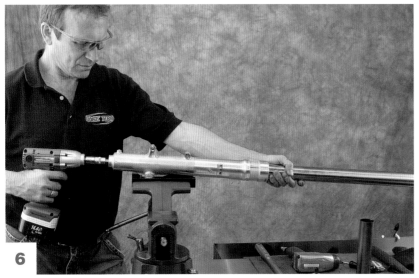

Loosen the compression bolt with an impact driver while pulling on the upper fork leg to keep it from spinning. If it continues to spin, you can reinstall the fork spring, spacer, and cap, then compress the fork. If it still continues to spin, you may have to make a holding tool for the damping rod.

If the compression bolt is stuck, hammer on the compression bolt with a properly sized socket to help break the thread loose. Again, if you do this be aware you can damage both the socket and the bolt. Wear safety glasses.

Remove the compression bolt.

Pour out the fluid and dispose of it properly.

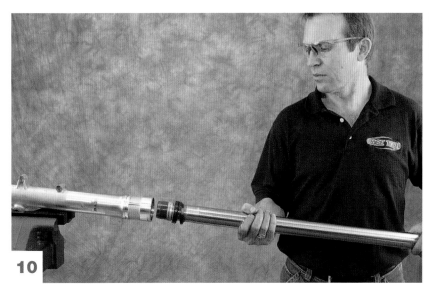

Slide hammer out the fork seals and bushings by vigorously extending the fork tube. Make sure the fork slider is firmly clamped in the vise. Make sure it is clamped on a strong area of the leg.

Remove the damping rod and top-out spring by inverting the fork tube.

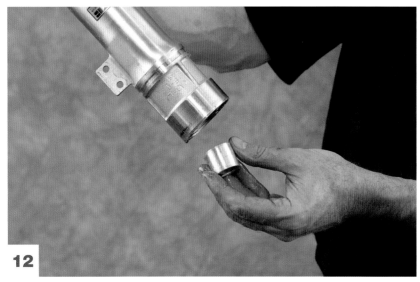

Remove the bottom-out cone from the slider. It is located on the damping rod, so it may be in the bottom of the fork tube.

Remove the outer bushing and seals from the tube.

Remove the inner bushing from the fork tube by spreading the bushing with your thumbnails. It may be easier to spread the bushing with a thin-blade screwdriver, but be careful not to damage it.

14

Inspect the Teflon bushing surfaces for embedded material and wear as well as possible damage done during disassembly. If the bushings have worn-out Teflon, check the lower fork leg for dents as these are the main cause of this kind of wear. If there are dents, the tubes may be able to be repaired by a competent professional. Otherwise the fork slider will need to be replaced. If there is embedded material, find the source before continuing. Inset: Here is an example of a new bushing next to an extremely worn-out bushing.

15

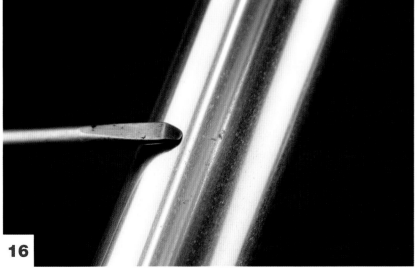

Inspect the fork tubes for pits. Minor pits can be polished out with 500-grit sandpaper. Major dings require tube replacement.

16

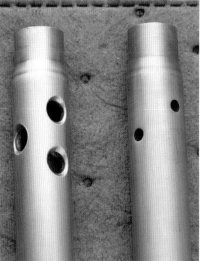

If you are installing Race Tech Gold Valve Cartridge Emulators, drill out the damping rod compression holes as described in your specific instruction sheet. Notice drilled damping rod next to the stock one on the right. Be sure to chamfer and deburr the holes.

Reassembly

Install a new inner bushing.

Install the top-out spring on the damper rod and insert the rod in the fork tube.

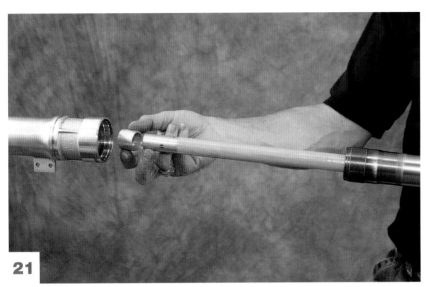

Install the bottoming cone onto the damper rod.

Install the inner fork tube into the outer fork tube.

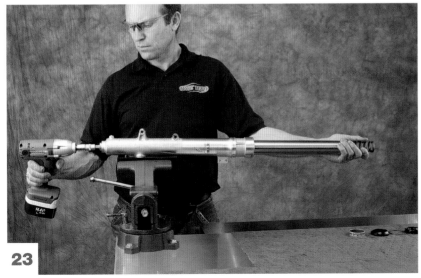

Tighten the damping rod bold to the manufacturer's specs. If the damping rod spins, install the spring and cap and compress the spring. If this doesn't work, you might have to use or even make a damping rod holding tool.

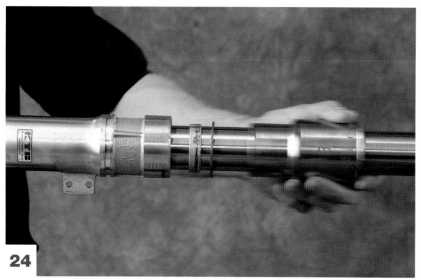

Install the outer bushing and seal washer with a seal driver.

Grease the seal. Normally we recommend seal replacement whenever the forks are serviced.

Slide the seal on the fork tube using a corner of a heavy gauge plastic bag (see inset) to protect the seal from being damaged by the end of the fork tube. Pull the bag taught to ease installation.

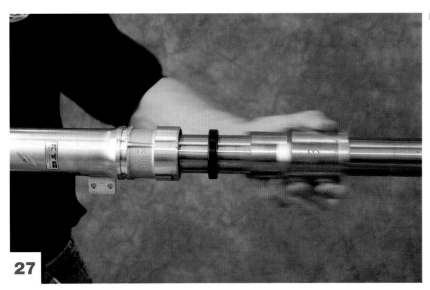

Install the seal into the slider with a seal driver.

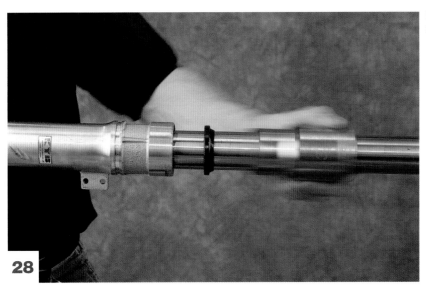

Install the dust seal with the seal driver. On some models, the retaining clip goes on before the dust seal.

Install the seal clip.

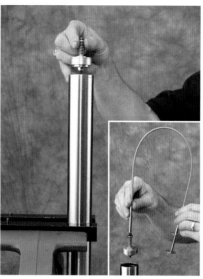

Drop in the Gold Valve Cartridge Emulator. Notice different types of Emulators on the left that cover a wide range of fork types and diameters. Check to make sure the Emulator is seated properly and in the proper direction. Many of the Emulator adapters for vintage models have a piston ring built into them to dramatically improve sealing and performance.

Drop in the spring, washer, spacer, and washer. Set the cap on the washer.

Check the preload by measuring the distance from the top of the fork tube to the sealing lip on the cap. The sealing lip is the portion of the cap that will contact the top of the tube when the cap is tightened. In this example we measure 38mm of preload with the existing spacer length. For this particular bike and rider we need 10mm, so we will shorten the existing spacer 28mm.

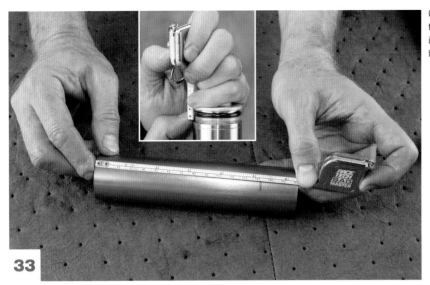

Cut the spacer to provide the correct preload. Make sure the spacer is cut squarely and deburred. If an Emulator is installed, this will procedure will compensate for its height. Inset: Re-measure the preload to check your work.

33

Remove the spring and spacers. Pour in the fluid.

34

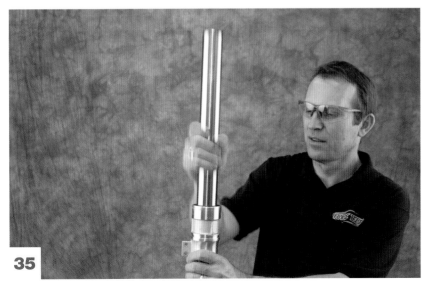

Bleed the fork by stroking the tube. Make sure there is an excess amount of fluid in the fork.

35

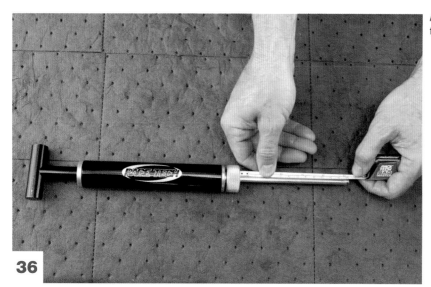

Adjust the tube extension on the oil sucker tool to equal the dimension of the target oil level.

36

37

If you are using an Emulator, install it before setting the oil level. Collapse the fork all the way and suck out the excess oil.

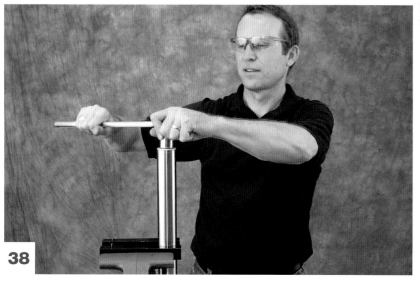

Install the fork cap and use a torque wrench to tighten it to manufacturer's specs.

38

PROJECT 2
Standard Cartridge Forks with Gold Valve Installation

 Skill Level:

 Time: B

 Tools: Basic Tools, Fork Cap Socket (TFCW Series), Fork Spring Compressor (TFSC Series) for street bikes, Cartridge Holding Tool (TFCH Series), Fork Seal Bag (TFSB), Shaft Holding Tools if Revalving (TFSH Series), Fork Seal Driver (TFSD Series), Cartridge Bleed Tools (TFBT Series), Oil Level Setting Tool (TFOL 02), Bike Stand/Jack

Standard cartridge forks are found on most late model sportbikes, some cruisers and tourers, mini MX bikes, and post-vintage MX bikes from the late 1980s to late 1990s. These can be conventional or inverted (shiny tube on bottom). This sophisticated fork design requires some special tools to work on. Care must be taken during service to avoid damage to expensive internal components and to ensure proper operation when completed. Most sportbikes have substantial installed spring preload, so be careful of sharp spring spacers under pressure so that you do not injure your hands or fingers! Use a fork spring compressor on those models for ease and safety.

Service Tip: Inverted-style forks require that the seals cross over sharp edges at the bushing grooves on the fork tube, which can easily ruin a new seal. Use a heavy gauge (4mm) plastic bag over the sharp edges or a thin piece of plastic wrapped inside the seals as you slide them over the groove. And always grease the seal lips!

Disassembly

Back off the rebound adjuster with a screwdriver.

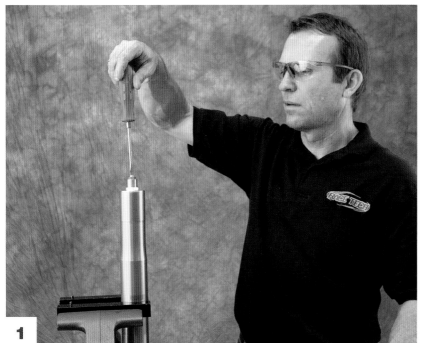

1

Hammer on the fork cap with a properly sized socket to help break the threads loose. This is not required but is quite effective for stubborn fork caps.

Remove the cap. On right-side-up forks keep significant downward force to control the cap in case it has an external top-out spring with lots of preload. Big touring and sport touring bikes typically have this issue. (Be sure to whistle while you work.)

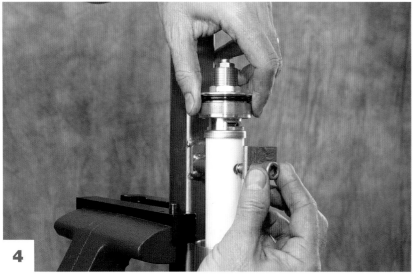

Clamp the fork spring compressor in a vise. Mount the fork in the fork spring compressor. Screw the thumb screw into the holes in the spacer.

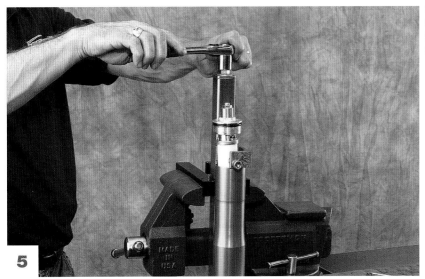

Compress the fork spring by tightening the compressor. Stop tightening when the tool hits the top of the tube or earlier if you have clearance or you will start destroying things.

Insert the holding tool. You may have to pull up on the cap to get the tool in.

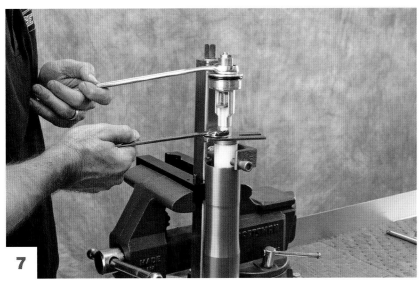

Break the jam nut loose while holding the in place with a second wrench.

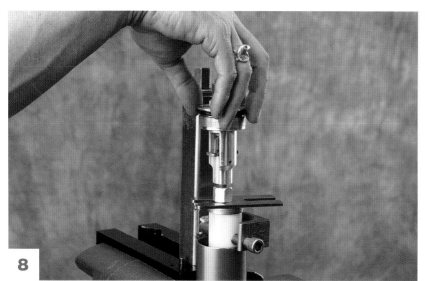

Remove the fork cap.

Thread on the bleeding tool, pull up, and remove the clip.

Release the preload.

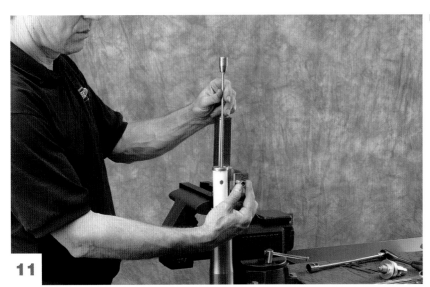

Remove the fork spring compressor.

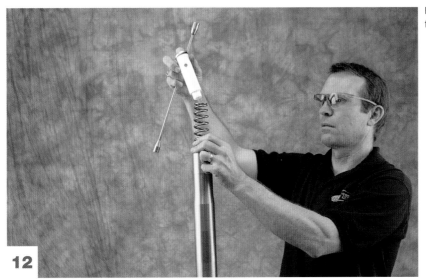

Remove the bleeding tool, washer, spring spacer, and fork spring.

Dump out the old oil.

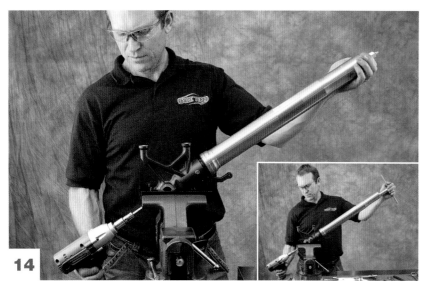

Remove the cartridge Allen bolt while pulling on the cartridge. Inset: If holding the cartridge by hand doesn't work, use the Race Tech Cartridge Holding Tool.

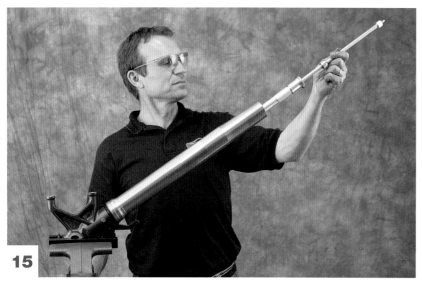

Remove the cartridge.

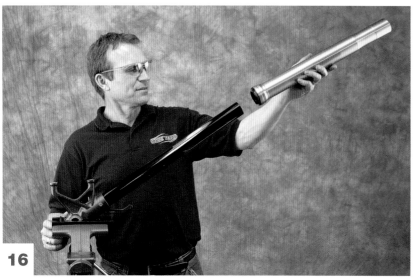

Remove the upper fork leg. The model shown has two outer bushings and slides off easily. Most models (particularly before 2003) have an inner bushing on the inner fork tube and must be "slide-hammered" off. If the outer fork tube does not slide off easily, remove the dust seal and clip then slide-hammer it apart. There are some models that are notorious for coming apart with difficulty. It is often helpful to heat the seal/bushing area with a heat gun before slide-hammering it apart.

Inspect the inner tube for pits or imperfections.

Remove the dust seal on the upper fork leg with a wood chisel.

Remove the seal clip.

On this style of fork with two outer bushings, the seal remains in the outer tube and must be pried out. Remove the seal and washer by prying it out with a wide tool to spread out the load. Be very careful not to damage the fork tube. You may need to pad the edge with a folded-up rag.

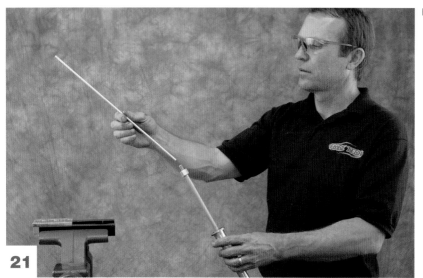

Remove the rebound adjusting rod from the cartridge.

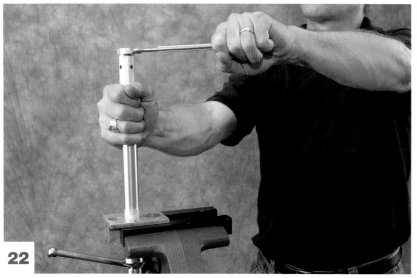

Clamp the cartridge assembly in the shaft holding tool and unscrew the compression base valve. Some models are held in with a clip. In this case push the base valve in far enough to expose the clip and remove it with a clip tool. Then remove the compression assembly.

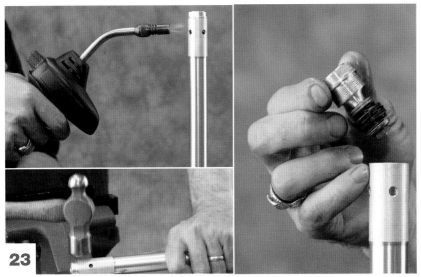

If the compression valve is stuck, heat the end of the cartridge at the compression valve with the propane torch or gently shock the threads with a hammer by tapping on the outside of cartridge at threads. If you tap on the thread be sure to hold the cartridge tube flat on the anvil surface of the vise. Hit the hammer squarely so as not to dent the tube. Only hit the cartridge tube on the very end where the thread is.

Clamp the compression base valve in a vise with soft jaws. On models that have the end of the valving shaft peened, file the end of the compression shaft down to the surface of the nut.

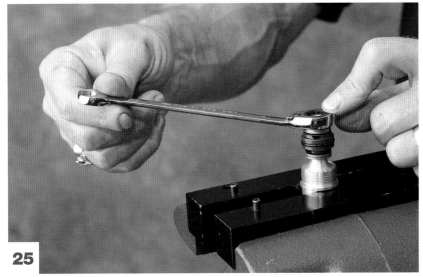

Remove the compression nut.

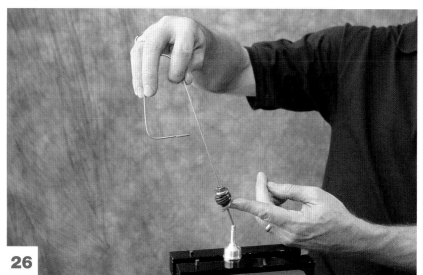

Remove the compression valving stack from the holder using a welding rod or a heavy wire. Notice this "special tool" has a hook so that the valving stack is captive for cleaning.

26

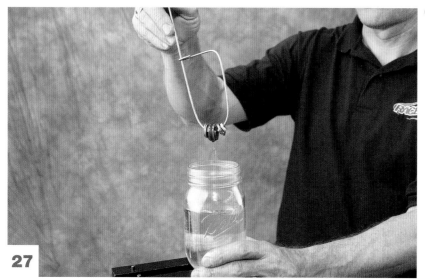

Clean the valving stack with contact cleaner.

27

Clean the center of the valving bolt with compressed air to remove filings and other debris.

28

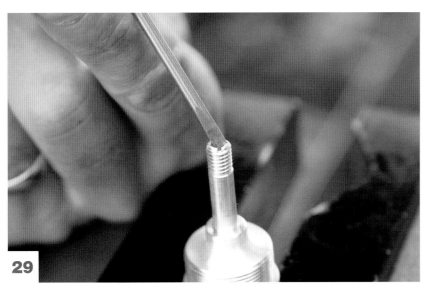

Clean out any debris in the stacking and on the shaft.

Chamfer/deburr the end of the cartridge bolt shaft slightly.

Finish both piston faces by sanding on 600-grit sandpaper over a plate glass base for a smooth and flat surface. Caution: sometimes the valving pistons are not intended to be flat all the way across. Refer to the valving section for preloaded piston types. On this type, do not surface the preloaded side of the piston.

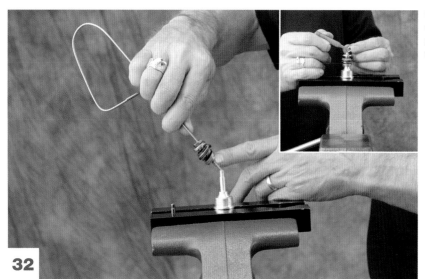

If you are installing a Gold Valve, follow the instructions with the kit. Install the new valving stack and use Loctite on the piston assembly nut (inset). Make sure the check valve is free before tightening the nut.

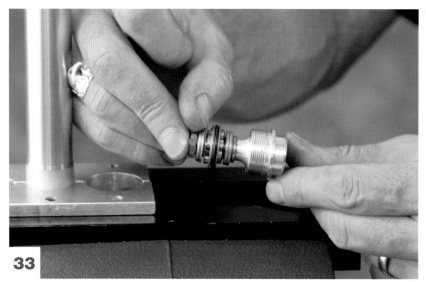

Check for compression check-plate freedom!

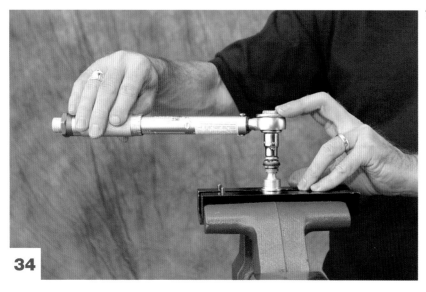

Torque the compression valving stack.

Heat the seal head to aid disassembly if needed.

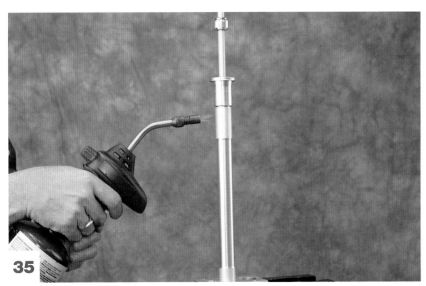

35

Or with a hammer, tap the seal head threads to help jar them loose. Sometimes the thread is "staked", in other words there are punch marks in the threaded area to insure they don't come apart. If this is the case, drill out the punch marks but only to the depth of the outer tube. Do not drill all the way through the seal head.

36

37

To access the rebound valving on models with peened-on bottom-out pistons, remove the cartridge seal head. To support the cartridge so that it won't crush in the shaft holding tool, temporarily reinstall the compression base valve in the cartridge. Clamp the cartridge tube at the compression valve assembly in the shaft holding tool. Next, using the cartridge holding tool, unscrew the cartridge seal head assembly. If it is stuck, use heat or tap the thread. *Note: Many models do not have a peened-on bottom-out piston. On this type you can simply slide out the damping rod assembly without having to remove the seal head.*

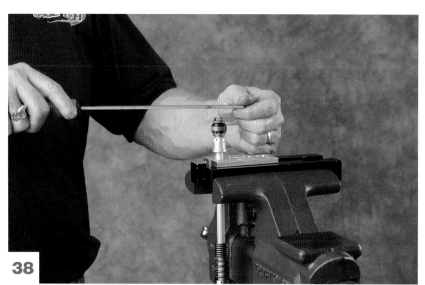

File the peening on the rebound valve.

Remove the rebound nut.

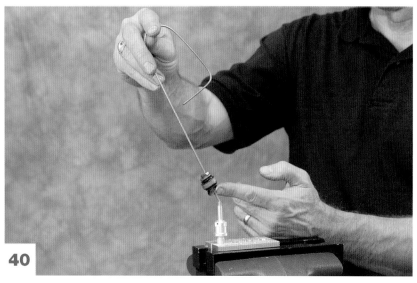

Remove the rebound valving.

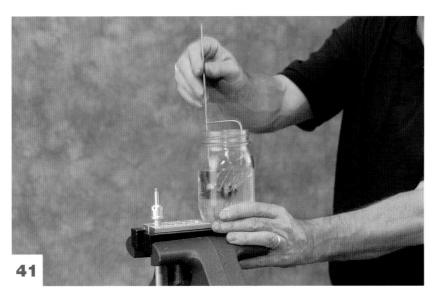

Clean the rebound stack with contact cleaner.

Chamfer the rebound shaft lightly. Dressing it on a wire wheel gives it the pro touch.

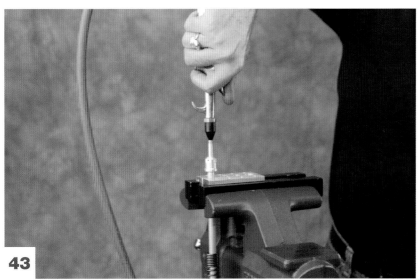

Blow any debris out of the inside of the low-speed shaft.

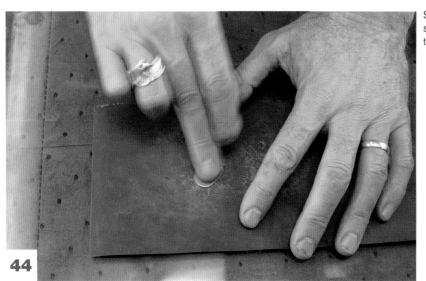

Surface the base plate to make sure it's flat. Again, use sandpaper on a plate glass surface. Use 280–320-grit for this steel base plate.

Surface the rebound piston next.

Reassembly

Follow the instructions for the Rebound Gold Valve if you are installing one. Install the rebound assembly.

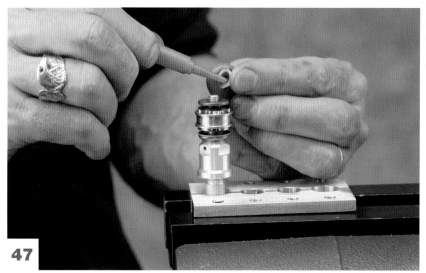

Make sure the thread is clean. Secure the rebound valve nut with a small drop of Loctite. Do not use too much as it can go down the center of the shaft and plug the adjuster. If any does get inside, immediately clean out the center of the shaft.

Make sure the check valve is free before tightening the nut.

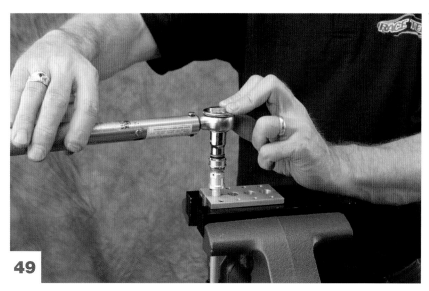

Torque the rebound valving nut.

Make sure the thread is clean and Loctite the rebound cartridge seal head.

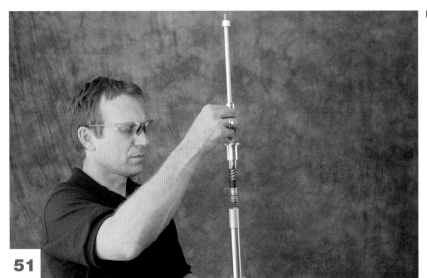

Insert the rod into the cartridge.

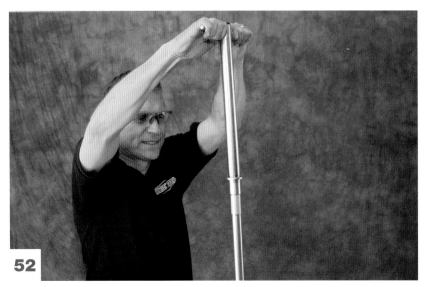

Tighten the seal head.

Use a small drop of Loctite on the thread (if it is the threaded type). Install the compression base valve assembly into the cartridge.

53

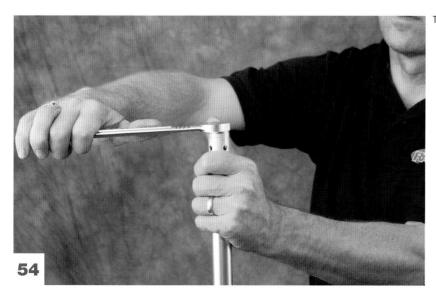

Tighten the compression valve assembly.

54

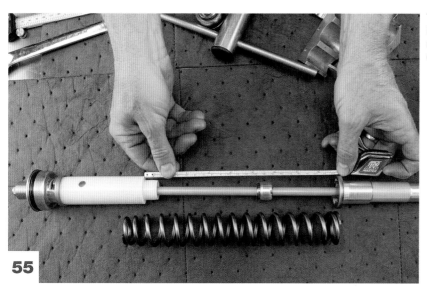

Temporarily install the preload spacer and fork cap. Back out the preload adjuster all the way and measure relaxed set length. Refer to the spring preload section in Chapter 2—Springs

55

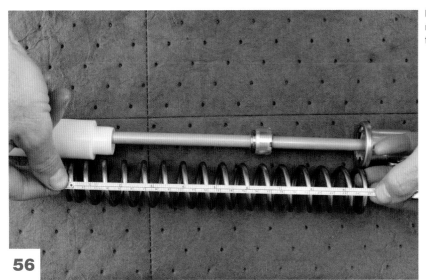

Measure the free length of the spring. Calculate the relaxed preload by subtracting the relaxed set length from the free length of the spring.

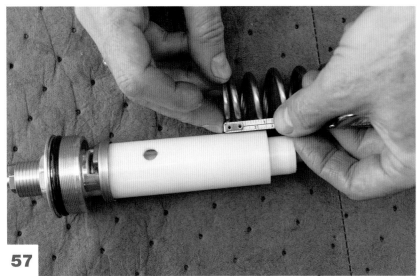

Optionally on this model you can line up one end of the spring with the spring seat and measure the relaxed spring preload directly as shown. Cut the preload spacer to set the proper preload. See setting preload section in the Springs Chapter.

Grease the fork seal.

Install the wiper and seal onto the tube. Use a 4mil thick plastic bag on the end of the tube to protect the seal. On models with an inner fork bushing groove pull the bag taut to aid in protection.

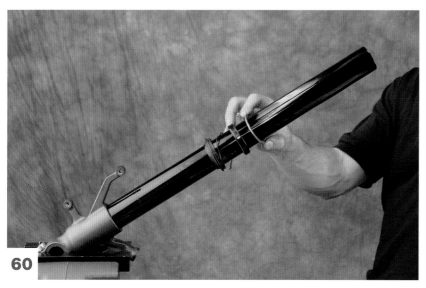

Install the seal washer and clip.

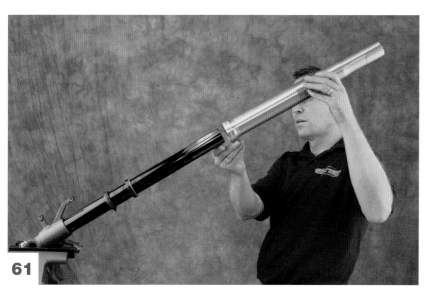

Slide the outer tube over the inner tube.

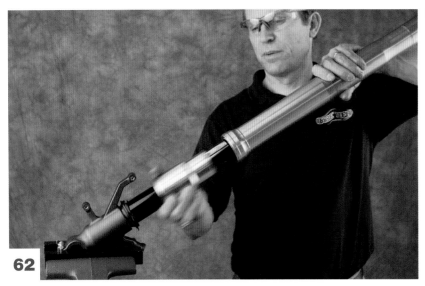

Install the seal by driving it with a seal driver.

Install the seal clip and then seat the seal clip with a screwdriver.

Install the wiper with the seal driver.

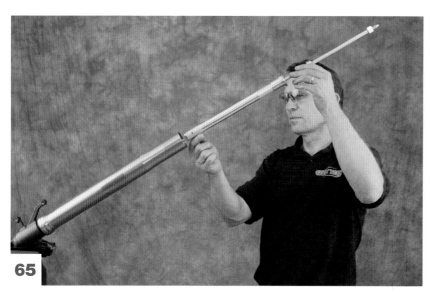

Insert the cartridge.

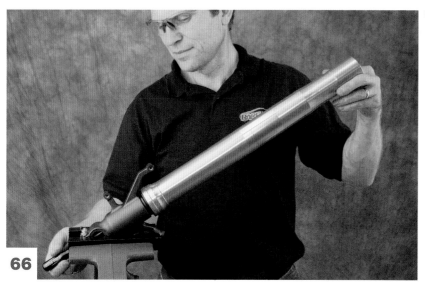

Screw in the compression bolt.

Install the compression bolt with an impact driver. If it spins, you will need to hold the cartridge with a Cartridge Holding Tool.

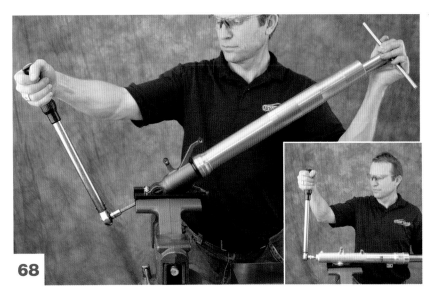

Torque the compression bolt to manufacturer's specs. If the cartridge spins, use a TFCH-Series cartridge holding tool (inset).

68

Add the proper suspension fluid.

69

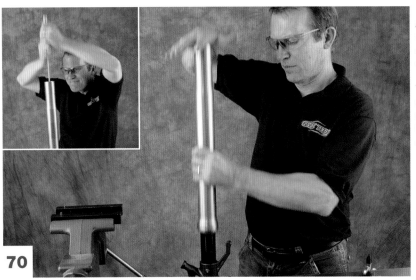

Tip: You can prime and speed up bleeding the cartridge by putting your hand over the top of the tube at full extension, then compressing the fork. The pressure will force oil into the cartridge. Then stroke the damping rod until the cartridge is bled.

There are two types of forks: those with and without a bleed hole in the inner tube. This hole equalizes the oil level in the area between the inner and outer tube. Forks without this hole must be extended all the way to evacuate this area before setting the oil level. It's good to notice which type you have before assembly.

70

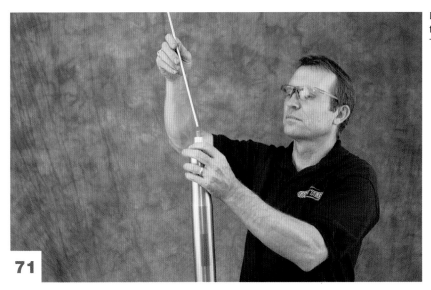

Drop in the rebound adjusting rod. Collapse the outer fork tube. Set the oil level by sucking out extra oil with the TFOL oil level tool.

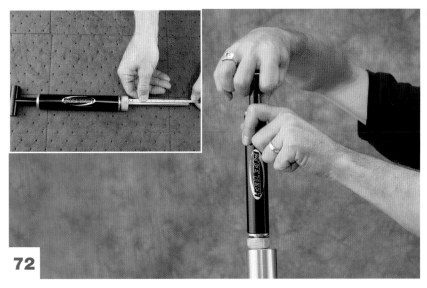

Collapse the outer fork tube. Set the oil level by sucking out extra oil with the TFOL oil level tool.

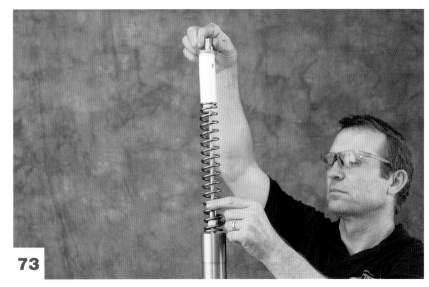

Add the spring, spacer, and spacer washer. Screw the proper TFBT bleeding tool onto the damping rod thread.

Clamp the fork spring compressor in a vise. Put the fork assembly into it. Gently tighten the thumb screw into the hole in the spacer. Compress the spring with the compressor enough to allow inserting the cup tool. *Note: You may have to pull up slightly on the damping rod to get the cup in. Do not use an impact on the spring compressor and be sure to stop tightening when it is fully compressed.*

74

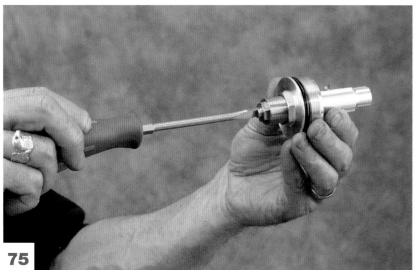

Set the adjuster screw. There are three types. The first two are the most common on street bikes. On these two types the cap must be screwed on the proper amount. One style has an adjuster screw that will stop as it is screwed in and the other will keep going and eventually fall out—along with the tiny detent ball and spring. Identify which type you have—first unscrew the adjuster all the way. If you screw it in more than seven turns (28 clicks) and it hasn't stopped you probably have the kind that comes apart. If this is the case, stop, back out the screw all the way, and screw it in four turns (20 clicks). On the type that stops, screw it in until it stops and back it out 2 clicks. Most dirt bikes (and a few street bikes) are the third type. This type is made so all you need to do is back out the rebound adjuster all the way and screw the cap on until it stops.

75

Use Loctite on the damping rod thread.

76

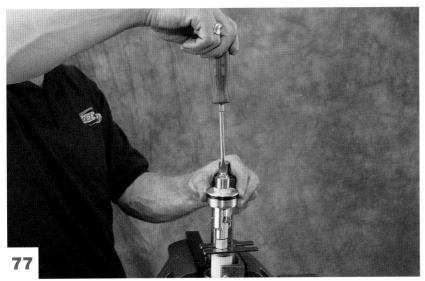

Screw down the cap on the damping rod until it is just snug. On the first two types, the rebound needle is now touching the seat. Tighten the jam nut up against the cap with your fingers. Hold the cap so that it doesn't turn. Now back out the adjuster screw ½ turn so that it is no longer seated.

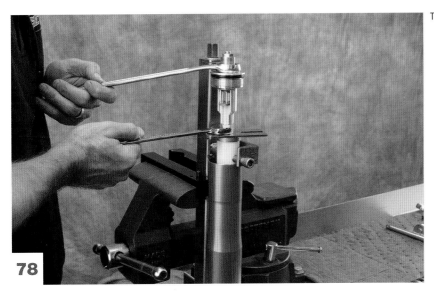

Tighten the jam nut to manufacturer's specs.

Tighten the fork cap. The torque on the cap is usually very low (around 10 lbs-ft. or 14 Nm). Consult manufacturer's specs.

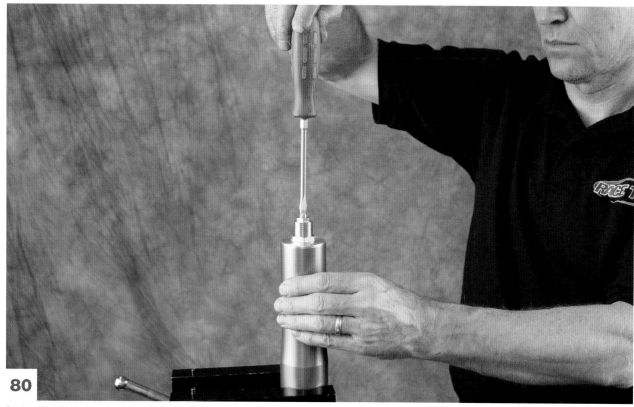

80

Set the rebound adjustment located on the fork cap. Count clicks or turns out (counterclockwise) from all the way in.

81

Set the compression adjustment, which is usually located on the bottom of the fork. Count clicks or turns out (counterclockwise) from all the way in.

82 Precisely align the sticker.

83 Make another goofy pose when someone has a camera. (Notice the form though.)

PROJECT 3
Twin-Chamber Forks

 Skill Level:

Time: C

 Tools: Basic Tools, Fork Cap Wrench (TFCW) Twin Champer Tool (TFCT Series), Damper Rod Holder (TFHP), Fork Seal Bag (TFSB), Shaft Holding Tools if Re-valving (TFSH Series), Fork Seal Driver (TFSD Series), Graduated Cylinder (TFGC), Nitrogen Station for Bladder Forks (see tools section), Bike Stand/Jack

Twin-chamber forks are used on late model MX bikes. Not always an inverted design, these forks may also have nitrogen bladders instead of pressure springs. They require some special tools and procedures. Great care must be taken on some models because of the sharp edges and threads at the base of the damping rod that can damage cartridge seals, resulting in lost damping.

Service Tip: When replacing only the fork seals (no re-valving), the inner chamber does not need to be disturbed or drained. If you do so, check for a full cartridge with the cartridge out of the fork, push the damping rod in, and watch to see that it re-extends fully on its own. Also make sure that no fluid leaks out around the shaft seal. Be mindful of bushing grooves when installing fork seals.

Disassembly

Loosen the compression valve assembly with a fork cap wrench. It is located on the inside of the outer hex. It may require a special wrench or socket.

1

Loosen the fork cap with the fork cap wrench but do not remove it completely.

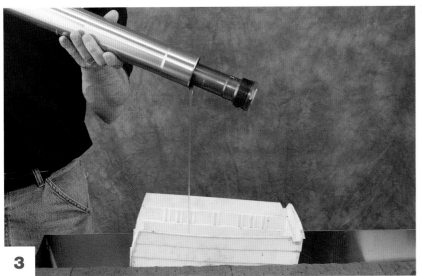

Pour out the oil and dispose of properly.

Loosen the damping rod bolt at the bottom of the fork. When clamping on the fork bottom, select the strongest location. Never clamp on brake arms or smaller tabs.

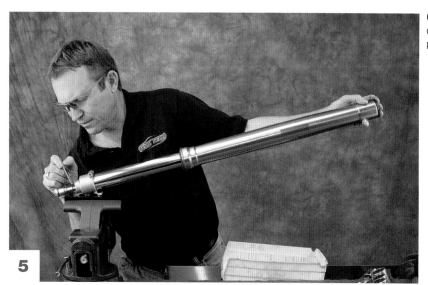

Compress the outer tube and insert a holding clip tool on the damping rod. Our new clips are made of special plastic, so there is no chance of marring the damping rod.

Loosen the jam nut.

Remove the damping rod bolt. *Tip: On Showas with a D-shaped rebound adjuster rod, hold the rebound adjuster in a fixed position with a screwdriver while you unscrew the bolt. This will keep the aluminum D-shaped rod from rounding out if the adjusting screw is corroded and tight.*

SUSPENSION SERVICE DEPARTMENT

This is a close-up of D-shaped rod.

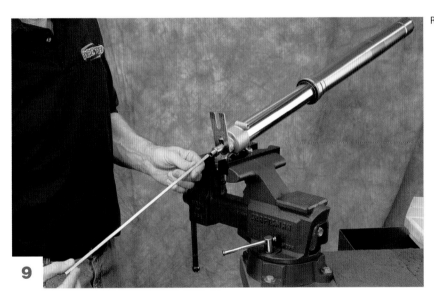

Remove the D-shaped rebound adjuster rod.

Compress the fork and remove the clip tool.

Remove the cartridge.

Inspect the cartridge for damage such as dents, wear, etc.

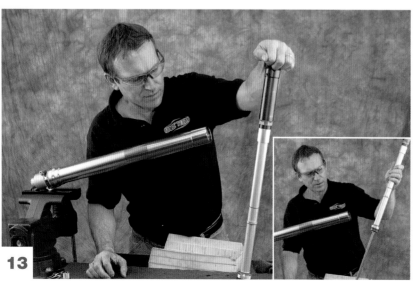

Check for evidence of good seals. Compress the cartridge all the way, and it should return to the fully extended position by itself. If it doesn't, the internal oil level may be low, possibly caused by leaking shaft or reservoir seals. If it is a 05 YZ, it will not return all the way as the pressure spring is too short from the factory. Also it may not extend all the way if there is only slightly too much friction.

Remove the spring from the fork tube.

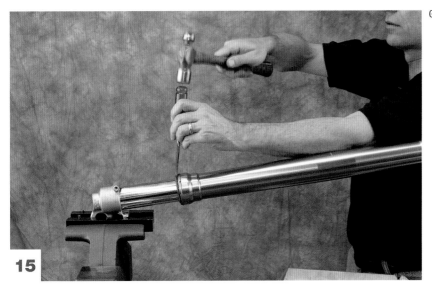

Gently remove the wiper with a sharp wood chisel.

Remove the seal retainer clip with a clip tool.

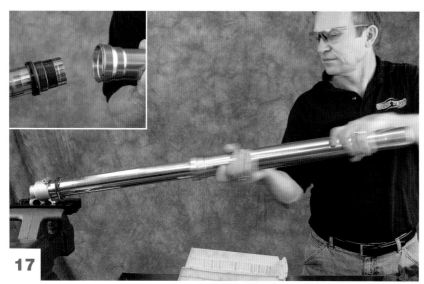

Slide hammer the fork seal and bushings out forcefully.

Tip: heat the seal/bushing area if the tubes don't come apart easily. On certain models, most notably KYB 46mm upside-down forks this is a good idea before slide hammering is done.

Some forks may suffer damage to the Teflon bushings during disassembly (as shown). This is common on 46mm KYBs. It's good to have extra bushings on hand.

Another way to remove the seal with a minimal chance of damage to the bushings is to completely fill the fork with used "work" oil, invert it, remove the wiper and clip, and put it into a hydraulic press to force the seal out.

Remove the inner fork bushing by opening up the bushing using your fingernails inserted into the gap. If the bushing is too stiff, use a screwdriver.

20

Remove the bushings and the seal washer.

21

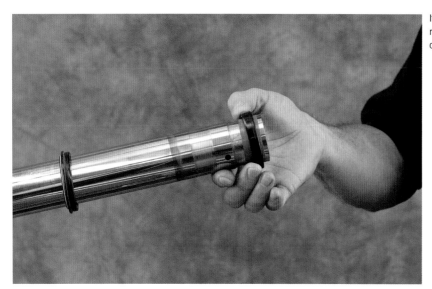

If you're not replacing seals (though it's always recommended), use boxing tape to cover the sharp edge of the bushing groove during removal.

Inspect the bushings for damage, including worn-down Teflon or embedded material.

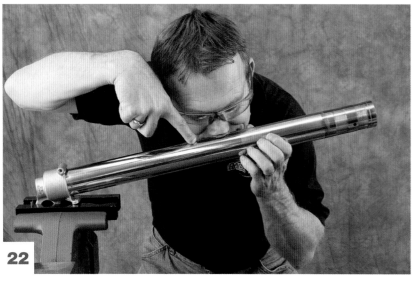

Inspect the fork tube for pits, dings, and straightness. Make another goofy pose that might offend a really near-sighted person.

22

Inspect the condition of the hard anodizing, looking for wear inside the outer fork tube with an inspection mirror and flashlight.

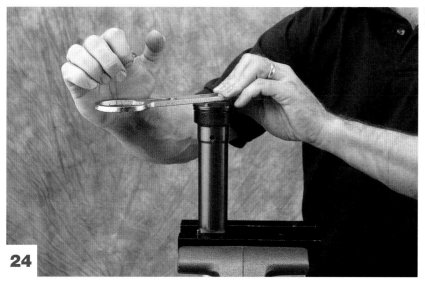

Gently hold the cartridge assembly in a vise and unscrew the compression assembly.

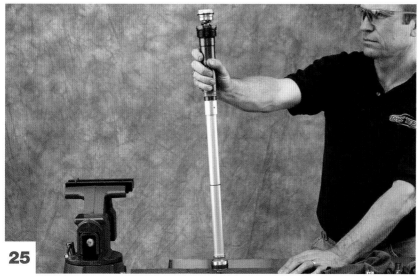

Compress the damping rod to lift the compression assembly.

Remove the compression assembly.

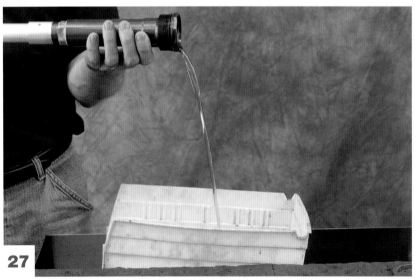

Empty the oil from the cartridge.

File the peening from the top of the compression shaft down to the nut surface if there is any.

Remove the compression valving nut.

Remove the compression valving assembly. It is helpful to use a welding rod bent into a special tool or a small screwdriver.

Chamfer the end of the compression valving shaft with a fine, flat file.

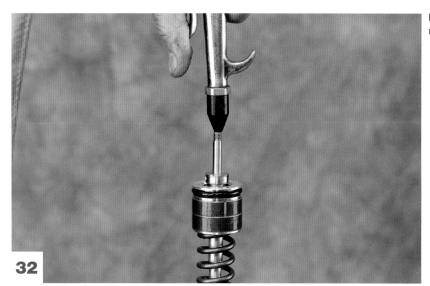

Blow out the center of the shaft with compressed air to remove filings.

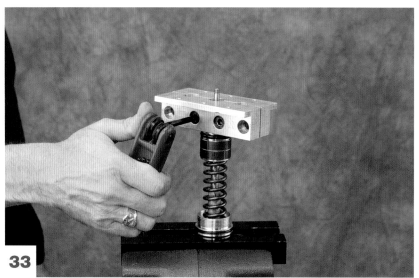

If you are replacing the pressure spring or reservoir piston seal, you must disassemble the reservoir. While maintaining pressure on the spring and reservoir piston, clamp the shaft holding tool on the shaft. Remove the compression valving holder by unscrewing it.

Disassemble the reservoir and pressure spring shaft. Inspect them for wear. Some models with aluminum shafts have severe wear problems. Inspect the seals and remove the clip. *Note: The necked-down area bleeds the cartridge during assembly.*

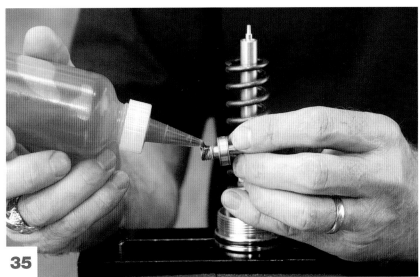

Add a small drop of red Loctite to the compression valving holder thread.

Install the pressure spring, reservoir piston, and compression valving holder. Tighten the compression valving holder with a shaft holding tool. Use an adjustable wrench to apply additional leverage.

Wash the compression valving stack in contact cleaner.

38

Surface the piston on 320-grit or finer sandpaper on a piece of plate glass.

Before

Halfway through, showing uneven surface.

Complete

SUSPENSION SERVICE DEPARTMENT

COMPRESSION PISTON ASSEMBLY

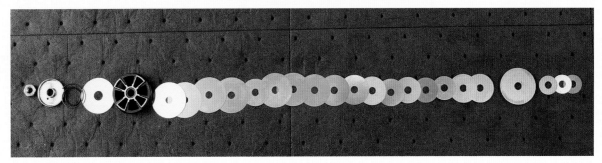

Stock compression stack components laid out in order.

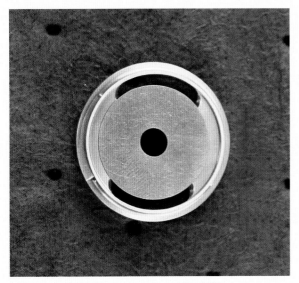

G2-R compression Gold Valve with restrictor valving stack.

G2-R piston showing refill ports on the side and the recess on the compression face for creating preload and restriction.

Race Tech G2-R Gold Valve compared to the stock piston.

Surface the base plate.

39

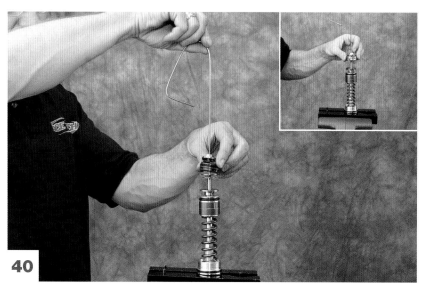

Install the stock compression stack or the Race Tech G2-R stack.

40

Apply a small drop of Loctite to the compression valving shaft nut.

41

SETTING PROPER STACK HEIGHT

Set the proper total stack height so that the nut gets full engagement and doesn't run out of thread.

Incorrect stack height on a G2-R

Correct stack height

Stock piston incorrect

Stock piston correct

Check to make sure the check valve is free.

Torque the compression valving shaft nut. (stock/G2-R)

Continue disassembling the cartridge. Remove the damping rod jam nut.

On Showas with 12mm shafts, the trailing edge of the last thread on the damping rod is razor sharp. This edge can easily tear the shaft seal. Carefully dress it up with a fine file.

Pack the thread with grease to help them get through the seal during removal from the cartridge.

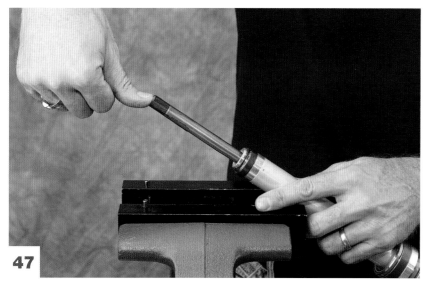

Push the damping rod out through the seal.

Put the rebound rod in the shaft holding tool and remove the peening by filing it down to the nut face.

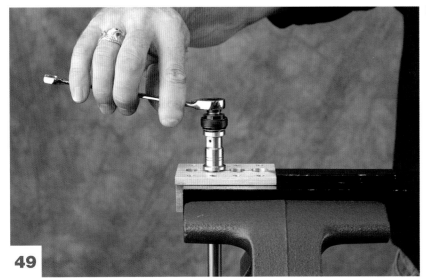

Remove the rebound valving nut.

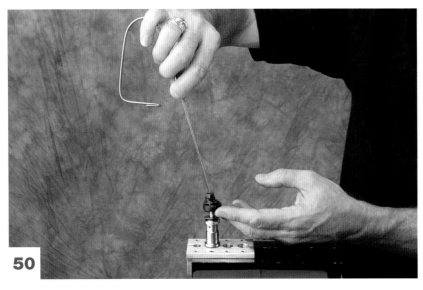

Remove the rebound valving assembly.

Chamfer the rebound valving shaft lightly. Use a wire wheel on the shaft end to smooth it.

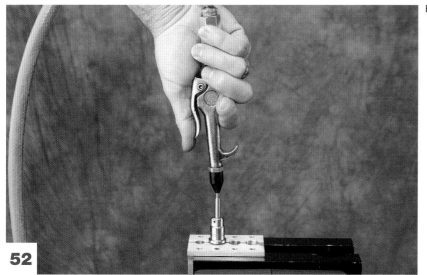

Blow out the center of the shaft with compressed air.

Inspect the rebound rod for pits, excessive wear, bends, worn-through anodizing, and so on.

REBOUND VALVING STACK

Rebound stack exploded view.

Every valve has two distinct sides. The piston on the left is showing the recessed side. This is the mid-valve/check valve side. The piston on the right is showing the flat side, which is the rebound valving side.

Surface the rebound piston on 320-grit sandpaper on a piece of plate glass.

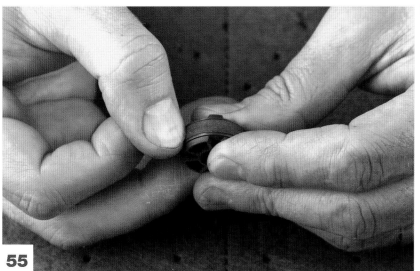

Use a fingernail to remove any embedded material.

Clean the rebound valving stack.

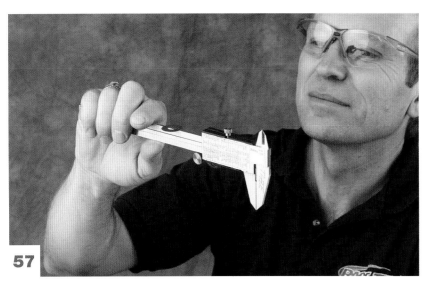

Inspect each shim for deformation.

Assembly

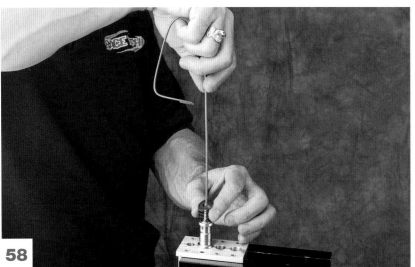

Install the mid-valve or check valve on the valving holder. The mid-valve consists of a cupped washer, sleeve, check spring, and mid-valve stack. A check valve consists of a cupped washer, sleeve, check spring, and check plate.

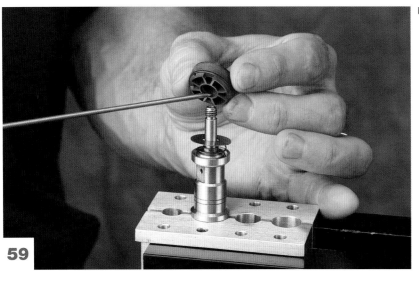

Install the rebound piston with the recessed side down.

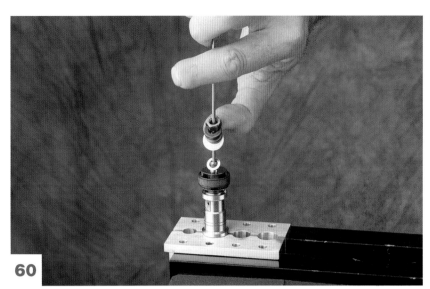

Install the rebound valving.

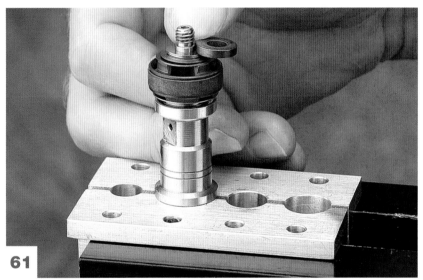

Make sure the valving stack height is correct. This means the nut has full engagement but doesn't run out of thread onto straight shaft. Refer to picture on page 173.

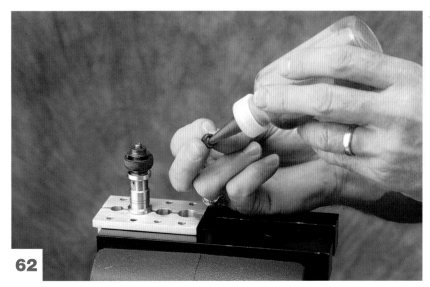

Apply a small drop of Loctite to the rebound valving nut.

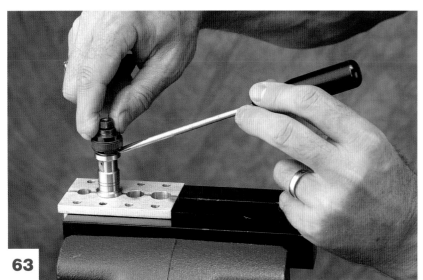

Make sure the mid-valve/check valve is free to move up and down.

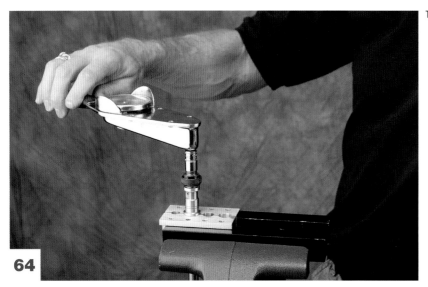

Torque the rebound valving nut

Fully pack the rebound rod thread with grease. Remove excess grease.

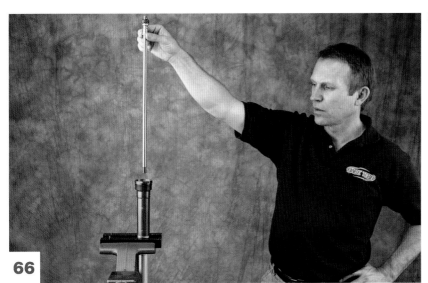

Insert the rebound rod into the cartridge.

Quickly push the end of the damping rod through the seal using a T-handle.

Fill with fluid about 100mm (4") from the top.

Bleed the cartridge by pumping the rod in and out of the cartridge. Make sure you stroke it slowly on compression to avoid causing cavitation.

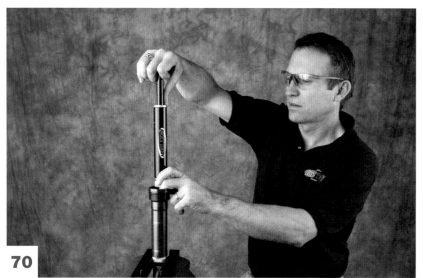

Replace the damping rod jam nut (see page 174) and set the oil level with a fork oil level tool.

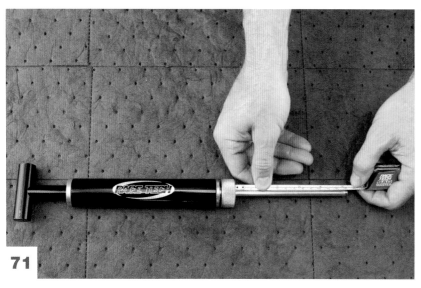

This amount of oil is actually too much oil. The excess will be removed further in the procedure.

Insert the compression valve assembly.

Push down on the compression assembly and tighten. This will take a bit of force because there is excess oil and you are compressing the pressure spring. Install the jam nut on the rebound rod.

Set oil volume by compressing the cartridge all the way. The reservoir piston will move up until the piston no longer seals on the shaft where the "necked-down" portion of the shaft is. This is called the "assembly groove" on figure 3.32. Extra oil will go past the reservoir piston.

Note: Some of the excess oil may drip out of the vent holes as the damping rod is compressed and excess oil is forced out through the assembly groove.

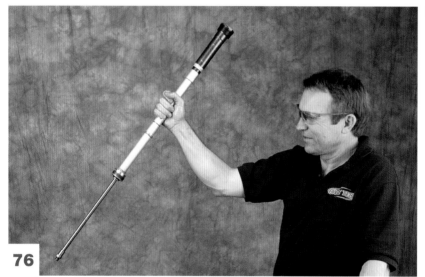

Release pressure—make sure the rod extends completely.

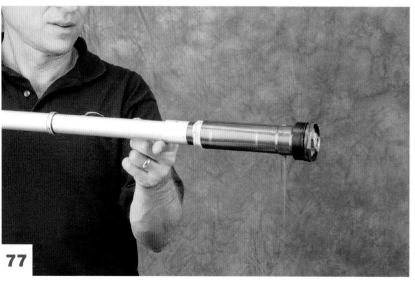

Pour out excess oil.

Grease the fork seal and wiper.

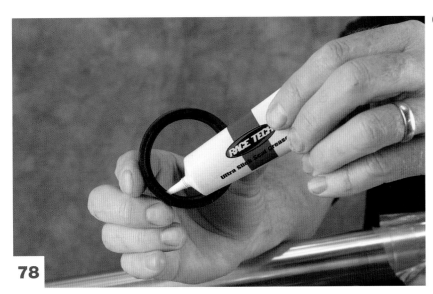

78

Use the corner of a heavy gauge plastic bag and place it on the end of the fork tube. This will protect the seal from the sharp edges of the inner bushing groove.

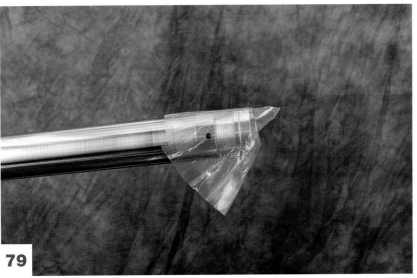

79

Slide on seal and wiper over plastic bag. Pulling the bag taut will further smooth the sharp edges, preventing damage. The seal and wiper are directional, so make sure they are on the right way with the dual-lipped part of the seal facing away from the fork bottom and toward the outer fork tube.

80

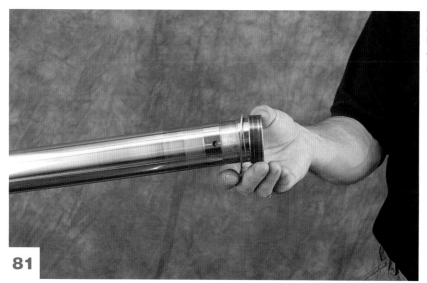

Install the seal washer and outer bushing. There is usually a sharp and a rounded edge on the washer. I like to put the sharp edge toward the bushing. Sometimes the seal washer is more elaborate than a plain washer. If it is a machined part, make sure it goes on in the right direction.

Install the inner bushing into its groove.

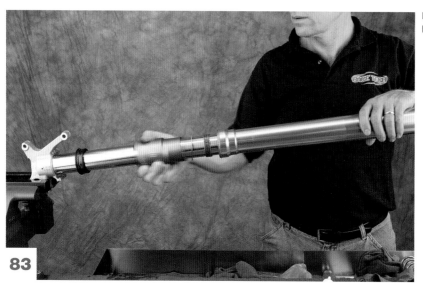

Install the outer bushing with the seal driver. You will be hitting on the seal washer, and it will drive in the bushing.

SUSPENSION SERVICE DEPARTMENT

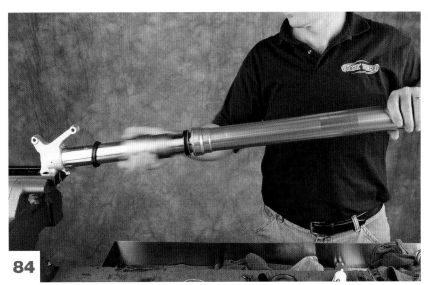

Install the oil seal with the seal driver.

84

Install the clip.

85

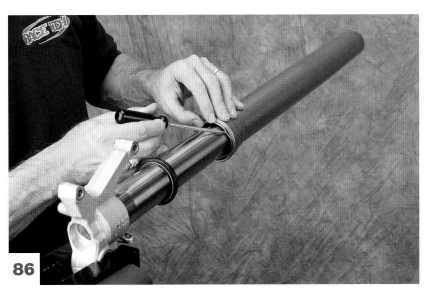

Seat the clip in the groove with the clip tool or a small screwdriver.

86

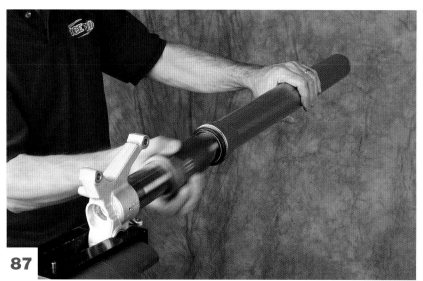

Install the dust seal with the seal driver.

Insert the D-shaped rebound adjusting rod. Spin it until it registers on the D-shaped pin.

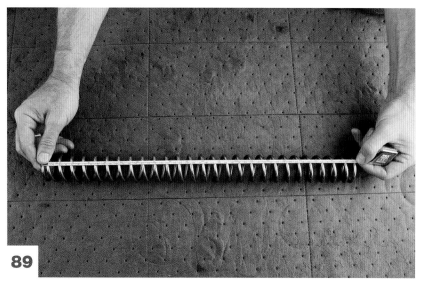

During the re-assembly we will calculate the preload. Measure the spring free length. (Ex: 493mm)

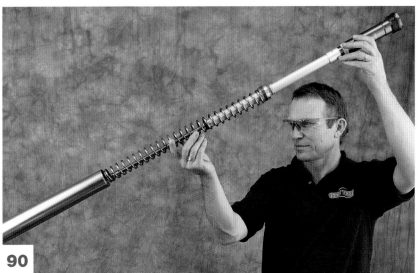

Slide the spring onto the cartridge and insert it into the fork tube.

The next step in measuring the preload is to gently rest the cartridge on the spring. Make a reference measurement between the end of the bottomed-out fork tube and any easily identified edge on the cartridge. (Ex: 105mm) This measurement will be drawn in when the bottom bolt is installed by the amount of the preload.

Compress the spring and insert the clip tool.

Put a drop of Loctite on the damping rod thread.

Screw on the rebound adjuster bolt. Use a screwdriver to hold the adjuster screw in position while turning the adjuster bolt. This protects the D-shape rod as we did during disassembly.

Tighten the jam nut.

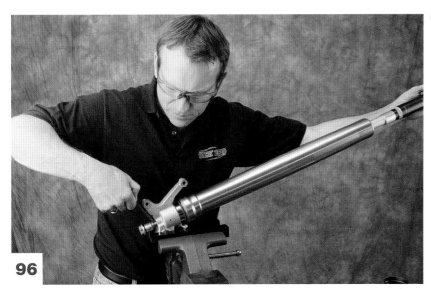

Compress the fork and remove the clip tool.

Put a drop of Loctite on the adjuster bolt.

Tighten the rebound adjuster bolt with a torque wrench to manufacturer's spec.

The last step in measuring preload. Now that we have tightened the cartridge, the spring is compressed to the set length. Re-measure the reference distance (ex: 99mm). If we subtract this from the first reference measurement, this gives us the preload (ex: 105mm - 99mm = 6mm of preload. We can also calculate the set length as it is the free length minus the preload (493mm - 6mm = 487mm set length).

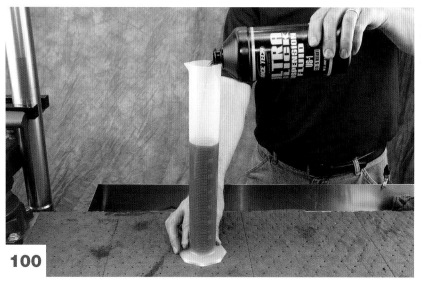

Continuing the assembly, measure oil volume with a graduated cylinder. For these forks we cannot measure the oil height, so volume is the only option. Do not use a large-diameter measuring device or one that is tapered as they are not as accurate as needed.

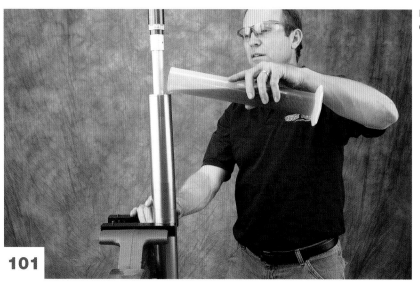

Pour oil into the open fork tube. Let the graduated cylinder drain completely.

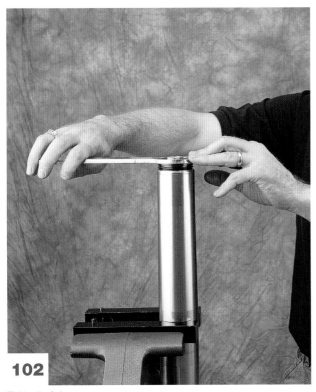

102

Tighten the fork cap.

103

Set the compression adjuster by counting clicks or turns outward (counterclockwise) from all the way in. Be careful to just gently bottom the needle in its seat as it is easy to damage the tapered needle.

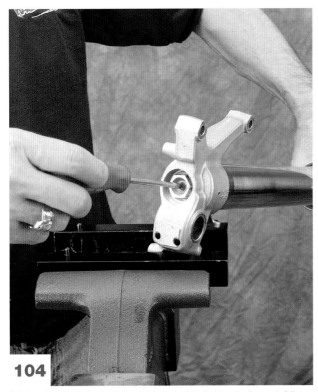

104

Set the rebound adjuster located on the bottom of the fork leg. Again zero is fully clockwise (all the way in.)

105

Let us not forget the essential last step. Install the protective sticker. Be sure orient the sticker as to properly locate the bleed screws on the fork cap.

PROJECT 4
Emulsion Shocks

 Skill Level:

 Time: A

 Tools: Basic Tools, Shock Spring Compressor (TFSC series), Pin Spanners (TMPS series) for some models, Shaft Holders (TFSH if removing shaft from eyelet clevis), Seal Head Tools (TSSS series), Clip Tool (TSCP), Seal Head Bullet (TSSB), Nitrogen Station (see tools section), Bike Stand/Jack

Emulsion shocks are found on all types of motorcycles and ATVs, dirt and street. They are typical on most vintage models as well as many modern bikes. This most basic shock design is fairly straightforward to work on, with no piston or bladder to separate the oil and nitrogen.

Service Tip: Inspect the bushings at the mounting eyelets carefully. Rubber bushings degenerate over time, resulting in a loose feel to the rider. Needle or spherical bearings can do this too. They can also seize up, causing binding and resulting in a harsh feel to the rider. Don't overlook them.

Remove the spring and depressurize the shock using the Shock Nitrogen Needle tool. It is also common to use a Schrader (tire) valve.

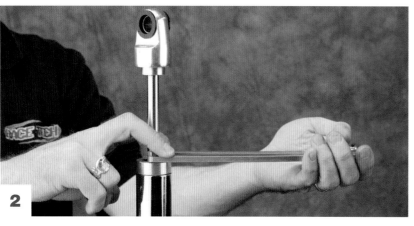

Unscrew and remove the seal head assembly with a RT Pin Spanner. Some models will have a hex instead of pin holes. Some models have a pressed on cap and a seal head held in with a clip as is shown in the reservoir shock section.

Remove the shaft assembly.

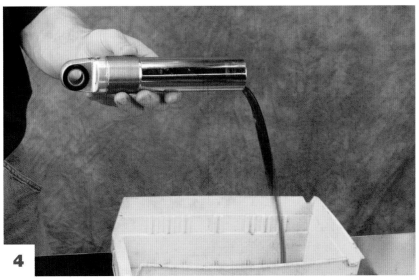

Dump out the oil.

Clean everything, replace seals if needed, and refill the shock body with oil.

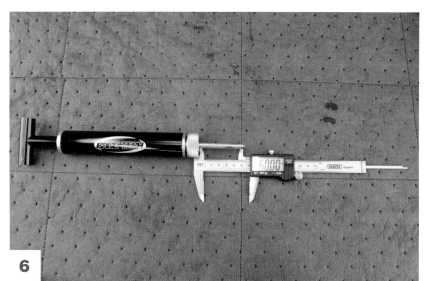

Adjust the tube extension on the Race Tech Pro Fork Oil Level Tool to the required oil level.

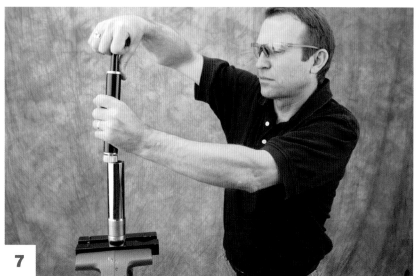

Set the oil level. This is critical as there must be more air space than the volume the shock shaft displaces (see Figure 3.34).

Insert the shaft assembly into the shock body.

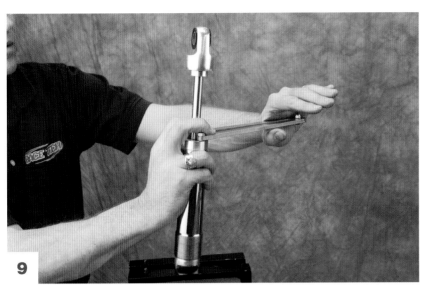

Tighten the seal head with Race Tech Pin Spanner.

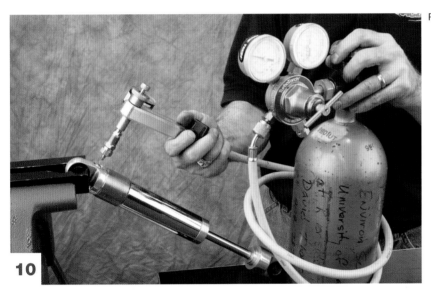

Pressurize the shock with the nitrogen needle.

Compress and make sure the shaft extends completely.
Note: Make sure emulsion shocks are mounted body up.

PROJECT 5
Reservoir Shocks

 Skill Level:

 Time: B

 Tools: Basic Tools, Shock Spring Compressor (TSSC series) on most models, Pin Spanners (TMPS series) for some models, Reservoir Cap Puller (TSCT 01), Shaft Holders (TFSH) if removing shaft from eyelet clevis, Seal Head Tools (TSSS series), Clip Tool (TSCP), Seal Bullet (TSSB), Nitrogen Station (see tools section), Bike Stand/Jack

Reservoir shocks are modern, high-performance designs used on all types of motorcycles and ATVs, both dirt and street. These shocks may or may not have an external reservoir. They may use either a bladder or a floating piston or even a diaphragm to separate the oil and nitrogen.

Service Tip: Aluminum-bodied shocks can suffer wear to the hard anodizing, resulting in oil contamination and body wear. Some aluminum body shocks come without any anodizing. If the oil is inky and black, carefully inspect the anodizing. In many cases they can be re–hard-anodized. Be sure to check hoses and fittings on remote reservoir models when inspecting for wear and damage.

Disassembly

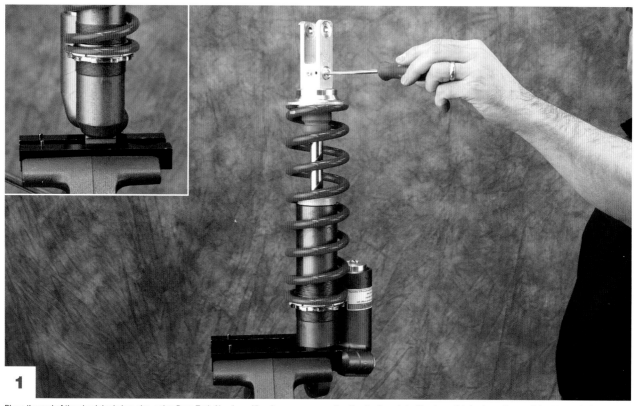

1

Place the end of the shock body in a vise, using Race Tech Aluminum Vise Jaws, or secure using the shock eyelet without special vise jaws. Be careful not to crush the shock body. *Hint: Check clicker positions on dampers and note settings.*

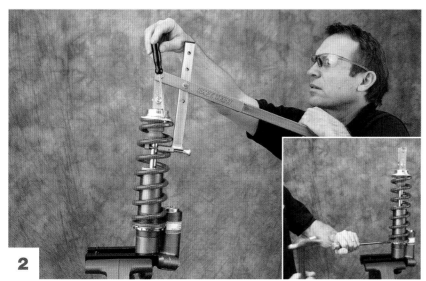

Remove the spring with a Race Tech Shock Spring Compressor or remove the spring by unscrewing the preload collars with an RT Shock Preload Adjusting Tool. For street bikes and shocks with high spring rates (10kg/mm or more), use TSSC 02 Spring Compressor.

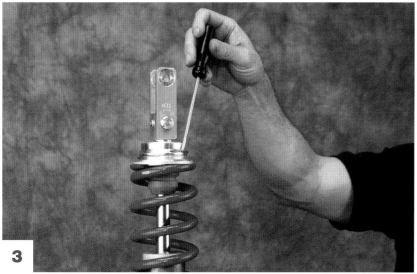

Remove the spring retaining clip with the Race Tech Shock Clip Pick Tool. There are other styles of retaining clips as well.

Remove the spring and collar.

Compress the shock and make sure it returns completely. If not, then there may be a blown shaft seal, a bad bladder, a low-pressure bladder, or an improperly located piston (on piston style shocks).

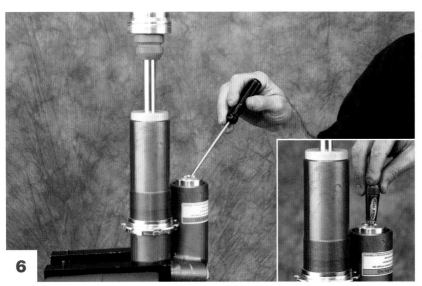

Remove the nitrogen pressure from the reservoir and remove the valve with a valve core removal tool. Sometimes a Nitrogen Needle Tool is required instead of a valve core tool. In this case the Nitrogen Needle Tool is inserted into the opening to bleed out the pressure.

Depress the reservoir cap using a socket and a hammer. Many YZs can use a TSRC 01 Reservoir Cap Setting Tool to protect the Schrader Valve. On some models the cap is threaded on instead of being held in with a clip. Unscrew this type.

Remove the reservoir clip with the clip tool.

Remove the reservoir cap with the Race Tech Reservoir Cap Removal Tool. Make sure the tool is screwed on all the way. (Alternatively you could use compressed air to blow the cap off.) For WP shocks with a threaded cap, use a pin spanner.

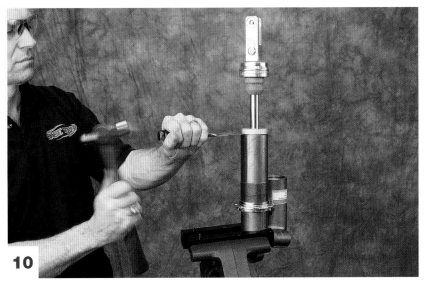

Remove the shock body cap with a sharp wood chisel. Some models screw on, so don't get too excited with the chisel unless you are sure. *Note: Most Showa, KYBs, and Öhlins are pressed on. Penske, Works Performance, and early Öhlins are screwed on.*

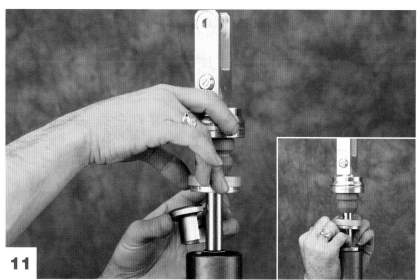

Compress the seal head to expose the circlip with the Race Tech Shock Seal Head Setting Tool. Some early WPs have a circlip underneath the seal head as do some Yamaha shocks. The WPs are easier as the top piece screws on. The Yamaha has a clip on the top and sandwiches the seal head assembly between it and the bottom one.

Remove the seal head circlip with the clip tool. For shocks with a threaded seal head cap, use a pin spanner.

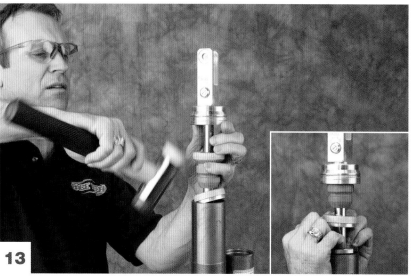

Remove the shaft assembly from the shock body by tapping with a plastic mallet. If it is stubborn, you can clamp the clevis in the vise and tap downward on the body.

Empty oil from the nitrogen reservoir and the shock body.

Remove peening with a flat bastard file (I just like saying flat bastard). File the outer diameter of the peened area down to the root of the thread. On Showas it is critical not to grind off the top flat as it holds in the rebound mechanism. Most KYBs can be ground flat.

Remove the shock shaft nut.

Remove the valving stack.

Chamfer the end of the shock shaft.

Wire wheel the end of shaft.

Blow out the center of the shaft to remove any particles.

Note the correctly dressed shaft end. Beeeeeeeautiful!

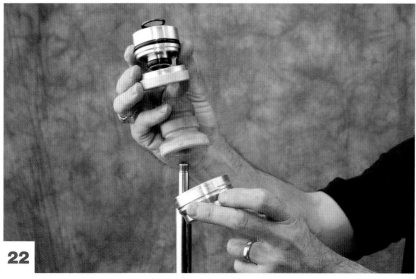

Remove the seal head, body cap, bottom-out bumper, and retaining cup. Some models have slightly different hardware.

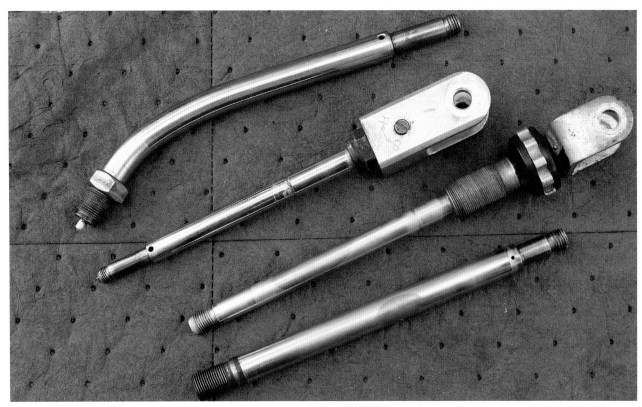

Behold the Shock Shaft Hall of Shame. From top to bottom: Bent shaft caused by ramming after linkage bolt came out; vise grips are *not* for holding the shaft end; and two examples of worn-through hard chrome from extreme use. *Hint: don't take off shock mud flaps.*

Note: A bottom-out bumper is a consumable item—only the one on the right is still usable. Always inspect your bumper and replace it if necessary.

Polish the shaft with 500- or 600-grit sandpaper.

23

If the seal is being replaced, begin by removing the top-out spring from the seal head (for shocks that have one.)

24

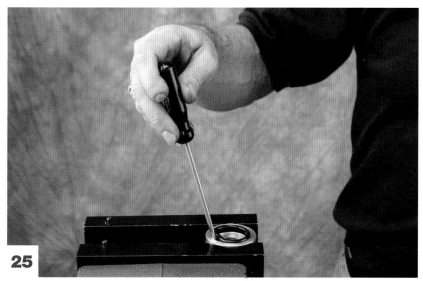

Remove the top-out bumper with a clip tool.

25

Remove the top-out bumper. *Note: Some models do not have these pieces.*

26

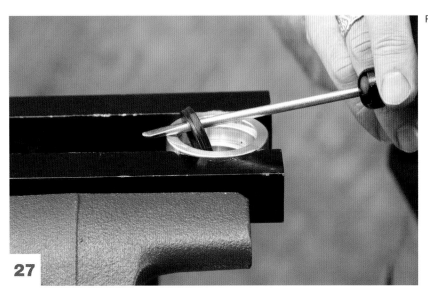

Remove the shock shaft oil seal.

27

Remove the dust seal. Note the notch in the vise jaws. If you hold the seal head with the top surface below the top of the vise jaws, you can pry on the edge of the jaws.

28

29

Inspect the shaft bushing and seal head O-ring. Replace them if they are damaged or worn. Bushing drivers are available.

This photo shows an exploded view of the seal head before assembly. Note the direction of the seal and other components.

Reassembly

Install the dust seat on the head with an appropriately sized socket.

Grease the seal with Race Tech Ultra Slick Grease.

Reinstall the seal head with the Shock Seal "Bullet" Tool.

Clean the valving assembly in contact cleaner.

Surface the base plate on 220–280-grit sandpaper on a piece of plate glass.

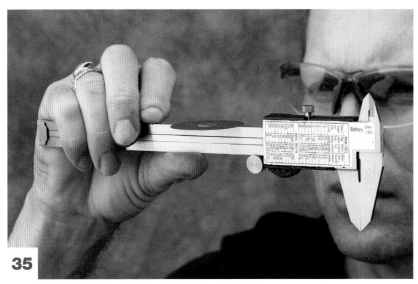

Inspect the valving stack for any warped, dished, or creased shims.

Install the compression valving stack.

Surface the piston on both sides. Inset: Note that the compression side of the piston is the one on the right. It has larger ports and larger diameter shims than the rebound side. Most, if not all, pistons are directional.

Install the piston and rebound valving. Use a Race Tech Gold Valve (inset) for improved damping action and tunability.

Surface the rebound top plate and install it on the shaft.

39

Use Loctite on the shaft nut.

40

Check for proper stack height with the shaft nut and add an additional spacer (inset) if needed. Torque the shaft nut. The rebound base plate should cover the step at the end of the thread. The nut must have full engagement and not run out of thread onto the straight shaft.

41

Pour Race Tech Ultra Slick Suspension Fluid into the reservoir first.

Reinstall the valve core and bladder onto the reservoir cap.

Make sure there is enough oil so that when the bladder goes into the reservoir it overflows.

Push down on the bladder cap until the circlip groove is exposed.

Reinstall the reservoir clip in the groove.

Use the reservoir cap tool to seat the reservoir cap on the clip. This can also be done without the cap tool by using compressed air. If you use this method, gently bring up the pressure and make sure the clip is properly located. Use compressed air to pressurize the reservoir to 20–40 psi to over expand the bladder.

Fill the shock body with oil up to about 50mm (2") from the top.

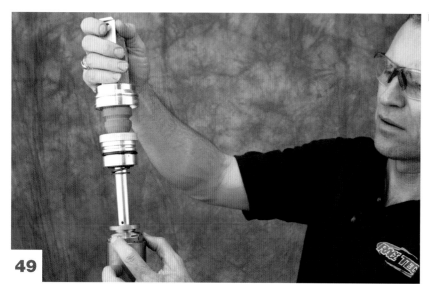

Install the shaft assembly into the shock body.

Top off the fluid to within 10mm of the top of shock body.

51

Pull up very slowly and then push down firmly until no more bubbles show up on the compression stroke. If you pull up too quickly, the fluid will cavitate and you will not remove the bubbles. Make it look like you are really working hard—even if no one is watching.

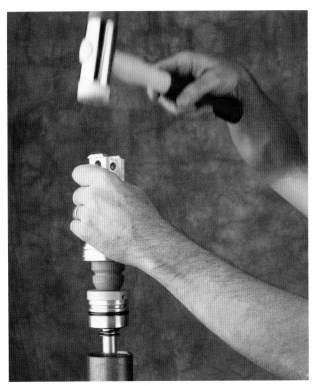

Tip: Use a plastic mallet for shocks with extremely high compression damping to open the valving stack and allow any trapped air past the piston.

52

Once it's bled, extend the shock and top it off with fluid. *Note: Make sure the low-speed rebound inlet port stays submerged at all times to avoid introducing air bubbles.*

Push in the seal head with the seal head setting tool until the O-ring seals.

Once the O-ring seals, depressurize the reservoir bladder while keeping downward force on the seal head. The volume displaced by the seal head will cause the overextended bladder to collapse back to its normal relaxed shape.

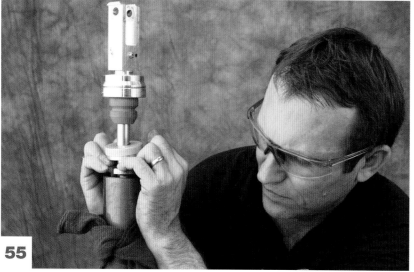

Push down the seal head until the circlip groove is exposed. An alternative to this method is to use a vacuum fill tool (TSVM 01). If used properly this will do an excellent job of removing trapped air and even some of the air that is in suspension in the fluid. With a vacuum filling tool the shock can be assembled dry. Be sure to follow the instructions carefully to trap the correct nitrogen volume.

Install the circlip carefully into the seat.

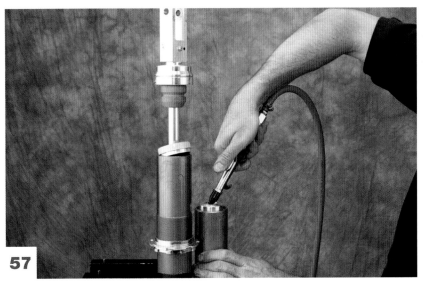

Gently pressurize the reservoir and make sure the seal head and circlip are properly seated. This method will also work for most piston reservoirs. Two-piece and threaded seal heads require positioning the piston before installing the seal head.

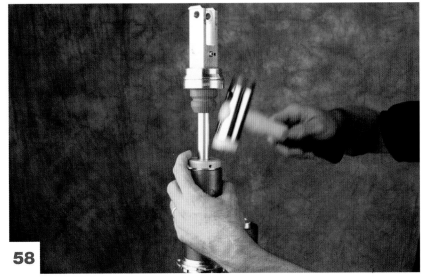

Tap in the shock body cap. *Note: The drain hole should be aligned with the shock body eyelet so that it will be at the lowest point when installed on the bike. Threaded-in seal heads should be torqued properly.*

Compress the shock while depressurizing the bladder.

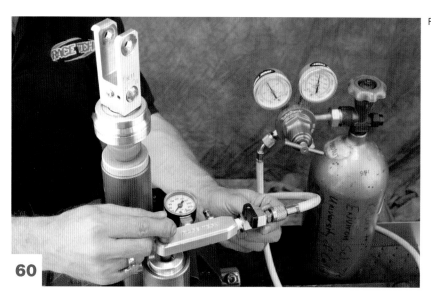

Fill up with nitrogen using the Pro Shock Nitrogen Gauge.

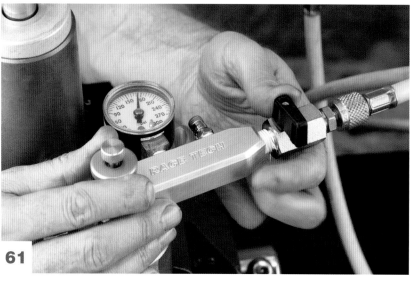

Bleed the shock to the proper pressure.

Stroke the shock shaft. The shock shaft should extend all the way. If it does not, the shock is probably underfilled or the shaft is bent. Check the body and shaft as well. Stroke the shock to feel for proper function and smoothness.

If the seal head does not displace fluid as it is installed it will not compress the bladder the proper amount (or locate the reservoir piston properly). In these cases the bladder pressure should be reset to 4-5psi before the seal head is installed. When in doubt, ask a pro.

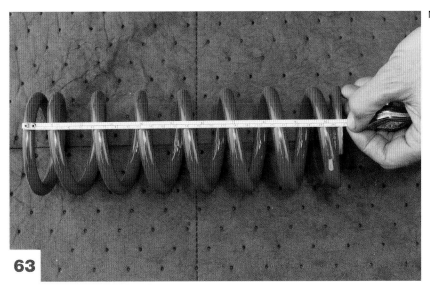

Measure the free length of the spring.

Install the spring, retaining ring, and circlip.

Adjust the collars to the desired set length for proper preload.

65

Tighten the lock ring with the shock preload adjuster tool. Grease the preload collar thread before installing the spring.

66

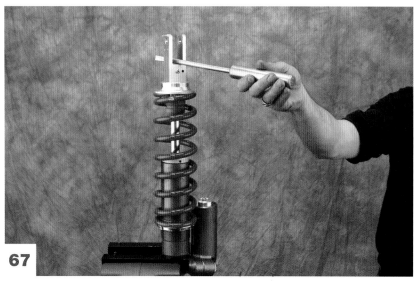

Line up the eyelets top to bottom. Make sure the adjusters are aligned correctly. Usually compression and rebound are on the same side but not always. Sometimes the shaft clevis has cutouts for linkage clearance. This is important.

67

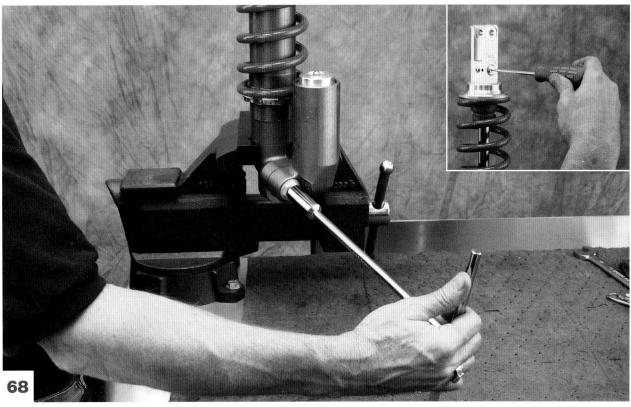

68

Adjust compression (high-speed adjustment shown) and rebound clickers. Normally zero is all the way in and clicks or turns are counted as the adjuster is unscrewed (counterclockwise).

69

Chicks dig stickers.

PROJECT 6
WP Progressive Damping System Shock

⭐ **Skill Level:**

🕐 **Time:** C

🗄️ **Tools:** Basic Tools, Shock Spring Compressor (TFSC series) on most models, Pin Spanners (TMPS series), Shaft Holders (TFSH if removing shaft from eyelet clevis), Seal Head Tools (TSSS series), Clip Tool (TSCP), Seal Head Bullet (TSSB), Nitrogen Station (see tools section), Bike Stand/Jack

Progressive damping system (PDS) shocks are offered by WP and Öhlins, generally on off-road models as well as snow machines. They are unique in that the damping increases as the shock compresses. To accomplish this they have some extra internal components. General servicing procedures are the same as reservoir shocks unless you are planning to remove or change the compression needle. We will show only the things that are unique about this design.

Service Tip: It is not necessary to remove the compression needle unless you intend to replace it with an upgraded high-performance unit.

Disassembly

1

WP PDS shaft (right) versus conventional shaft (left). Notice how the PDS shaft utilizes dual pistons.

SUSPENSION SERVICE DEPARTMENT

Note shaft inner diameter size of the PDS shock. This needle will plug the shaft as it is approaching bottom.

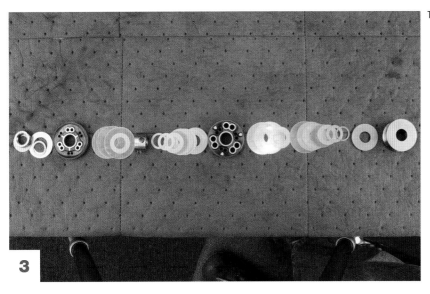

This is a PDS valving layout.

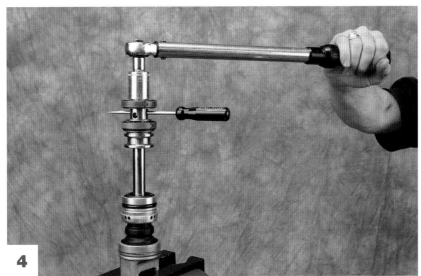

When reassembling the valving assembly, position the spacer so that the feed ports on the sleeve are aligned with the ports on the shaft while the shaft nut is torqued.

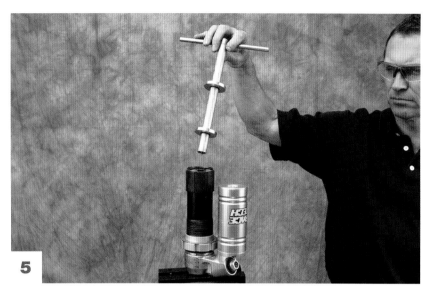

If charging the telescopic needle, use one of the RT TSST Series tools. There are three sizes.

This is the stock metering needle assembly.

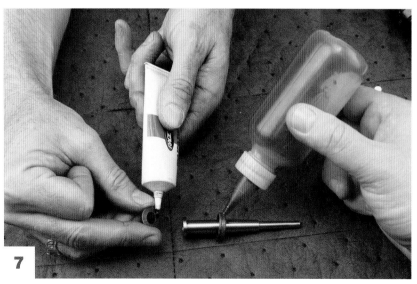

This is the Race Tech Telescopic Needle. Apply thread locking compound on the retaining collar and a small amount of Race Tech Ultra Slick Grease on the Bellville washer during installation. The grease temporarily sticks the washer to the end of the needle.

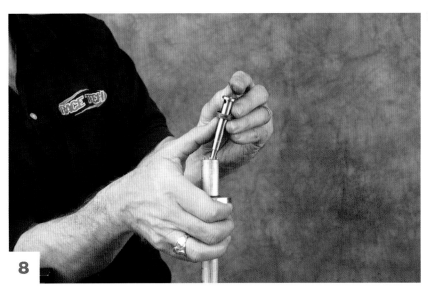

Insert the needle assembly into the tool.

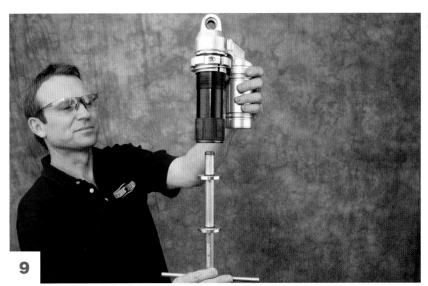

Insert the tool with the needle assembly into the shock. Tighten the needle assembly to specification.

Remove the reservoir cap with the Race Tech Pin Spanner. Use the largest pins that will fit into the pin holes.

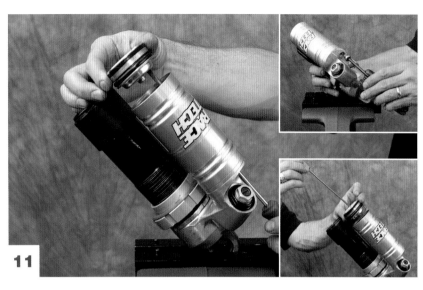

To remove the piston from the reservoir there are two options. Option one: remove the piston by pushing a small screwdriver through the bleed port at the top of the reservoir. Option two: remove the piston with the WP special tool that threads into the piston.

Reassembly

After reinstalling the bleed port screw, make a sleeve tool by cutting a piece of .12mm (.005") shim stock and wrapping it around the inside of the reservoir. This is because there is a threaded area with a lip that will tend to catch the piston band, keeping it from slipping into the reservoir. Pour the proper suspension fluid into the reservoir until it is full. If the piston is being replaced with a RT Bladder Conversion, the shim stock is not necessary.

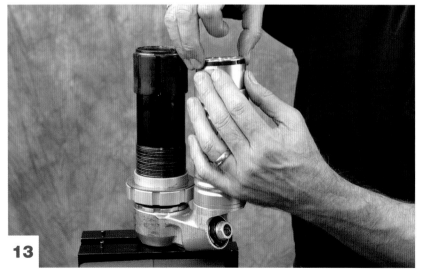

Install the reservoir piston using your new sleeve tool. Instead of making a sleeve tool you could try holding the piston ring into the groove with a bit of heavy grease.

Push the piston down until the piston band engages the reservoir.

Bleed all the air from the reservoir. Invert the shock and push the reservoir piston into the body. Trapped air will be pushed out. Be sure to collect and re-use this new oil.

Pour oil into the body with the reservoir positioned below the shock body, as shown.

Fill the shock body with oil to a height of 40mm (1½").

Lightly grease the O-ring and install the reservoir cap.

With the Allen bolt loosely installed, attach the Race Tech WP Nitrogen Charging Tool. Push down on the tool as you tighten the holding clamp.

Charge the reservoir with nitrogen to approximately 50 psi. Tighten the Allen bolt.

Fill the shock body with oil to about 40mm (1½") from the top.

Insert the shaft assembly into the shock body.

Rapidly and forcefully compress the shock shaft.

Tip: When installing a heavy compression damping stack, tap the end of the shock clevis to open the compression valve to allow trapped air past the piston.

Top off the oil.

Install the seal head with the Shock Seal Head Setting Tool (TSSS 02) until it can no longer go in. Maintain downward force on the tool while simultaneously releasing nitrogen pressure from the reservoir.

Install the retaining clip.

Pressurize the shock to the manufacturer's specification.

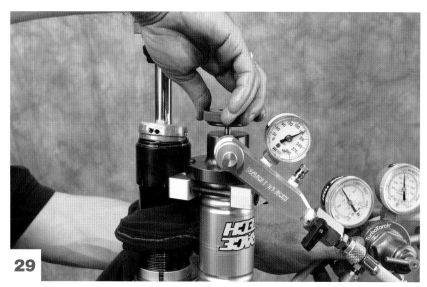

Tighten the Allen bolt with the knob on the tool.

Install the end cap by tapping it with a soft-faced hammer. The drain holes should be aligned with the shock body eyelet so that it will be at the lowest point when installed on the bike.

There are two alternatives to using the Race Tech or original equipment WP Shock Charging Tool. The first is the SPNV 0512 Nitrogen Valve Bolt. It replaces the stock Allen screw (left) and is charged with a Nitrogen Needle (shown). Second is a SWBL Series shock bladder conversion kit with a reservoir cap that uses a Schrader valve (right).

32 These two photos show the piston displacement prior to and after the seal head installation. Notice that in this case the displacement of the seal head into the shock locates the piston in the reservoir automatically.

33 Verify the piston height after the seal head has been installed.

Appendix 1

LOWERING

Lowering can be required for a number of reasons: touching the ground, wheelie control (such as in drag racing), converting a bike from one genre to another (MX to flat track, supermoto, or road race), and geometry changes are the main ones.

In some cases lowering is as simple as the addition of special spacers in both the forks and shock. In other cases it is quite involved, including changing or modifying springs and custom machining.

Suspension lowering can be done on all rebuildable suspension—some models have suspension that is not rebuildable. This is more of a problem with the rear suspension components, though some forks have sealed cartridges.

In some cases the solution on the rear is to build shorter custom shocks with less travel. Lowering the suspension can also be done internally using spacers. Ultimately, lowering a bike means shortening the shock and forks. Lowering is reversible, so if you don't like it, you can always return to the stock height.

In general when lowering a motorcycle, both the front and rear end should be lowered the same amount. G.M.D. Computrack is a good resource to check for proper geometry. As an added benefit, chassis alignment is measured at the same time.

If the bike is being lowered so that the rider can touch the ground, I normally recommend lowering 25mm (1 inch) to begin with. Riders are constantly surprised how much of a difference this amount makes. The reason only 25mm is recommended is that the loss of ground clearance, cornering clearance, and suspension travel (the ability to deal with bumps and holes) becomes more of a problem the lower you go.

However, if the rider is willing to deal with those shortcomings, bikes can be lowered significantly more. The absolute limit to lowering is the original bottom-out point. Keep in mind that the more a bike is lowered, the more likely new springs will be required (more on this in a moment).

Some street models are already lowered. On these models further lowering should be considered carefully before proceeding, as ground and cornering clearance is a bigger issue.

Let me make this next point in the strongest terms I can: *I do not recommend lowering links!* They do nothing to decrease the travel, meaning that the tire can bottom out through the fender. This has the potential to stop the rear wheel from turning and, if this happens, it can cause a crash. Lowering links can sometimes be used if the shock travel is shortened the appropriate amount with external travel limiters. However if the shock has to be taken apart, the lowering can be done inside the shock without the added expense of the lowering link.

Keep in mind that shortening the shock by 5mm does not lower the rear end 5mm. This is because of the leverage ratio of the linkage or geometry of the shock mounting. In general, most modern dirt bikes have an initial leverage ratio ranging from 3.1 to 4.0. With a 3.1 leverage ratio, a 3mm spacer would lower the rear end 3.1 times the spacer length, or 9.3mm at the wheel. This relationship is important in making the proper length spacer.

One easy way to measure required shock spacer length is as follows: remove the spring and slide the bottom-out bumper up all the way until it contacts the shock body end cap. Then compress the rear wheel to create the desired lowering amount—this will move the bottom-out bumper. You can then measure the required length of the internal spacer: as it is the distance the bumper has moved. The spacer is then installed internally between the top-out plate and the seal head. The spacer should be made in such a way as to allow oil flow to the low-speed rebound adjuster. Race Tech produces spacers in 2 and 3mm increments that can be stacked in 1mm increments. If you'd rather do it yourself, a single, solid spacer can be machined.

Shorter springs may be required for the reduced length of the forks and shock. For example, if the fork does not have a spring spacer or the shock preload collars cannot be backed off far enough to create the proper preload, you're going to need new springs.

If the rider wants to have the stock spring force, the spring rate must be increased. Here's how to calculate the rate required: take the original correct spring rate times the original travel divided by the new travel. $k_2 = k_1 \times (d_1/d_2)$ The "correct" spring rate is affected by personal preference, and many riders prefer the decrease in bottoming resistance.

Keep in mind that the compression damping's contribution to bottoming resistance will be diminished with decreased travel. This means that more compression damping is required to resist bottoming, but this will result in a harsher ride. Once again, this is affected by rider preference, as many riders don't want it harsher. On rear shock street applications, lowering 25mm may not cause much of an issue as bottoming resistance is rarely a problem.

F450 Moto Conversions (converting a motocross bike into a road race bike) require both lowering and bottoming point changes. This means the bottom-out bumper is shortened and moved as well. The spring rates are radically changed and the geometry is set up, so this is a job for experts.

Another solution for gaining inseam clearance is shortening and/or re-contouring the seat. This can be done for dirt bikes as well as street bikes. Seat re-contouring is relatively inexpensive as well. The width of the seat is also important: the wider the seat, the harder it is to touch the ground. If altering the seat does the trick, it might be the best solution.

Appendix 2

SWINGARM LENGTH

Let's look at the effect swingarm length has on spring rate. The equation for it is as follows:

$$(L2 / L1)^2 \times K1 = K2$$

L1 - Length Swingarm Stock
L2 - Length Swingarm Modified
K1 - Correct Spring Rate for Stock Length Swingarm
K2 - Correct Spring Rate for Modified Length Swingarm

It is fairly common to increase swingarm length for drag racing, sand dunes or drags, hill climbing, and so on. When the rear axle is moved back (or even when changing gearing), many other things change. First, the leverage ratio increases (I define leverage ratio as the wheel travel divided by the shock travel). This increase in leverage means the effective rear wheel spring rate is decreased.

Note that most of the time tuners think in terms of shock spring rate, but altering the shock spring is simply a way to change a rear wheel spring rate. The rear wheel spring rate is the shock spring rate divided by the leverage ratio. To maintain the rear wheel spring rate of a lengthened swingarm, the shock spring rate must be increased. The formula above can be used to calculate the required change in shock spring rate.

It is important to note that K1 is the correct rate for the stock length swingarm and not necessarily the stock spring rate.

When the swingarm gets longer, the wheel travel also increases. It is a linear relationship, meaning if you double the swingarm length, you'll double the wheel travel. This means if you want the original wheel travel, the shock shaft travel must be shortened. The shock travel can be shortened two ways: first the shock can be shortened with internal spacers. Second, external spacers can be installed on the shock shaft between the bottom-out bumper and the eyelet or clevis. This second method lengthens the collapsed length.

A combination of both these methods is usually the best answer for extended swingarms. Here's why: swingarm length will affect rear end ride height. If the swingarm length is increased and the swingarm angle is positive (the swingarm pivot is above the rear axle), the rear end ride height is increased. If you want to keep the rear end at the original height, the shock must be shortened. The amount the shock needs to be shortened is determined by the leverage ratio of the linkage.

If the swingarm angle goes negative as it gets close to bottoming, increasing the swingarm length will decrease ground clearance at bottoming. This means the tire-to-fender clearance will also decrease and may even cause the tire to contact the fender (this has the unwanted side effect of stopping the wheel and pitching the rider off the bike). The solution is to shorten the bottoming point (shorten the travel by increasing the collapsed length of the shock with an external spacer placed between the bottom-out bumper and the eyelet).

Increasing swingarm length will also decrease the weight on the rear wheel, decreasing rear wheel traction.

The spring rate calculated with this formula will create the same rear wheel force at the original wheel travel. This means that if you decreased shock travel to compensate for the increase in leverage and ended up with the original rear wheel travel, you would have the same spring force at bottom out.

Keep in mind that the increase in leverage ratio created by extending the swingarm also requires more damping, for two reasons. First, the increase in leverage requires an increase in damping for the same reason as the spring rate. Second, for a given rear wheel velocity the shock is moving slower. This decrease in shaft velocity has the added effect of decreasing damping when *more* is actually required. This is usually best remedied with an internal valving change.

In addition, changing swingarm length will affect anti-squat as well. See the geometry chapter for more details.

Sometimes increasing swingarm length is done at the same time as lowering the motorcycle. Lowering a motorcycle has its own set of considerations that should be carefully considered. I do not recommend lowering links, as they generally give no consideration for decreasing wheel travel and can therefore cause ground clearance and tire-to-fender contact problems. See Appendix 2 for further details.

Appendix 3

GLOSSARY

anodizing
A coating on aluminum. It can be cosmetic in nature, as with color anodizing, or it can be functional as with hard anodizing.

anti-high side device
A long, soft, top-out spring used in road race shock absorbers instead of a top-out bumper. Developed by Öhlins.

anti-dive system
A mechanical or hydraulic device intended to decrease the amount the front end dives under braking. The hydraulic types vary in design but all increase the compression damping when the brakes are applied. Most are actuated by the braking force on the wheel cylinders or the hydraulic pressure in the brake lines. Quite common on large bikes in the 1980s, they are now rare because they create even more harshness on the square-edge bumps. As of this printing this type of system is still used on Gold Wings.

axle offset
The distance between the centerline of the fork tube and the center of the front axle perpendicular to the centerline on offset axle forks (mostly used on dirt bikes).

base plate
A thick washer or plate that the valving shims rest on.

base valve
The compression valve assembly on cartridge forks or older style twin-tube shocks.

bladder
A flexible membrane separating the suspension fluid from the nitrogen in a shock absorber. Allows the shock to be pressurized to eliminate cavitation.

bladder reservoir
A style of reservoir where the fluid and the nitrogen are separated by a flexible membrane.

bleed (or bypass)
A free-flow orifice that allows fluid to pass easily at low flow rates. It is usually the lowest speed circuit.

bottom-out bumper
A rubber or urethane bumper commonly used in shocks to cushion the shock when it uses up all the travel on compression. This functions as a second spring in parallel with the main spring and adds to the total spring force. Typically made out of rubber or urethane, they are prone to break down after awhile and should be replaced.

bottoming
Using up the total available travel of the suspension system.

bottoming cone
A hydraulic device designed to give additional damping resistance when the fork or shock reaches bottoming.

cartridge fork
A more sophisticated type of fork than a damping rod fork. It utilizes pistons with shims that bend to create compression and rebound damping. The basic design allows the manufacturer to produce a less progressive damping curve than a damping rod fork. Note: Some cartridge forks with poorly designed valving create very similar curves to damping rod forks.

cavitation
Cavitation is the formation of vapor bubbles in a flowing liquid caused by a decrease in pressure (specifically in an area where the pressure of the liquid falls below its vapor pressure). This is the same phenomenon as boiling however not due to the addition of heat but to a decrease in pressure. Cavitation creates loss of both compression and rebound damping.

center of gravity
The location at which the entire mass of an object can be represented by a single force acting on that point.

check valve
A one-way valve that easily opens in one direction and shuts off completely in the other direction.

clamping shim
The last shim in a valving stack, farthest away from the piston and closest to the base plate. All the other shims must bend on the clamping shim.

clickers
External damping adjusters. These usually control low-speed rebound damping or low-speed compression damping on forks. On shocks the clickers usually control low-speed rebound and high-speed compression damping. Many bikes have no clickers. Note: Some clickers don't click so you would count "turns" instead. Unless otherwise marked, most adjusters create maximum damping when they are screwed all the way "in" (clockwise), and therefore counted as clicks (usually quarter turns) "out" (counter clockwise from all the way in).

compression
Suspension movement when the wheel hits a bump and compresses. Also known as the bump stroke.

compression bolt assembly
The complete compression valve assembly. Also known as the base valve in a cartridge fork.

compression damping (aka bump or jounce damping)
Damping created on the compression stroke as the suspension is collapsing. Because damping is sensitive to velocity, the terms low-speed compression damping and high-speed compression damping are often used.

crossover shim
The small diameter shim in a two-stage valving stack that separates the low-speed stack from the high-speed stack.

cylinder valve
An additional compression damping circuit located at the top of the cartridge on some 1998 through 2004 KYB dirt bike forks (most notably on YZs and CR125).

DLC
See diamond like carbon

damper
See shock absorber

damping
(a.k.a. dampening which the purists don't like to use as it also means to make something wet.) Fluid resistance to movement. The force is created as oil passes through holes or other types of valving systems. The amount of damping force is dependent on the particular valving configuration and the viscosity of fluid used. Key points: The amount of damping created is determined by the speed at which the suspension is compressing or extending. Damping turns mechanical energy into heat.

damping circuit
A physical path for suspension fluid that creates resistance. There may be five or more compression circuits and three or more rebound circuits in a shock or cartridge fork. The effect of each circuit generally overlaps, creating massive flexibility, while sometimes making for complex adjustments, as well.

damping piston
The valve that the shims are stacked on. It is sealed on its outer diameter with a piston ring or o-ring. The piston ring is usually made of a Teflon composite if the piston is sliding in a chamber (as with a shock or the rebound piston on a cartridge fork). On a compression piston on a cartridge fork it is stationary and therefore is sealed with an o-ring.

damping rod fork

A simple type of fork that utilizes a tube with holes in it to create compression and rebound damping. The basic nature of creating damping by shoving fluid through holes produces a damping curve that is excessively progressive, resulting in harshness and bottoming.

DeCarbon shock

A high-pressure monotube shock absorber invented by Christian Bourcier de Carbon in 1953. It uses a floating piston to separate the oil from a high-pressure gas (usually nitrogen) to minimize cavitation during high-velocity suspension movement. This term has loosely been referred to any shock with a piston or membrane that separates the oil from the gas.

Delta Valve

An aftermarket fork valve from Race Tech that has externally adjustable low-speed and high-speed compression damping, used primarily on dirt bikes.

diamond like carbon

An impressively hard surface coating with an extremely low coefficient of friction. Commonly used on fork tubes and shock shafts.

diving

The phenomenon of the front forks compressing during braking. Many linkage-type alternative front ends control dive mechanically. The term usually implies excessive diving.

dual-rate

Typically refers to a spring that has closely wound evenly spaced coils, as well as evenly spaced, wider-gapped coils. As the spring compresses, the tight coils contact each other and are "blocked out," thus reducing the effective number of coils and creating a stiffer rate. This results in one spring with two rates. Dual rate spring setup can also be created by stacking springs and controlling the crossover.

dynamic friction

Friction where there is movement between the surfaces.

Emulator

See Gold Valve Cartridge Emulator.

emulsion

A mixture of oil and air. Emulsion shocks do not have a membrane or piston between the fluid and the nitrogen. They are less expensive to produce than a reservoir shock. They are expected to foam up and create consistent damping. These are not high-performance shocks.

fork bushing

A low friction, load-bearing sleeve. Modern fork bushings consist of a steel band with a coating of bronze and a layer of Teflon bonded on it. Most forks require two per leg. Early telescopic forks did not have these bushings and therefore suffered from even more friction than current designs.

free length

The length of a spring fully extended (not mounted on the shock or in the forks, with no load on the spring).

free sag

aka bike sag, unladen sag – The amount the bike settles under its own weight (with no rider). If static sag is correct and there is too much free sag, the spring is too stiff (not too soft).

friction

Mechanical sliding resistance. Friction turns kinetic energy into heat. Its magnitude is calculated using the formula:

$$F = u \times F_n \text{ where:}$$

F – Frictional force.

u – Coefficient of friction. (This depends on which materials are in contact with each other. For example, rubber on steel will have a higher coefficient than steel on steel.)

F_n – Normal force (the force perpendicular to the surfaces in contact).

Gold Valve

Replacement high-performance pistons for shocks and forks. Made by Race Tech.

Gold Valve Cartridge Emulator

An aftermarket valve made by Race Tech used in a damping rod fork that creates the compression damping curve of a cartridge fork. A.K.A. Emulator.

hard anodizing

An electro-chemical process that deposits a very hard layer of aluminum oxide on an aluminum surface. The layer builds up as much as it penetrates. Therefore a .002" coating penetrates .001" and builds up .001". It can be applied in a limited number of colors as well.

harshness

An uncomfortable jolt that occurs on the compression stroke. It can be caused by many different factors, including too much high-speed compression damping, too much friction, too much low-speed rebound damping causing packing, too high of a spring rate, too much preload, binding from things like bent fork tubes, excessive friction, poor suspension fluid, and poor suspension linkage bearings. It can also be caused by excessive bottoming.

headshake

An unnerving phenomenon where the forks oscillate back and forth rapidly and sometimes violently. It can be caused by various factors, including a frame that is out of alignment or twisted, too little "trail", underdamped rebound, overdamped high-speed compression, anything that causes a bind, chassis flex, and swingarm flex.

high-speed compression damping

Compression damping created by fast vertical wheel movements. This occurs when hitting anything that has a square edge, such as pot holes, expansion joints, Bots Dots, some railroad crossings, or braking bumps particularly when the vehicle is traveling at high-speed.

high-speed rebound damping

Rebound damping that occurs when the vertical wheel movements are fast. Since the force that extends the suspension is primarily due to the spring, high-speed rebound occurs when there are large wheel movements. High-speed rebound is often produced when hitting big dips or gullies at speed. Of course, chain forces and the terrain will affect the rate of extension as well, so it is not solely determined by the amount of travel used.

inner bushing

Also known as an RU bushing (as well as many other names), it fits onto the inner chrome fork tube and has Teflon on the outer surface.

kicking

Serious harshness that actually throws the wheel off the ground. This can occur when hitting square edge bumps like pot holes or large expansion joints. Any of the factors that cause harshness can also cause kicking, but it is generally caused by too much high-speed compression damping and/or friction or severe bottoming.

leverage ratio

The mechanical advantage of the wheel on the shock. It is the ratio of the travel of the wheel to the travel of the shock. It is also the ratio of the force on the shock to the force on the wheel. The higher the leverage the less the shock moves for a given wheel travel. This requires higher damping and spring rates. (NOTE: It can also be defined as the opposite, i.e. as the ratio of the travel of the shock to the travel of the wheel.)

leverage ratio curve

The plot of how the leverage changes through the travel of the rear wheel. This change is caused by the mechanical linkage. Normally the leverage decreases as more travel is used up, creating more resistance due to the shock spring and the shock damping.

linear

Straight line (not necessarily flat).

low-speed compression damping

Compression damping that occurs when the vertical wheel movements are slow, such as when going through a dip or gully or on the forks during braking particularly at low vehicle speeds.

low-speed rebound damping

Rebound damping that occurs when the vertical wheel movements are slow. Because the force that extends the suspension is primarily due to the spring, low-speed rebound occurs when there are small wheel movements.

mid-valve

An additional compression circuit placed where the rebound check valve is usually located. Often used in dirt bike applications. If overdone it can add harshness and cavitation.

nitrogen

An inert gas used to pressurize shock absorbers to help eliminate cavitation. Argon or any inert gas could also be used.

normal force

The force perpendicular to the surface.

oil level

A way to measure the amount of oil in a fork leg as opposed to measuring volume. The oil level affects the force created by air pressure as the fork compresses. The oil level is the distance from the top of the fork tube down to the top of the oil with the fork completely collapsed and usually with the springs removed.

outer bushing

Also known as a DU bushing (as well as many other names), it fits onto the outer fork tube and has Teflon on its inner surface.

offset

A distance between two centerlines, typically referring to triple clamp or axle offset. Total Offset is the combination of Triple Clamp Offset and Axle Offset.

offset forks

An external fork design where the axle is off set from the centerline of the fork. This is most commonly used on dirt bikes.

orifice

A hole commonly used as a bleed in shocks and cartridge forks. It is generally the major source of damping in damping rod style forks. Orifices create velocity-squared style force vs. velocity curves. In other words, when the velocity is doubled the damping force increases with the square of the velocity (at a rate of four times). This is the most progressive type of damping found in standard shocks and forks.

packing

When hitting a series of bumps the wheel extends too slowly after being compressed that it does not return completely when the next bump is encountered. It is caused by excessive low-speed rebound damping.

piston reservoir

A style of reservoir where the fluid and the nitrogen are separated by a floating piston.

piston ring

A sealing ring on a shock piston or a cartridge fork rebound piston. Usually made of a Teflon composite or a Teflon-coated steel band. It seals because of the pressure behind it similar to the piston ring in a motor.

piston ring energizer o-ring

The o-ring underneath the piston ring that provides an initial load against the inner wall of the shock body.

piston rod (Aka damping rod or rebound rod)

The rod in a cartridge fork that attaches to the fork cap and usually also carries the rebound piston.

pogoing

Uncontrolled rebounding.

preload

The term preload has two meanings (length and force). In the motorcycle industry it usually refers to preload length.

preload adjuster

A method of externally adjusting the preload. These can be ramped, threaded or hydraulic. Hydraulic preload adjusters on shocks allow remote adjustment of the preload. Note: When the preload adjusters are backed off all the way, they do not necessarily have zero preload. With forks in particular there is usually some preload at the minimum external preload setting.

preload force

The amount of force on the spring when it is at its preload length.

preload length

The amount a spring is compressed from full extension when installed with the fork or shock fully extended.

preload spacer

Material used to set the preload in a fork. Thin-wall steel or aluminum tubing is commonly used. Many aftermarket spring companies use PVC as spacer material, which works fine if the ends are finished flat and a steel washer is used on both ends of the spacer.

progressive

Usually refers to spring rates, leverage ratio curves or damping curves. As travel or velocity is increased, the resultant force increases slowly at first and more rapidly as it goes up.

race sag

See static sag.

rake

The angle of the steering axis from vertical, measured in degrees. For a given offset, there is more trail if there is more rake. (NOTE: Some manufacturers [KTM] measure rake from horizontal.)

real trail (also see trail)

The self-straightening characteristic built into front-end geometry. It is the perpendicular distance between the steering axis and the center of the point of contact of the front wheel with the ground. This method is far superior to standard "Ground Trail" or "Trail". Trail is usually measured in millimeters.

rebound

Suspension movement when the wheel extends. Also known as tension.

rebound damping

Damping created on the rebound stroke as the suspension is extending. Because damping is sensitive to velocity, the terms low-speed rebound and high-speed rebound are often used.

rebound rod

Aka damping rod in a cartridge fork.

rebound

Suspension movement when the wheel extends. Also known as tension.

rebound damping

Damping created on the rebound stroke as the suspension is extending. Since damping is sensitive to velocity, the terms low-speed rebound and high-speed rebound are often used.

reservoir

A canister or portion of a shock absorber with a membrane or piston separating the fluid from a compressible gas. Usually filled with high-pressure nitrogen. This allows for displacement of the fluid by the shock shaft because oil is incompressible.

revalving

Changing the internal valves that create damping.

rising rate

Usually refers to a leverage ratio curve. The leverage of the wheel on the shock decreases as the wheel goes through its travel.

sag

See static sag.

set length

The length of the spring installed in the forks or on the shock with the shock fully extended. Free length minus preload equals set length.

shim (Aka valving shim)

A thin washer made out of spring steel used in a damper to create hydraulic resistance. It is typically stacked up in combination with other shims of various thickness and diameters on a damping piston to create the required damping curve.

shock absorber

A hydro-mechanical device that uses a fluid to create resistance. Key point: The damping force is sensitive to velocity. The kinetic energy is converted to heat.

shock body

The outer cylinder of the damping unit. Usually made of aluminum or steel.

shock bumper

A mechanical cushion made out of rubber or urethane, designed to give additional spring-type resistance when the fork or shock reaches bottoming.

shock linkage

A series of mechanical levers designed to change the leverage the wheel has on the shock as it goes through its travel.

shock shaft

The main shaft in a shock absorber. The valving is on one end and the eyelet is attached to the other. It is typically hard chrome plated for durability.

single stage

A single stage valving stack consists of a single continuous straight or tapered stack and an end on the clamping shim.

spring

A mechanical device that stores energy as it is displaced. It usually is in the form of a coil design but sometimes is a leaf design. Chrome silicon steel is typically used, but titanium and carbon fiber have been used as well. Air can also be used as a spring. Key point: Springs are position sensitive and store energy.

spring rate

The stiffness of the spring (see also dual rate, linear and progressive). It is the slope of the load deflection curve.

$$K = \_F \, / \, \_D$$

K – Average Spring Rate (measured in kilograms/millimeter or pounds/inch)
$\_F$ – Change in Force (in newtons, kilograms or pounds) between two measurement points.
$\_D$ – Change in Displacement (in millimeters or inches) between two measurement points.

sprung weight (aka sprung mass)

The weight of the motorcycle above the spring. It includes part of the spring weight.

static friction (aka stiction)

Friction where there is no movement between the surfaces. Static friction is typically higher than dynamic friction though slight slippage can have the greatest friction.

static sag

The amount the bike settles vertically with the geared up rider on board in the riding position.

stiction

See static friction.

straight stack

In this type of valving stack all shims are the same diameter until the crossover or clamping shim, which is smaller in diameter.

stressed member

A part in a system that bears the load. This term is commonly used when referring to an engine that is a structural load-bearing part of the chassis as in most Ducatis.

suspension fluid

Used inside a shock absorber for two purposes: to create damping when forced through orifices or valving, and to lubricate. Viscosity and viscosity index are important quantities. Key point: Oil is incompressible (not exactly, but close enough for our discussions).

swapping (Aka pogoing)

A disconcerting phenomenon where the rear end of the bike oscillates back and forth with large amplitude. It can be caused by a number of non-suspension related causes, such as a flexible chassis or swingarm, low tire pressure, and misaligned chassis or wheels. Excessive high-speed compression or spring rate, or extremely underdamped rebound could also be the cause.

tapered stack

The valving shims gradually decrease in diameter as their position gets farther away from the piston face. This is primarily designed to reduce the chance of the shims becoming permanently distorted or creased.

Teflon®

From DuPont (polytetrafluoroethylene or PTFE), a low-friction, dry-film lubricant.

three stage

This valving stack is similar to the two-stage stack but has two crossover shims, resulting in a low-speed, mid-speed and a high-speed stack.

titanium nitride

An extremely hard coating commonly used to create long-wearing tool bits, applied microns thick to hard chrome fork tubes and shock shafts to lower friction. It does not adhere to aluminum.

top-out bumper

A rubber or urethane bumper commonly used in shocks to cushion the shock when it becomes fully extended.

top-out spring

A coil spring commonly used in forks and some shocks (see anti-high side device) to cushion the fork when it becomes fully extended.

top-out valve

A hydraulic top-out device.

topping out

When the forks or shock extend to the limits of travel. This can occur when the wheel gets airborne, but it can also happen during acceleration or in a series of turns when the bike is flipped from side to side. It can also be caused by too much preload on the spring. This can happen when the spring used is too soft and therefore requires excessive preload to get the correct sag. Too much rebound damping can mask the problem.

trail (aka ground trail) (see real trail)

The self-straightening characteristic built into front-end geometry. It is the distance between two specific points. One point is the intersection of an imaginary line extending through the centerline of the steering stem and the ground. The second point is the center of the point of contact of the front wheel with the ground. Trail is usually measured in millimeters.

triple clamp offset

The distance between the centerline of the steering stem and the front axle perpendicular to the steering axis. The more offset that is used, the less resulting trail will be for a given fork geometry. It's usually measured in millimeters.

triple rate

See dual rate. Same concept as dual rate but with three rates. The three distinct rates are usually achieved by stacking three separate springs on top of each other.

twin chamber

A cartridge fork design where the cartridge is inverted and separated from the rest of a fork utilizing a spring-loaded, piston-type reservoir manufactured by Showa. The term is also loosely used to cover other brand of spring pressurized or air pressurized bladder forks.

twin tube shock

A style of shock that is very similar in design to a cartridge fork. The air space is located between the shock body and the outside of the cartridge. It is the most common type of shock in use in automobiles today.

two stage

This valving stack has a "crossover shim" in it. The crossover shim is a small diameter shim upon which the low-speed shims bend. This allows the low-speed stack to open until the fluid flow increases enough that it hits the high-speed stack. When this occurs, the total stack stiffness is the combination of the low-speed and the high-speed stacks.

unladen sag
See free sag.

unsprung weight aka unsprung mass
The weight of the chassis that must go up and down with the wheels as it compresses and extends. This includes everything below the springs, such as the wheels, axle, brakes, part of the spring, and a portion of the swingarm. The swingarm is more effectively measured as the rotational mass moment of inertia with respect to the swingarm pivot instead of the unsprung mass.

valving
The mechanical hardware that creates damping. This can be a combination of holes, ports, shims, springs, check valves, etc.

valving stack
A set of shims. Some examples of valving stacks are compression and rebound stacks. These may have subsets like low-speed compression, mid-speed compression, high-speed compression, low-speed rebound, and high-speed rebound. The configuration may be single stage, two stage, three stage, etc., and may be tapered or straight.

viscosity
A fluids resistance to flow or more precisely it's resistance to shear. How thick the oil is. It must be measured at a specific temperature because the thickness is sensitive to temperature. The test equipment contains a specific volume of oil and is held at a specific temperature. It is then allowed to flow through a specific size orifice and timed. The longer it takes, the thicker the oil. SAE 20, SAE 30, etc., refer to a range, not a specific viscosity.

viscosity index (VI)
A number that indicates how much a fluid thins out as it heats up. A higher number means the viscosity is more temperature-stable. A mineral base fluid typically has a VI of 100. Fork fluid is usually around this number as well. High quality suspension fluids for rear shocks have a VI of 200 or can be in excess of 400.

weight bias
Typically front to rear weight bias. Can be laden or unladen (rider on or off). The percentage of front wheel weight to rear wheel weight. There is also a sprung weight bias that is used to calculate dynamic response of vehicles.

Appendix 4

RACE TECH MOTORCYCLE SUSPENSION BIBLE TESTING LOG

DATE		TRACK	
BIKE		CONDITIONS	
RIDER		WEATHER	
WEIGHT/SKILL		TEMPERATURE	
TUNER		ALTITUDE	

FRONT

	TEST 1	TEST 2	TEST 3	TEST 4	TEST 5
Spring Rate (kg/mm-n/mm-lbs/in)					
Preload (mm)					
Free Sag (mm)					
Static Sag (mm)					
Stiction Zone (mm)					
Oil Brand/Viscosity					
Oil Level (mm)					
Low-Comp Adj (clicks-turns)					
Hi-Comp Adj (clicks-turns)					
Rebound Adj (clicks-turns)					
Fork Height Adj + / - (mm)					
Tire Brand / /Model					
Tire Size					
Tire Pressure (cold / hot psi)					

LAP TIMES

RIDER COMMENTS

RACE TECH MOTORCYCLE SUSPENSION BIBLE TESTING LOG

DATE	TRACK
BIKE	CONDITIONS
RIDER	WEATHER
WEIGHT/SKILL	TEMPERATURE
TUNER	ALTITUDE

REAR

	TEST 1	TEST 2	TEST 3	TEST 4	TEST 5
Spring Rate (kg/mm-n/mm-lbs/in)					
Preload (mm)					
Free Sag (mm)					
Static Sag (mm)					
Stiction Zone (mm)					
Oil Brand/Viscosity					
Oil Level (mm)					
Low-Comp Adj (clicks-turns)					
Hi-Comp Adj (clicks-turns)					
Rebound Adj (clicks-turns)					
Fork Height Adj + / - (mm)					
Tire Brand / /Model					
Tire Size					
Tire Pressure (cold / hot psi)					

LAP TIMES

RIDER COMMENTS

Appendix 5

RACE TECH TOOL LIST

Item Number	Description
TCPN 4301	SWINGARM PIVOT NUT TOOL 4301
TFBT 02S	FORK BLEED TOOL SET
TFBT 1010	FORK BLEED 10x1.0 & 10x1.25
TFBT 1010	FORK BLEED 10x1.0 & 10x1.25
TFBT 1212	FORK BLEED 12x1.0 & 12x1.25
TFCA 01	FORK CLICKER TOOL - THIN
TFCA 02	FORK COMPRESSION SOCKET - R6
TFCH 01	FORK CARTRIDGE HOLDING TOOL 01
TFCH 03	FORK CARTRIDGE HOLDING TOOL 03
TFCH 04	FORK CARTRIDGE HOLDING TOOL 06 R6
TFCH 06	FORK CARTRIDGE TOOL - BPF 33/35mm
TFCT 35	FORK TWIN-CHAMBER TOOL 35mm KYB
TFCW 02	FORK CAP WRENCH WP 48 - 4 PIN
TFCW 243241H	FORK CAP WRENCH 24/32/41mm HEX
TFCW 4549	FORK CAP WRENCH 45/49 OCTAGON
TFCW 4650	FORK CAP WRENCH 46/50 OCTAGON
TFCW 50H	FORK CAP WRENCH 50mm HEX WP
TFGC 500	GRADUATED CYLINDER 500cc
TFHD 1724	HEX AXLE WRENCH 17,19,22,24mm
TFHP 01	FORK ROD HOLDING CLIP 10/12/12.5
TFOL 02	FORK OIL LEVEL TOOL-PRO
TFPA 14	FORK PRELOAD SOCKET 14mm
TFPA 17	FORK PRELOAD SOCKET 17mm
TFPC 2328	REBOUND P-RING COMPRESSOR-WP 23/28
TFSB 01	FORK SEAL INSTALLATION BAGS (5)
TFSC 01	FORK SPRING COMPRESSOR PORTABLE
TFSC 02	FORK SPRING COMPRESSOR FOOT OPERATED
TFSC A01	FORK SPRING COMPRESSOR ADAPTER H-D
TFSD 30	FORK SEAL DRIVER 30mm
TFSD 33	FORK SEAL DRIVER 33mm
TFSD 35	FORK SEAL DRIVER 35mm
TFSD 37	FORK SEAL DRIVER 36/37mm
TFSD 39	FORK SEAL DRIVER 38/39mm
TFSD 41	FORK SEAL DRIVER 40/41mm
TFSD 43	FORK SEAL DRIVER 43mm
TFSD 46	FORK SEAL DRIVER 45/46mm
TFSD 48	FORK SEAL DRIVER 47/48mm
TFSD 50	FORK SEAL DRIVER 49/50mm
TFSH 10	SHAFT HOLD TOOL 10,12,12.5,14
TFSH 14	SHAFT HOLDING TOOL 14,16,18mm
TFSH 20	SHAFT HOLDING TOOL 20,24,29mm
TFSH 32	SHAFT HOLDING TOOL 32,35mm

Item Number	Description
TFSH S500	SHAFT HOLD TOOL 1/2"
TFTT 01	FORK TUBE DISASSEMBLY TOOL
TMDB 08	DEBURRING TOOL
TMPS 01	PIN SPANNER 4.0 & 4.5mm
TMPS 02	PIN SPANNER 5.0 & 5.5mm
TMPS P01P	SPANNER PINS 4.0 & 4.5 PAIR
TMPS P02P	SPANNER PINS 5.0 & 5.5 PAIR
TMVJ 065	VISE JAW SET
TSBD SET	BUSH DRIVER SET 12.5,14,16,18
TSCA 01	SHK COMP ADJ SOCKET YZ
TSCA 19	SHK COMP ADJ SOCKET 19mm
TSCA 21	SHK COMP ADJ SOCKET 21mm
TSCA 24	SHK COMP ADJ SOCKET 24mm
TSCP 01	SHOCK CLIP PICK TOOL
TSCT 01	RESERVOIR CAP REMOVAL TOOL
TSNC 02	NITROGEN CHARGING TOOL - WP
TSNG 02	SHOCK NITROGEN GAUGE-PRO
TSNH 48	NITROGEN HOSE 48"-HI PRESSURE
TSNN 01	SHOCK NITROGEN NEEDLE
TSNR 01	SHOCK NITROGEN REGULATOR
TSPA 01	SHOCK PRELOAD ADJUSTING TOOL
TSPS 1524	SHOCK NEEDLE TOOL-WP PDS 1.5x24d
TSPS T1524	SHOCK NEEDLE TOOL-PDS PRO 1.5x24d
TSPS T16530	SHOCK NEEDLE TOOL-PDS PRO 1.6x30d
TSPS T20	SHOCK NEEDLE TOOL-PDS PRO 20-2009
TSRC 01	SHOCK RES CAP SETTING TOOL YZ
TSSB 125	SHOCK SEAL BULLET 12.5x10mm
TSSB 14	SHOCK SEAL BULLET TOOL 14x12mm
TSSB 16	SHOCK SEAL BULLET TOOL 16x12mm
TSSB 18	SHOCK SEAL BULLET TOOL 18x16mm
TSSB 1812	SHOCK SEAL BULLET TOOL 18x12mm
TSSC 01	SHOCK SPRING COMPRESSOR-LEVER TYPE
TSSC 02	SHOCK SPRING COMPRESSOR-SCREW TYPE
TSSM 01	SAGMASTER TOOL
TSSS 01	SHOCK SEAL HEAD SET TOOL 40-50mm
TSSS 01S	SHOCK SEAL SET TOOL 40-50mm SHORT
TSSS 02	SHOCK SEAL HEAD SET TOOL WP 50mm
TSSS 03	SHOCK SEAL HEAD SET TOOL 33-36mm
TSVM 01	SHOCK VACUUM FILL TOOL
TTHS 02	T-HANDLE SET 8,10,12,14,17mm
TTHS 03	T-HANDLE SET8,10,12,13,14,17mm
TTHS 13	T-HANDLE 13mm ONLY

Appendix 6

RESOURCES

G.M.D. Computrack
www.gmd-computrack.com
chassis geometry and alignment

Intercomp
www.intercomp-racing.com
spring testers

K & L Supply
www.klsupply.com
lifts, stands, tools – dealers only

Lee Parks Design
www.leeparksdesign.com
bike stands, gloves and accessories

Öhlins Suspension
www.ohlins.com
suspension components

Penske
www.penskeshocks.com
suspension components

Pit Bull
www.pit-bull.com
stands

Race Tech
www.racetech.com
suspension components, valving kits, tools, seminars

Roehrig
www.roehrigengineering.com
shock dynos

Scotts Performance
www.scottsperformance.com
steering dampers

Tony Foale
www.tonyfoale.com
chassis design

Total Control
www.totalcontroltraining.net
Lee Parks' Total Control Riding Courses

WP Suspension
www.wpsuspension.com
suspension products

WPC Treatment Co, Inc.
www.wpctreatment.com
friction reduction surface treatment

Index

INDEX

MOTORBOOKS WORKSHOP
Sheet Metal Fabrication
- Forming Compound Curves
- Building Forms and Mock Ups
- Preparing Metals
- Choosing and Using Tools
- Identifying Types of Metals
Eddie Paul

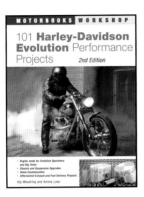

MOTORBOOKS WORKSHOP
101 Harley-Davidson Evolution Performance Projects **2nd Edition**
- Engine mods for Evolution Sportsters and Big Twins
- Chassis and Suspension Upgrades
- Aftermarket Exhaust and Fuel Delivery Projects
- Home Customization
Kip Woodring and Kenna Love

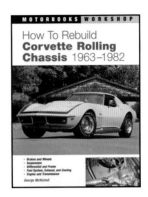

MOTORBOOKS WORKSHOP
How To Rebuild **Corvette Rolling Chassis** 1963–1982
- Brakes and Wheels
- Suspension
- Differential and Frame
- Fuel System, Exhaust, and Cooling
- Engine and Transmission
George McNicholl

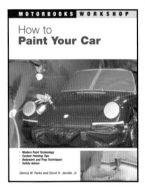

MOTORBOOKS WORKSHOP
How to **Paint Your Car**
- Modern Paint Technology
- Custom Painting Tips
- Bodywork and Prep Techniques
- Safety Advice
Dennis W. Parks and David H. Jacobs, Jr.

Other Great Books in This Series